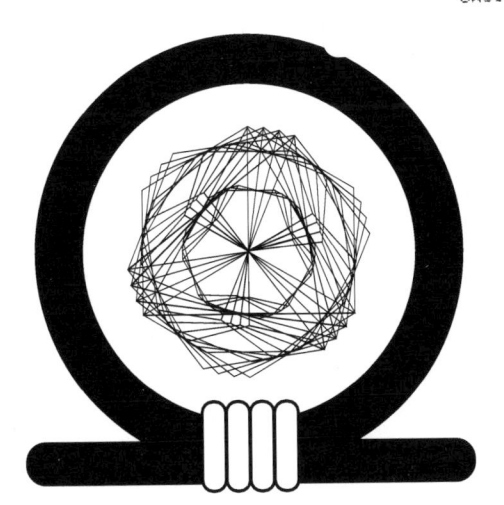

FORBIDDEN KNOWLEDGE

"Revelations of an multi-dimensional time traveler"

JASON QUITT & BOB MITCHELL

Copyright@2016 by Bob Mitchell and Jason Quitt
All rights reserved. No part of this work covered by the copyrights hereon may be reproduced or used in any form or by any means – graphic, electronic or mechanical, including photocopying, recording, taping or information storage and retrieval systems – without the prior written permission of Bob Mitchell or Jason Quitt.

All rights reserved.

ISBN-13:
978-1530570195

ISBN-10:
1530570190

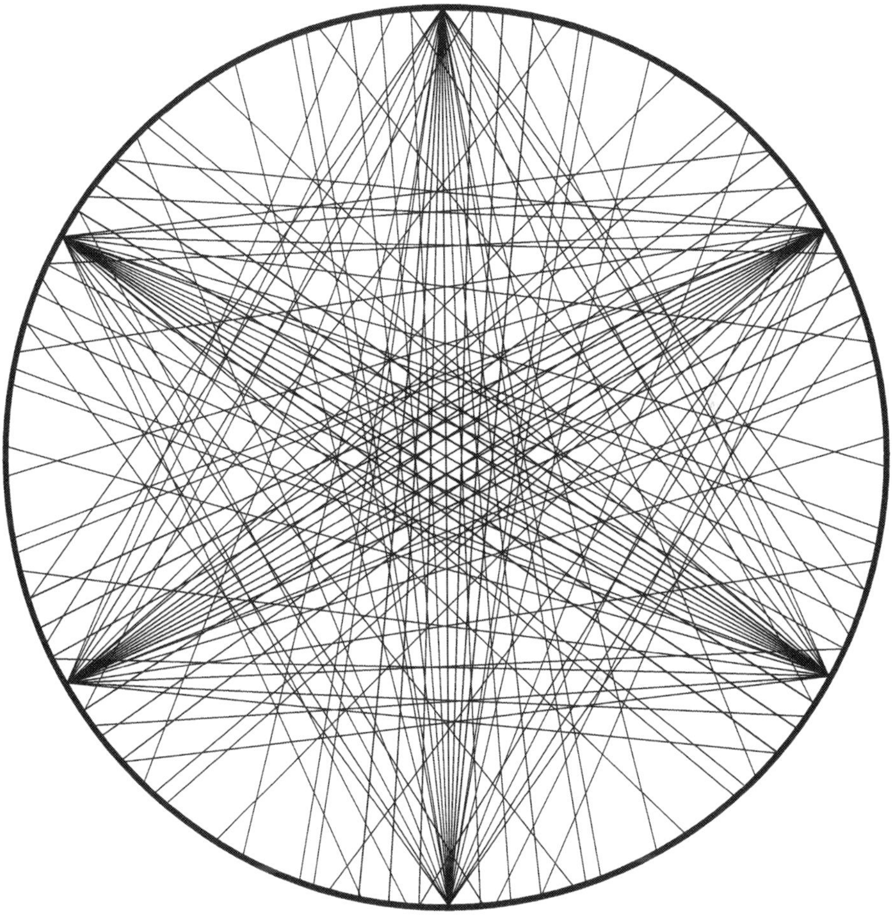

DEDICATION

To all our families and friends through time, space and dimensions.

ACKNOWLEDGMENTS

Our appreciation to the following people and organizations that made this book possible.

Saundra Arnold, Dennis Barnett, Peter Bernard, Bob Connolly, Canadian & American Society of Dowsers, LD, Dr. Javier Cabrera Darquea, Dr Sabina Devita, Robert Dean, Klaus Dona, Jo-Anne Eadie, Laura Eisenhower, Alien Cosmic Expo, Eagle Feather, Stanton Friedman, Mary & Dean Hardy, Dr. Magda Havas, Paul Hellyer, Kathleen Marden, Josh Mandell, Norval Morrisseau, Cinta ej Narat, Dr. Madi Nolan, Howard Pilsmaker, Lorne Quitt, Monika Quitt, Geoffrey Riley, Mark Russell, Aaron Singleton, Rick Strassman, Whitley Strieber, Sri Sri Sri Ganapati Sachchidananda Swamiji, Michael Tellinger, Nikola Tesla, Tesla Magazine, Kathy Wilson, Nora WalksInSpirit, August Worley.

CONTENTS

Statement From Jason Quitt..7
Introduction - From Bob Mitchell..8
Chapter 1 - Being Reborn..11
Chapter 2 - Astral Experiences Begin...17
Chapter 3 - A New Being Emerges...25
Chapter 4 - Visions of an Apocalyptic Future...31
Chapter 5 - The Healing Begins..39
Chapter 6 - Meeting Thoth...55
Chapter 7 - The Spiders Web...69
Chapter 8 - The Shaman Factor...83
Chapter 9 - Where Did He Go?..97
Chapter 10 - We Are Not The Voices In Our Minds...103
Chapter 11 - Astral Teachings..109
Chapter 12 - The Peru Experience...121
Chapter 13 - All Roads Lead To Tesla...137
Chapter 14 - Tesla's Hidden Medical Devices..145
Chapter 15 - Pyramids and The Great Galactic War..157
Chapter 16 - Tesla's Hidden Technologies, Government Secrets & Alien Treaties....167
Chapter 17 - Attacked..175
Chapter 18 - The Ancient Serpent Gods..189
Chapter 19 - Time Travel and Mind Control..205
Chapter 20 - Atlantis: The Untold Story..213
Chapter 21 - The Living Crystals...225
Chapter 22 - The Crystals Speak..235
Chapter 23 - The Reality of Our Reality..243
Chapter 24 - Life in Another Body..253
Chapter 25 - Forbidden Archeology..259
Chapter 26 - Unacknowledged Artifacts..275
Chapter 27 - Our Anunnaki Connection...283
Chapter 28 - The Greys...293

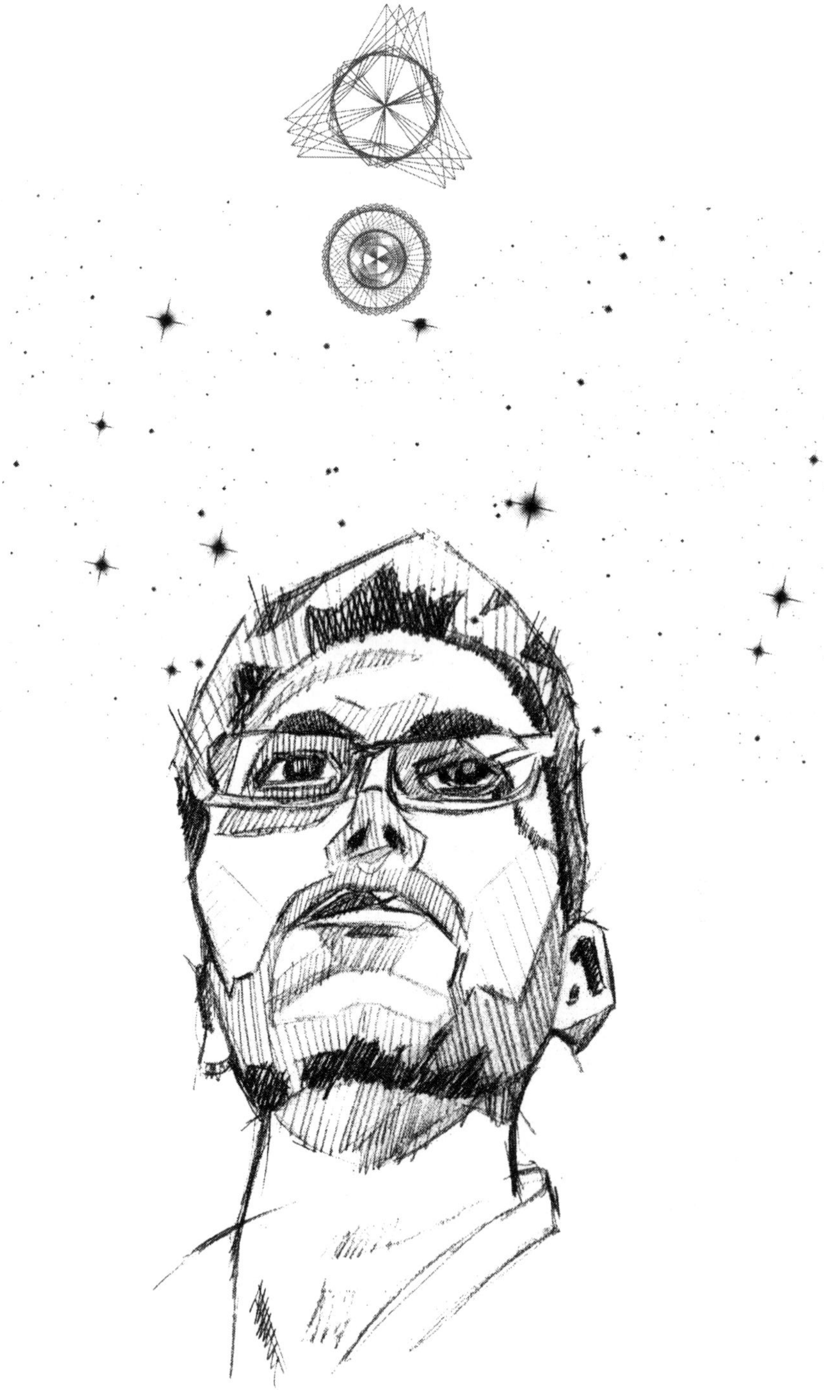

STATEMENT FROM JASON QUITT

I'm not connected to any government or military office.
I'm not associated with any secret society.
I'm not bound by any oaths or contracts.
I'm simply an individual with an incredible story to tell.

Within these pages are true stories of events and information that has been made available to me. All of these accounts and the information provided come directly from my own personal experiences and journeys.

Other information has come from various insiders, Experiencers and whistleblowers – information that provides context to some of my personal experiences and knowledge.

I can neither confirm nor deny the authenticity of their stories based on my first hand experiences.

It will be up to the reader to decide what fits and what doesn't fit with their personal belief system and their own personal search for the truth.

The information contained within this book will open many doors that have never been fully been explored.

Collectively, we must tread gently forward without fear to ask the right questions, allowing us to peer into the nature of our reality.

As our perception of this reality widens with it comes a new awareness providing all of us with the ability to change the way we see ourselves and our place in this world.

May we go forward with peace in our hearts.

FROM BOB MITCHELL

I first met Jason Quitt at the Alien Cosmic Expo in Brantford, Ontario during the summer of 2015.

We instantly connected.

At the time I had no idea why we did but over the next several months I began to understand the connection.

Even though we had just met, I was so fascinated by his lecture and his affinity to ancient Egypt that I approached him afterwards and told him I wanted to write a book about his incredible life and his other worldly experiences.

We later decided to co-write this book.

My wife Kim also seemed to have a connection to Jason when he was introduced to her at the Expo.

Interestingly, while I have never been drawn to ancient Egypt, Kim has always felt as if she had a past life in the days of the Pharaohs. Perhaps she does. After co-writing this book that idea doesn't seem so strange any more.

Before collaborating with Jason on this book I wrote "What If? Close Encounters of the Unusual Kind" where I posed the question – What if the world we live in isn't what we think it is?

Essentially, if the Experiencers in my book really did have alien encounters in the way they absolutely believe they did then the world we think we're part of really isn't what we believe or have been told it is.

In some ways, "Forbidden Knowledge" is an extension of "What if? Close Encounters of the Unusual Kind" but in a far more enlightening way.

In fact, although I'm obviously biased, I believe "Forbidden Knowledge" might just be one of the most important books you'll ever read.

It's a life-changing work.

For many, it will be a game changer.

Of course, we're sort of preaching to the choir so some of the revelations of this book will be understood by some readers better than others. However, for others, it's going to take a tremendous leap of faith to believe some of what Jason is revealing within these pages.

He tells an extraordinary story.

You'll be taken to places you never thought possible.

It's a story that if Jason is correct, then our world, our recorded history, and how we got to where we are today has been one enormous fabricated lie.

If Jason is right, then planet Earth has never been and isn't what we have been taught it is.

In one sense, this book is about aliens and the control various species have had for millions of years and continue to have over planet Earth and the third dimensional species known as mankind.

It's also a book about astral traveling and who we are and who we will become when we are able to ascend to our rightful spot in the universe as multi-dimensional beings.

It's also a book about what reincarnation really is and why life on Earth is only one stage of existence in one of the lower realms in the Universe.

Jason doesn't claim to have all the answers, but his journeys have provided an insight and deeper understanding of the role all of us play in the cosmos and our connection to alien species both good and bad, some truly helpful to humankind and others in a diabolical conspiracy that has been under way for decades with an elite group of humans.

So find a comfy chair and relax and keep an open mind as you delve into a world that might seem implausible.

Enjoy the ride folks. Your life might never be the same again.

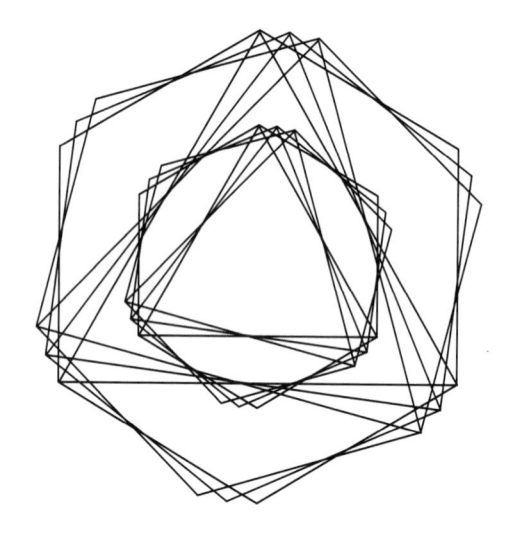

"Reality is merely an illusion,
albeit a very persistent one."

- Albert Einstein

Chapter 1
"Being Reborn"

Before Jason Quitt incarnated on Earth he got to choose and view his parents.

"We all do. Most of us just don't remember."

But Jason isn't like most people.

He's a multi-dimensional, planetary time traveler.

He has lived many lives, visited several different planets, communicated with numerous species, battled benevolent forces, and possesses forbidden knowledge that has put his life in danger.

He is one of the few incarnated humans with this knowledge. Most die or are killed before they reach maturity by beings and dark forces, who don't want humanity to know their true place in the world.

They made an unsuccessful attempt on his life in May 2015 after Jason publicly revealed secret information about what he knew.

The circumstances surrounding what happened to him when he nearly died and the astonishing secrets he possesses about humanity – what and who we are and what really is happening on Earth - will be revealed throughout this book through first hand accounts of his journeys and experiences since his last incarnation on Earth.

While most of us have trouble remembering our early childhood, Jason has many vivid memories of his past.

Not only does he remember his childhood but he also recalls a time from another plane of existence before he was physically born into his current life.

So where was this other plane of existence?

It's a concept that for most will be difficult to comprehend.

Essentially, it's another realm of existence, but not one to be confused with the place many call Heaven.

"It's a transitional place that our consciousness exists in before we incarnate again," Jason explained. "It's not a physical place. It's more akin to the astral world."

Jason recalls his pre-birth memories.

"Early on in my childhood I believed we all had the opportunity to choose our parents before we incarnated here," Jason said. "These were my first memories when I entered into this world."

Jason remembers crawling along a hallway with many other infants around him. It sort of reminded him of being in a 1980s airport with carpeted flooring.

"Leading us down these hallways were different women," Jason said. "From my perspective now, these women resembled airline stewardesses. They wore uniforms and were very official looking.

"There were many of us, all different races, naked and crawling down these hallways. The women were directing the flow of babies like it was some kind of baby highway."

In this recalled memory, the infant Jason seemed to be only a couple months old.

"I'm in a physical human body," he said.

In his current incarnation Jason has no memories of what happened immediately before he realized he was crawling down a hallway.

"The only memory before this was being in darkness and then moving out of the darkness through a doorway and suddenly being in the physical form of a baby," Jason said. "I'm crawling on my hands and knees.

"But this memory of crawling as a baby might not be what it actually was. But from a baby's mind with no real perspective of what

"Being Reborn"

life and death is, this is what I was allowed to perceive.

"But I was now in human form. It was the concept my baby mind could understand."

As he crawled with the other children one of the women directed him to go down another hallway and said to him, "It's time for you to choose your parents."

An overwhelming feeling of joy and happiness came over him.

"It was as if I was happy to be doing this trip again," Jason said. "I was super excited."

The woman then guided him to one of many doors in this hallway. She then opened the door for him. This door was very small and built so that only a child could enter.

"This room reminded me of a movie theater. It was very big and dark with high ceilings," Jason said. "As I looked in front of me a circular portal of light opened and I sat down in front of it."

Various images and scenes of his soon-to-be parents suddenly appeared within the portal.

"I was able to view my parents before they were married," he said. "I saw them before their wedding and at their wedding. I already had the knowledge that I had selected them before this moment. That I had chosen them to be my parents."

Once again he felt nothing but love and happiness.

"I felt so happy to see my future family," he said. "I felt very connected to them."

After watching them for some time he suddenly found himself being pulled towards them.

"It was as if I was being pulled right through the portal," he said.

But this wasn't the moment of his birth, or more accurately, his rebirth.

None of the images he saw showed his mother pregnant. Instead, his consciousness, his soul, was being implanted within the fetus his mother was carrying.

Once he was old enough to talk Jason would often tell his mother, "Aren't you happy I chose you?"

His mother would smile and tell him that she was even though

Forbidden Knowledge

Jason's pre-birth memory of the portal where he viewed his parents.

she was understandably unaware of the significance of what he was actually saying to her.

"It was always on my mind as a young child," he said. "My mother just thought it was something sweet that her child was saying to her without any deeper understanding of where it was coming from."

Now you must remember that as a young child Jason thought these memories were completely normal. He thought everybody chose their parents.

"I thought it was something everybody did," Jason said. "That everybody knew and experienced."

As he grew into adulthood he would start to recall many past

"Being Reborn"

lives and many rebirths.

His rebirth wasn't instantaneous most of the time although he recalls one memory of life, death and then rebirth all occurring at the same moment.

It involved an ice world.

"It could have been somewhere in the Arctic as far as I know," Jason said. "I remember I was running on the ice and it was cracking beneath me.

"I was terrified. And then suddenly the ice cracked open and I fell into the water. The current was so strong that it pulled me down very quickly.

"I remember thinking that this was it, I was going to die. But then my entire body was filled with warmth. Then everything turned black."

The next thing he experienced was the sound of him crying as a baby.

He was in his next incarnation.

"I had experienced an almost direct transition from death to life again through my birth," he said. "But what I have learned is that instantaneous incarnation is rare.

"It happens but it can take many years, even hundreds of thousands of years for those who choose to incarnate or be reborn although time isn't the concept that we think it is."

Jason would later learn that we all choose our parents based on very specific reasons.

"But genetics and location are the most important," he explained. "Our essence is looking for the right vessel in order to access specific genetic traits. Once found these traits can be activated and enhanced as we age.

"We are also looking for the right type of life-stream and experiences to work out the karma that we carry forward from our past lives and ancestry. This is to allow for our consciousness to evolve with our given life path.

"We also incarnate in soul groups. All the people I have close contact with today such as my family and my friends have all had past lives together. It's almost like having familiar energy around you right from the start."

Jason would also learn that our consciousness can insert itself in the past as well as in the future.

"Time doesn't exist in the way we perceive it to," Jason said. "Time is more like a physical object than a concept. The past has already happened and so has the future.

"But we just don't realize it."

When we are reborn our memories are wiped clean so that we can experience our new lives. But certain people retain some memories in order to put them on the right path.

"We choose our entire path in this world before we are even born," Jason explained. "At specific points in our lives memories will appear, gifts will awaken and events will unfold that will shift us and guide us on the path we have chosen to walk. This is to keep us in the right direction for us to fulfill our purpose here.

"There is also a higher awareness guiding us down our paths that gently or not so gently help us along even when we stray from the path."

Jason was raised Jewish although his family wasn't particularly religious.

"I never really had any religion imprinted on me," he said. "But I always knew that all of us were reincarnated souls. That everybody had past lives and that we are all connected to a source. Nobody needed to tell me this. I just knew.

"For me this was normal and that's why despite this knowledge as far as I was concerned I lived a normal childhood."

However, his adult life would be anything but normal.

Chapter 2
"Astral Experiences Begin"

Like many youngsters Jason was afraid of what went bump in the night.

He was afraid of what lived under his bed and was particularly scared of what lurked inside his bedroom closet. It was where the bogeyman hung out.

But you see, in Jason's closet, he did.

"There were many nights when I would hear my closet door open," Jason said. "I would be so frightened that I would pull the covers over my head."

One night he somehow summoned the strength to peak into his closet.

He couldn't believe his eyes.

"The only way I can describe what I saw was a dehydrated person," Jason recalled. "It was very dark inside the closet but I could see him. It was like some scarecrow type of being."

Fortunately for him this being didn't do anything but watch him.

"He just stared at me," Jason said. "I think I was about 4 years old."

Jason ran to his parents' bedroom. They consoled him. It was just a nightmare. There was nothing in his closet.

But Jason knew different. There was definitely somebody or

some "thing" in his closet. Jason did not really know what the thing was – or what the other beings he would soon encounter were - but this was the start of his explorations into the astral world.

Being just a child he simply thought he was dreaming.

In these dreams he would leave his body and play around in this house. He would even travel to the park behind his home.

"It was summer outside and people would be playing baseball in the park. I would go and sit in the outfield and watch them," Jason said. "I would hear the sounds and feel the ambiance of the outdoors. But I just thought I was dreaming. I just thought that every kid did this.

"I had no reason to believe that I wasn't dreaming."

But his dreams would soon dramatically change.

At night Jason would feel a being guiding him out of his body. He never saw this being but just felt a presence always behind him. This being took him to different places in his home although in this reality it wasn't the home he currently lived in. It was a home from a different time line.

"It was as if this being wanted to show me their life or their past life," Jason said. "It was like they were time traveling with me."

In this time line, there was no park behind his house. Instead, it was a corn field and a farm house stood near the spot where his recently-built home had been erected.

"This being started showing me that they were dead," Jason said. "He would take me down to the basement and show me a coffin with a body inside of it. I assumed this being was the man in the coffin."

Jason peered into the coffin.

"It looked like a mummified body," he said.

Jason knew the coffin was in the basement of his childhood home but despite being so young he still realized that he wasn't in the same home where he had gone to sleep. He was in the home the being once lived in.

As Jason grew into adulthood he realized he had never been dreaming. He was actually astral traveling.

"I was able to travel back in time and experience that time with

"Astral Experiences Begin"

these beings," he said. "I was an observer.

"I was still dressed in my pajamas. I felt as if I was there in my physical body even though I wasn't."

But his astral traveling soon took him to another past life. This time it wasn't theirs. This time it was one of his.

"It wound up being one of the most horrible experiences that ever happened to me," Jason said. "I was being exposed to the worse things possible at such a young age. But I later learned they were preparing me for what was to come."

Jason recalled waking up one night to very loud noises.

"They were very animalistic sounds," he said. "There was a lot of grunting and screaming and it was coming from outside my bedroom."

The scary sounds wouldn't stop.

He recalled getting out of bed and peering out into the hallway just outside of his bedroom.

Suddenly, he wasn't in his home and what he saw wasn't his hallway.

"I saw two men brutally fighting each other. They were tearing each other apart with their bare hands," Jason said. "They were fighting to their death.

"Neither of them had weapons. They were just using their hands and they were tearing each others flesh off. It was incredibly gruesome."

Where were these men fighting?

What time period was he observing?

Jason didn't know.

There didn't appear to be anybody else around or watching them. He was the only one observing the bloody scene.

But as he stood there watching the horrific scene unfold in front of his young eyes another gruesome thought entered his mind.

"I realized that I was actually watching my own death in a past life. That I was one of these men," Jason said. "You can only imagine what this was like for me, witnessing this horrible event from a child's perspective."

Jason also had a recurring 'dream' that always affected him psychologically.

Forbidden Knowledge

The Skeksis are a fictional species which act as the main antagonists in the 1982 fantasy film The Dark Crystal by Jim Henson.

"In the dream my parents handed me over to another race of beings," Jason recalled. "These beings were very scary looking. Their features were half reptilian and half birdlike. They reminded me of the Skeksis from the movie 'The Dark Crystal'"

These fictional species were the main antagonists in the 1982 fantasy film.

"I cried hysterically. I begged my parents not to give me to them," Jason said. "My parents just looked at me with so much hate in their eyes. They told me they didn't want me and how they never wanted to see me again.

"I also think this dream was based on deep trauma of actual events that occurred in multiple past lives."

As Jason grew many other past life experiences resurfaced.

When he was 11 his parents enrolled him in a new elementary public school in a community immediately north of Toronto. By then his parents had divorced. Even though his mother raised him he still had close contact with his father.

He didn't have many friends but one day he met another boy his age and they instantly hit it off.

"We became best friends. It was as if we had this connection," Jason said.

"Astral Experiences Begin"

Soon memories long buried in his mind started to come back. He completely remembered a past life that he and his new friend shared.

"I became very emotional," he said. "I tried to get him to remember us from our past life. I kept asking him; don't you remember who we were?

"Don't you remember that I killed you in another life?"

He then told him the story.

His memories led him back to medieval times when he and his friend were members of a King's elite protection force. They were always by the King's side.

"We had grown up together," Jason said. "We trained together. We were closer than brothers."

Jason has no idea who this King was or in what country or even if this life occurred on Earth.

But one day the King received word about a plot against him and the leaders of the conspiracy were alleged to be him and his friend.

"Of course it wasn't true but the King gave us two choices," Jason said. "Either we both would be killed on the spot or we could fight each other to the death with the winner being allowed to live."

The two men decided to fight each other.

"But before the fight my friend told me that he didn't intend to kill me," Jason said. "He wanted me to kill him so that I would live on.

"So we fought and when he was ready he gave me a signal and I took my dagger and stabbed him in the side of his head. I held his head while he was dying. He actually smiled at me just before he died."

These memories lasted for days and bothered him for quite some time.

"My friend never had any recollection of our fight or any part of our past life," Jason said.

Today, they remain close friends.

"I think on some level he wanted to believe me," Jason said. "He never thought I was crazy. But it really wasn't important to him.

"The interesting thing is that today he's a very strong person.

Forbidden Knowledge

He's into martial arts and has a black belt while I don't have any interest in things like that. We were once elite soldiers and today he's still an elite soldier but I don't have the stomach for it anymore."

Strange things would continue throughout his young years. His younger brother Lorne also experienced incidents.

"Lorne ran into my room one night and hit me with his pillow," Jason said. "He was very upset. He told me never to come into his room again."

Lorne was about 5 at the time. It seems he had been sleeping when his pillow was ripped out from under him and somebody was hitting him with it.

"He managed to fight back and when he did the pillow flew across the room and hit the wall," Jason said. "He was so scared and angry that he ran into my bedroom to get me back.

"But I had never been in his bedroom. It wasn't me hitting him with his pillow."

Another time Lorne recalled being awoken by a strange feeling that something was in his room.

"As he turned over to see what it was he noticed that his night table lamp was floating in the air next to his bed," Jason said. "He was really scared but he just turned around went back to sleep thinking that he was just dreaming.

"The next morning he awoke to find his lamp a couple feet away from his bed broken on the floor."

Was their home haunted?

Were the time traveling beings now also interacting with Jason's younger brother?

"I'm not sure but I always thought our house was haunted even though it was a new house," Jason said. "I remember my mother was doing some renovating in the house and the contractors had to open up my bedroom wall to fix the plumbing. When they removed the drywall they found the remains of a gigantic crow. This was a mystery to them and I remember them saying that this bird must have gotten stuck in here during construction.

"It was freaky to learn that all this time I was sleeping with a

"Astral Experiences Begin"

dead bird in my wall. I'm not sure this had anything to do with my experiences but Native Americans and Canadians believe the totem of the crow opens us up to the gifts of ancient wisdom and the sacred laws. The Crow is also believed to bring the gift to see into the spirit world."

Another case of haunting involved their basement television always turning on by itself.

"My mother would yell at me for leaving the TV on in the basement, "Jason said. "I would run down to turn the TV off and right when I got to it the set would turn off by itself. That always freaked me out.

"Many times when I walked past the basement I would hear people talking down there. I would proceed to follow the voices and they would just disappear."

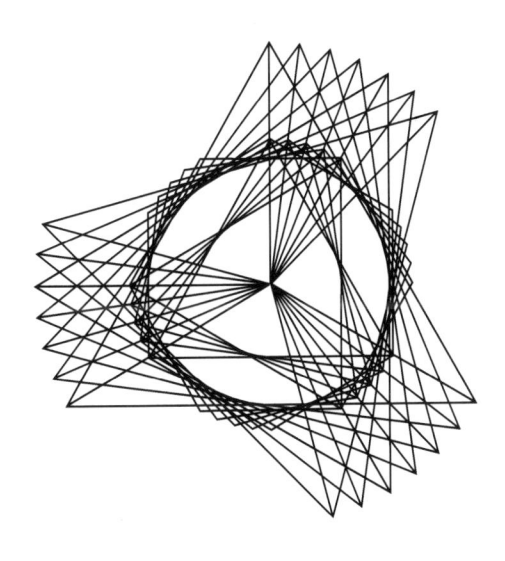

Forbidden Knowledge

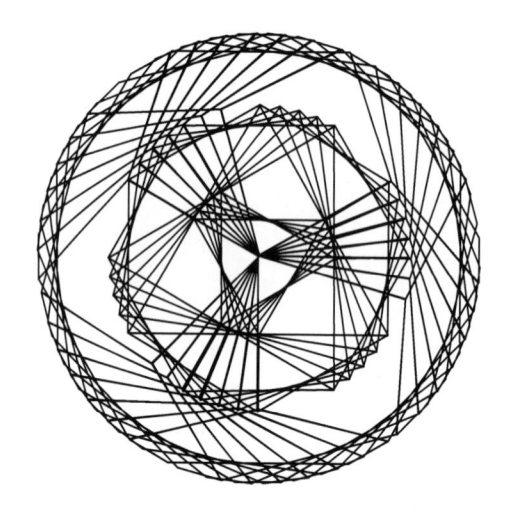

"The problem is not to find the answer, it's to face the answer."

- Terence McKenna

Chapter 3
"A New Being Emerges"

Growing up Jason suffered from a health issue called irritable bowel syndrome.

"This was a constant battle. Everything I ate just made me sick and passed right through me," Jason said. "I was always in incredible pain."

The illness took so much out of him that during his high school years a friend dubbed him with the nickname "Jack Skeleton."

Jason is 6-foot-5 and he weighed 150 pounds in high school. So you get the picture.

"You could literally see my bones sticking through my body," he said. "I was white as a ghost. This affected everything in my life.

"I was in really bad shape. I definitely wasn't healthy."

To make matters worse, he was dyslexic and also stuttered.

"I always had a problem with reading and spelling and when I spoke I stuttered constantly," Jason said.

At 16 he was prescribed codeine for his pain after undergoing surgery. He would never forget the experience.

"Instantly my clairaudience would take over," Jason said. "By that I mean I would hear things that weren't there in a physical state. It was an extremely frightening experience."

Forbidden Knowledge

His pain subsided but the sounds didn't end.

"It was as if there were hundreds of people standing in my room and they were all talking at the same time and trying to talk over each other," Jason explained.

"They're all trying to have a conversation with me all at once. There was depth to their voices. I could hear where each voice was coming from in the room. I couldn't see them but they were all yelling at me at the same time.

"I felt as if I was going insane."

The same strange occurrence happened every time he took codeine.

"Even today my hospital chart says I'm allergic to codeine with audio hallucinations in brackets," he said.

Jason's initial experiences with the strange beings that had visited him in his home ended when he was about 11. Nothing really happened again until he was in his 20s.

"After high school I was accepted into a very good university for business studies," Jason said. "I was actually pretty excited that I got into this school and so was my family."

His father took him to the university to register for his courses.

"I remember standing in line and looking around," Jason said. "There were other students with their parents doing the same thing."

Then something took over his mind and turned to his father.

"We are leaving. I'm not going to this school," Jason blurted out defiantly.

For some reason Jason knew he had to leave the university and fast.

"There was just a sudden urge to get out of there as fast as I could," Jason said. "I felt like this was not the path for me."

But Jason still understood just how disappointed his father was at that moment.

So what was he going to do with his life?

He was always interested in graphic design, music and art so he enrolled at a design college. He had fun and made lots of new friends.

"After graduation a friend had a crazy idea to open a music studio and graphic art house," Jason said. "I loved that idea so much

"A New Being Emerges"

that I jumped on the opportunity and within a couple months we were running our own business."

It was an incredibly fun time in Jason's life. But this business path was short lived.

"During my time at the studio I started to suffer from a sleeping condition called sleep paralysis," Jason explained.

He would wake up and be totally aware of his surroundings but his body would be frozen.

"I would be screaming inside my head for my arms and legs to move but it was like I was in a coma," Jason said.

Initially, Jason experienced sleep paralysis about once a month. Then it would happen about once a week. Eventually, it was happening every single night.

It was a difficult time for him but his sleep paralysis would eventually transform his life.

While experiencing sleep paralysis one night he suddenly became aware that he wasn't alone in his bedroom.

"I sensed somebody or some thing was walking around the room," Jason said. "It was quite frightening."

This uneasy feeling continued each night.

"My mind was alert but everything else was frozen and I knew I wasn't alone in the room," he explained.

Although Jason wasn't into UFOs or aliens at the time his mind went to the absolute worse place and fear.

"I thought this was the beginning of an alien abduction," he recalled.

"Whatever was in my room had to be an alien or demonic."

One night Jason couldn't take it any more.

He needed to find out "who" or "what" was in his room.

"I was so angry. I was trying to forcefully shake myself out of my frozen body," Jason said. "As I desperately tried to wake my body up something suddenly happened. I shook myself so hard that I popped right out of my body.

"I was now floating above my bed and could see my physical body below me lying on my bed. My physical body was straight as

Forbidden Knowledge

Tall shadow being Jason witnessed during his sleep paralysis.

a board and my eyes were wide open."

Then he noticed the being.

It was standing at the foot of his bed and was very tall. Its head almost touched his nine-foot ceiling.

"There was no detail to it," he said. "It was like looking at a shadow with a strong outline. This being looked as if it was cloaked. The best way I could describe what it looked like was your classic grim reaper. This face to face experience shocked me to the core because I wasn't expecting any of this to happen."

The experience was so startling that Jason felt himself immediately sucked back into his body.

"I woke with my heart pounding and was out of breath," he said.

What the hell had just happened?

"A New Being Emerges"

What had he just seen?

One thing was certain. He definitely knew what he had experienced wasn't a nightmare.

"It was a completely different feeling," he said. "Popping out and seeing yourself and feeling as if you're no longer in your actual body.

"It's hard to explain but being out of your body actually feels more real than life itself. It's more genuine than even being alive. It's more real than existing in our third dimension."

Essentially, it's all physics.

"The third dimension reality we live in vibrates at a certain rate," he said. "But as this vibration increases we can then shift our consciousness into another reality that exists just beyond our field of vision.

"When we're in our astral body we're able to access this fourth dimension because our consciousness is now embodying our astral body.

"So when I returned to my physical body in the third dimension it appeared as if nobody was in my bedroom. This was because the beings are occupying space in our fourth dimension. I can't see them with my third dimensional eyes.

"They're invisible to us but they can still see us. Beings living in other dimensions can consciously connect to the third dimension when needed."

That night memories long buried resurfaced.

Jason began to recall some of his childhood experiences. He now realized that what he had thought were simply dreams of him flying to the park behind his house were really out of body astral traveling experiences.

After this experience all unintentional sleep paralysis ended, but Jason discovered how he could put himself into a state of sleep paralysis and control when and how to leave his body.

"Now, I was doing it to myself. I wasn't having it done to me," he said. "I believe the being had been deliberately causing my sleep paralysis to show me how to leave my body. Now I was able to put my body to sleep and keep my mind fully awake."

Forbidden Knowledge

At first, Jason would simply roll out of his body.

"It was difficult to do because it took a lot of practice," he said. "But suddenly I found myself floating above my bed.

"It was like being in a body but not in a physical body. It was like you were just energy. And you have 360 degree vision. You can see everything completely around you. You don't have arms or legs. You're not breathing. You're just floating energy but you can see and experience things."

Jason then discovered other methods, which produced the same effects.

"I found there were multiple ways I could leave my body and enter into this state," he said. "At first the only method I knew was to put myself to sleep and forcefully push myself out. I also found that if I put myself in the right state there would be a very warm tingling sensation starting to build in my stomach. This sensation would be accompanied by a low, vibrating, humming sound. I would tune my awareness into this sound.

"As I would do this the frequency and intensity of sound became greater until the sound literally popped me out of my body."

Over time Jason became quite good at both methods.

"Eventually I didn't need any of these methods," Jason said. "Soon it would simply just start to happen unconsciously. I would go to sleep and suddenly I would feel myself leaving naturally without any effort whatsoever."

Chapter 4
"Visions Of An Apocalyptic Future"

Jason's experiences changed as he became more adapt with his astral traveling.

Soon he would be visited by other beings, who took him on out of body journeys.

These beings came to him at night and pulled him out of his body. They took him on journeys into the past and to the future.

"I was an observer," he said. "I could only watch. I couldn't interact."

The beings were still outlines to him but they now appeared more humanoid in shape.

"They were tall but always just behind me out of view and there were always two of them," Jason said. "They touched my shoulders and directed me. I felt their physical touch."

There was very little direct communication and when there was it was always telepathic.

His initial journeys were anything but pleasant.

"I would be taken up through the ceiling and out the roof of my house and shot up into outer space," Jason said. "I would go higher and higher and I would see the Earth below me. We would then travel further and further into outer space."

Eventually, they would stop and Jason would be directed to go back.

Forbidden Knowledge

"I was told to look at a specific point on the Earth and then they would shoot me back down and I would land at that location," Jason said.

He was overwhelmed by what he saw.

"I knew I was somewhere in the United States but I had no idea what time period it was," Jason said. "The sky was completely blood red orange in color. It was as if the sky was burnt. It was as if the sky was on fire.

"The Earth was completely scorched. There were no standing trees. Any tree that I saw was just a few inches off the ground and just black cinders. The soil was orange and red as well. Like the sky, the soil also had been burned."

Jason scanned the desolate landscape. It was mesmerizing.

"Then suddenly my consciousness was pulled under ground inside a bunker of some kind," Jason said. "I saw a man; He was wearing leather and had goggles on.

"But he was dying in this bunker. Whatever had happened, the bunker didn't protect him. He was suffering."

Burnt landscape Jason was shown in one of his time travel experiences.

"Visions Of An Apocalyptic Future"

He was then quickly taken back into outer space and then transported back to his bedroom.

What had he seen?

What time period had he been dropped into?

Jason racked his brain.

"It looked as if a nuclear war had occurred because everything was completely devastated…There was nothing left." Jason said. "There were no buildings. No humans other than the dying man in the bunker."

Why was he being shown this?

Why weren't the beings explaining anything to him?

"It was as if they just wanted me to see it," Jason said.

Jason was about 22 when this first view of an apocalyptic future was presented to him.

About six months later he was taken again.

Again, he was dropped at a specific location in what he assumed was the United States.

It was another time period in the future.

And another horrific scene unfolded in front of him, again simply as an observer.

He was inside a children's prison camp.

"It was sickening," he said. "There were military soldiers and tanks and they were shooting at kids and running them over with their tanks.

"It was horrible and very, very gruesome."

The camp resembled a concentration camp from WWII but the children weren't dressed like the children of those camps would have been dressed. They were wearing modern day clothes.

"The soldiers didn't look like German soldiers so I knew I hadn't been dropped into WWII," Jason said. "I was totally immersed in the scene.

"I could hear the bullets flying and the screams of the children. It was horrific. There were hundreds of kids all between 5 and 13. And they were of different races.

"I was standing in the middle of everything. I was experiencing

Forbidden Knowledge

Prison camp that Jason was shown in one of his time travel experiences.

it as if it was happening right then in front of me."

As Jason looked around he realized the camp was surrounded by concrete walls and barbed wire.

"I remember looking up into the sky and it was similar to what I had seen before," he said. "It was red. Something was definitely wrong with the planet."

This experience affected him for days

"I was sick when I returned from this journey," he said. "I barely talked to anybody for several days. I was as white as a ghost. What I had seen was truly awful."

In fact, Jason didn't want to go on any more journeys.

"I was being shown the worst things imaginable," he said. "I started not to like my new found abilities."

But they didn't stop.

The next time he was dropped off in what appeared to be a type of FEMA (Federal Emergency Management Agency) camp.

"Visions Of An Apocalyptic Future"

Interestingly, conspiracy theorists maintain mass internment facilities operated by FEMA will and have been secretly built throughout the U.S. to house dissidents once martial law is declared in the future for preparation of a one world government.

According to Jason, the camp he saw consisted of many tents filled with families. It was night and the tents were guarded by soldiers.

"I sensed that everybody living in these tents were actually grateful to be there," Jason said. "They felt lucky to be in these camps."

But Jason also sensed tension between the families and the soldiers.

"There seemed to be some mistrust," he said. "The soldiers didn't talk to the people. I sensed even the soldiers were scared.

"Everybody talked a lot under their breath. But I still sensed they were grateful to be there."

In another journey Jason wound up hearing one of the loudest explosions he has ever experienced. He had no idea where he was. All he knew was that he was being allowed to experience the noise of what was happening.

"The ground literally shook," he said. "It felt as if my ear drums were going to be destroyed. I really thought I was going to lose my hearing.

"When it ended and I was back in my bed I was still holding my ears."

Jason experienced numerous other journeys involving this post-apocalyptic theme. One such experience was very profound for Jason. This involved a visitation in spirit from Norval Morrisseau, an Aboriginal Canadian artist known as the "Picasso of the North."

Jason has always admired his work.

Also known as "Copper Thunderbird," Morrisseau's work depicted the legends of his peo-

Aboriginal artist Norval Morrisseau

35

Forbidden Knowledge

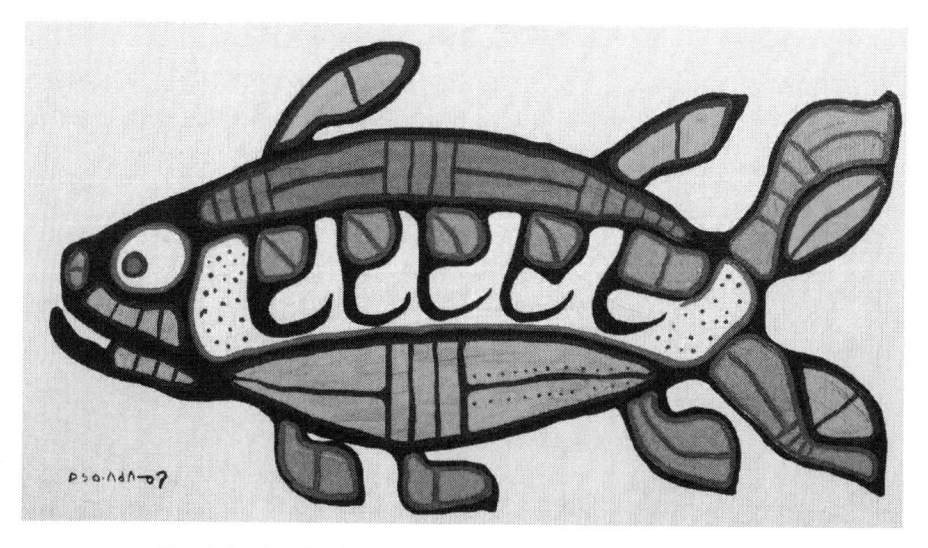

Aboriginal artist Norval Morrisseau's painting of a fish.

ple, their cultural, and the political tensions that existed between Native Canadian and European traditions, his existential struggles and his deep spirituality and mysticism. He founded the Woodlands School of Canadian art and was a prominent member of the "Indian Group of Seven."

Morrisseau died in Toronto in December 2007. He was 76.

Jason insists his spirit visited him one night soon after his death.

"I had always been drawn to his artwork so when he visited me I knew exactly who he was," Jason said. "He then took me to his art gallery in the spirit world. While in this gallery he showed me hundreds of his paintings hanging on the wall and all these painting involved fish swimming in beautiful Technicolor done in the style he was famous for. It was quite a beautiful scene."

Jason was then taken down a hallway and into another gallery but none of his paintings were hanging there.

"Instead, he showed me a painting of a soldier, who looked like a U.S. Marine," Jason said. "It was very realistic. And as we explored the gallery further we wound up entering another room.

"This one contained paintings of the visions similar to the ones

"Visions Of An Apocalyptic Future"

Duke Redbird

the beings had shown me. The sky was red. It looked like the aftermath of a nuclear explosion. There was also a mushroom cloud. I think the message Norval was showing me was the deep contrast between the beauty of nature and the destruction of man. These images still haunt me."

An interesting synchronicity with this story is years after this experience Jason had the opportunity to meet Duke Redbird, another influential Native Canadian elder.

"We ended up at Duke's house talking all night about the nature of the spiritual journey, the past and the future," Jason said.

"It was a very enlightening talk. I shared with him my story about the journey I had with Norval in the gallery. Duke looked at me with wide eyes and smiled.

"I had no idea that Duke was one of Norval's closest friends."

Duke confirmed that Norval always talked to him about his gallery in the spirit world, Jason said.

"This was the gallery where Norval saw the paintings before he painted them," Jason explained. "At that moment we felt Norval's spirit fill the room. It was as if he brought the two of us together so we could share these stories. It was an amazing experience for me."

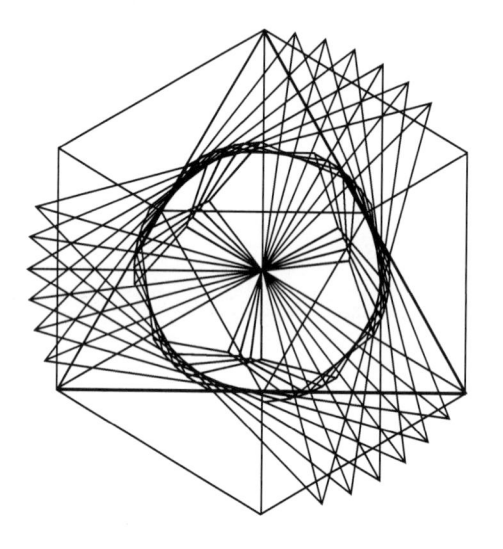

"The key to growth is the introduction of higher dimensions of consciousness into your awareness."

- Lao Tzu

Chapter 5
"The Healing Begins"

Jason's journeys suddenly changed after pleading with the beings to stop showing him such horrible visions.

The beings returned but this time they had a message for him.

"Before you go on your journey and before you can become who you will become, you have to heal yourself."

Despite his astral travels, Jason still suffered from IBS and literally looked as if he was on death's door.

"My father was very scared of my health so we decided to see a doctor to see if they could figure out whether something else was wrong with me other than just IBS," Jason said. "I was literally skin and bones."

Jason underwent a series of tests, including blood tests. They took x-rays and ultra sounds. Just about every test that could be done was done.

"We got the results back and the doctor basically told me that I was not only healthy but I was healthier than the average person," Jason said. "To me, it was the biggest joke. I felt as if I was dying and he's telling me I'm healthier than the average person.

"They couldn't find anything wrong with me. They said my IBS was just stress related and that I would eventually out grow it."

Forbidden Knowledge

Jason knew at that moment the traditional medical industry wouldn't be his avenue to health.

"I knew going to a doctor wasn't what the beings meant when they said I needed to heal myself," he said.

So what did he need to do to heal?

He then started to receive more messages.

Initially, they were only about the environment.

"They told me that our food and water had been compromised and laced with many chemicals and toxins," Jason said. "They said I needed to make an effort to eat only organic non-processed food and drink only the purest sourced water that I could find."

He was also provided with information pertaining to the "energy" existing in all food and water.

"They told me how the food we eat picks up the energies of the places and people it comes in contact with," he said. "By the time the food reaches the consumer its energy is highly compromised and essentially sick.

"This is why we must learn how to change this energy before we consume it. We need to learn how to extract the sick energy and replace it with healing energy."

Jason recalled a story he once heard about a guru in an Ashram in India. He would walk around the kitchen and watch the help prepare and cook the food.

"If he sensed someone was cooking with negative thought forms or emotions he would immediately kick them out of the kitchen," Jason said. "This was done to maintain the purity of the energy of the food".

Have you ever eaten something in a restaurant that later made you sick?

Perhaps the food was bad. Absolutely, sometimes we get ill because of contamination.

Or perhaps it's something else.

"Maybe you're just picking up on the chef's energy that has been transferred to the food," Jason said. "In fact, this is a very ancient practice. It is called the sacrificial lamb.

"The Healing Begins"

"In Biblical times when someone was sick they would conduct a ceremony to transfer this sickness to a new host. This new host was an animal. The animal was then ceremonially sacrificed so this sickness would die with the animal."

If someone found that animal and ate it they would in turn inherit that sickness.

"This energetic quality of the food and water is quite important for our spiritual growth, vitality and health," Jason said.

"This quality actually comes from the Sun. It's the amount of light collected during the growth of the food. When we consume the food we are capturing this light stored within it.

"This is essential and it is mostly missing from our food. This light feeds our energetic bodies and awakens our spirit."

Water is the same.

"In fact, water is like little solar batteries collecting and storing light," he said. "When we drink the right water we are actually drinking pure light energy.

"Once we disconnect from nature we disconnect from source, which manifests here through light. That's why the Egyptian god Ra is known as the sun and the source. This is why Akhenaten made Aten, the solar god, the prime deity.

"This is why the ancient gods where called "Sun" Gods."

Even the air we breathe has been compromised.

"They told me that powers in the world (government or the military industrial complex) have been putting chemicals and metals in the air that are creating turmoil with our environment and biological systems," he said.

Jason was also taught about the silent waves of energy that are also being used to compromise us.

"This is what we know as EMF, ELF, and other broadcast bands," he said. "These frequencies are affecting our mind and have also been altering our biological system right down to the cellular level."

One night Jason was taken out of his body so that he could witness a broadcast signal.

"This was the weirdest thing," he said. "It was like my conscious-

Forbidden Knowledge

ness was ascending through an EMF band or broadcast frequencies like a radio.

"We stopped at a broadcast that I was supposed to witness. It sounded like I was listening to a radio show with two hosts rambling back and forth. The content of what they were saying was the lowest of the low brow content. It was like hearing the ramblings of 4-year-old child, who just learned how to swear. They were making fart jokes and burping and saying the weirdest things.

"When I came out of this experience the first thing I thought was, 'no wonder there are so many idiots out there.' It was like they were purposely broadcasting the lowest mental consciousness possible out into the world to subliminally program the population."

One of the biggest problems we now face is the massive infrastructure of millions of cell towers set up around the world.

"Frequencies being sent by these towers can do quite a lot of damage to us," Jason said. "These silent weapons can manipulate our brain waves and emotions."

Who knows what other capabilities these towers hold?

"But many people are starting to figure this out," he said.

Jason suggests readers should examine the work of Dr. Magda Havas, an Associate Professor of Environmental and Resource studies at Trent University near Peterborough, Ontario. Her work centers on the biological effects of environmental contaminants.

Since the 1990s, her research has concentrated on the biological effects of electromagnetic pollution, including radio frequency radiation, electromagnetic fields and dirty electricity.

The beings also told Jason there were other conscious forms of energy living underground.

"As we walk on the Earth these beings have access to pull down our energy to feed them," Jason said. "It's like underground vampirism."

Although Jason never received any more information about the underground beings, one day he found himself traveling through the dimensions below his feet.

"As I was passing lower through the dimensions I passed a level of very dark beings," he said. "They almost resembled black tar that

"The Healing Begins"

was moving and conscious.

"I just got a sense of it and continued my decent deeper into the Earth's realms."

After learning about these problems Jason was shown how to strengthen himself so he could step away from these lower energies.

It was at this point when Jason received another message.

"You need to learn Qigong."

Jason didn't have to look very far. At that time his cousin Saundra was practicing and taking classes in Qigong.

"I jumped at the opportunity to attend these classes with her because I knew this was my first step at healing," Jason said.

Saundra is actually Jason's mother's first cousin and she is the gifted clairvoyant of the family. She has the ability to channel messages and visions.

On day Jason received a very strange but illuminating message from Saundra. It was around the same time his controlled astral journeys began.

"We went for a family lunch and I sat across from her at the table," Jason said. "Saundra knew nothing about my experiences at the time."

As they sat suddenly Saundra stared at him and then began to channel.

"She told me that I was being awakened," Jason said. "Then she said that I was a being from another star system and that I was at war with a race of beings called the Reptilians."

Jason just stared at her and listened to her message. It was mind blowing.

"She didn't know anything about what I had been through," he said. "I looked at her and told her she was the coolest person in the family."

Jason then confided in her. He told her what had been happening to him. His 23rd birthday was coming up so Saundra decided to take him to a local Psychic Fair.

At the fair, she offered to buy him a spirit photo for his birthday gift. This was not the typical aura photo booth. Your picture was

Forbidden Knowledge

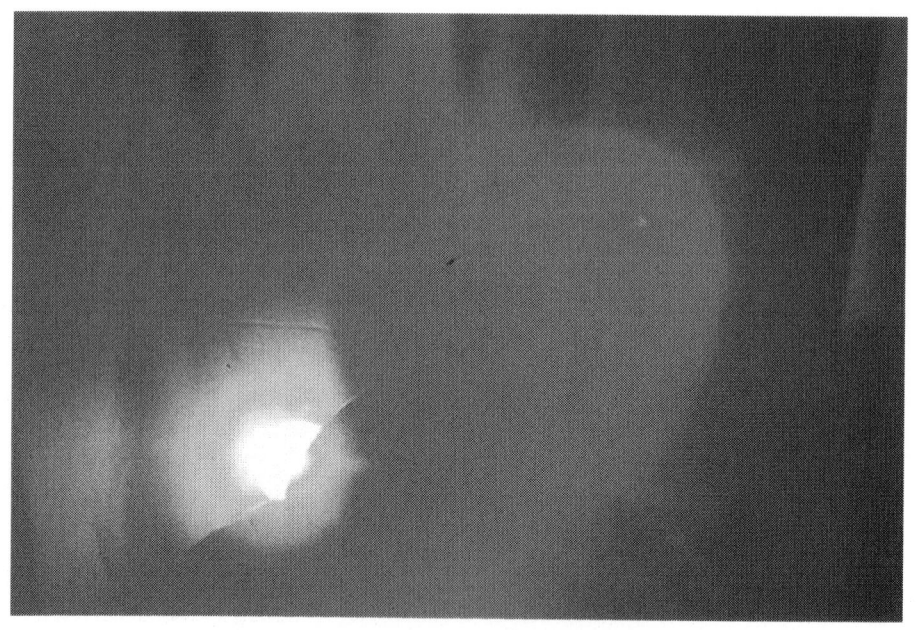

Original picture of Jason's spirit photo.

taken in a dark room using various filters on the camera to catch energies in the room with you.

The booth where the spirit photos were taken was basically a dark room covered with very thick velvet draping so zero light could enter. The booth's framing was done in heavy copper pipes so no energies could enter or leave the enclosure.

"The photographer used a really expensive camera with special filters that allowed you to see the energies around you when your photo was taken," Jason said. "You're supposed to see sparks or outlines of beings behind you."

Jason entered the booth and the woman snapped his picture.

"She looked at her camera and told me that she needed to take another photo because her camera wasn't working properly," Jason said.

The woman snapped another photo and then stared at it when it was developed.

"She asked me to leave the booth so another person could have

"The Healing Begins"

Enhanced picture of Jason's spirit photo showing a smiling being.

their photo taken," Jason said.

The woman looked at the picture taken of the other person and it was fine.

"She apologized and said her camera was now working again so I went in for another go," Jason said.

Once again she looked concerned and asked him to step out of the booth because she needed to talk to him.

"Now remember we're complete strangers but the first thing she asked me was if I heard voices," Jason said.

He jokingly replied, "Don't we all."

The woman then asked him if he meditated.

"Then she asked, 'Who are you? What do you do?'"

Jason told her that he really didn't do anything.

Then she showed him the photo she had taken of him.

"The photo showed the entire room inside the booth but you couldn't see any detail of anything," Jason said. "I wasn't even there.

Forbidden Knowledge

"Every other person, who went into the booth, had their picture taken and you could clearly make out every detail of their face and body with the addition of sparks around them. But there was nothing in my photos. They were completely blanked out with energy.

"She then told me that in all her years of taking spirit photos she had never seen a picture like this. She asked me if she could keep one of them and she gave me another copy."

It was at that moment that Jason realized that he might actually be different than most people. More life changes would soon happen once Jason began doing Qigong.

Interestingly, by the time "Forbidden Knowledge" was being written Jason took another look at the photo and decided to use Photoshop technology to enhance it. To his amazement, a peculiar funny face of what appears to be a smiling being could clearly be seen in the photo.

Also, although it's impossible to see this in the photo, using other variations of light and contrast enhancements of the original photo, there appears to be several different Egyptian-like figures within it. At least there seems to be when you make an effort to relax your eyes.

Qigong translates to 'Energy Movements' or 'Life Energy Cultivation'. This ancient martial arts practice comes from China and utilizes postures, meditation and breath work for health and spiritual growth. As the body and the mind enter into this practice you become connected to the life force energies of the universe. You allow this force to flow through your body, which stimulates your biological and spiritual systems.

Jason practiced every day. He became obsessed with it. In fact, Qigong basically took over his life.

"I practiced every single day, morning, noon and night," he said

Finally, after about a year, something clicked.

"I began to actually feel energy moving through my body," he said. "When I put my hands together it was like they were two magnets. I felt the energy moving between them.

"I was sensitized to the energy that was flowing through my

body. I could feel the acupuncture points running through my body. If I ate something that didn't agree with me I could feel various points on my body start to react with pain.

THE STRANGE TEXT

When Jason first started receiving the messages about our food, water, EMF, Aliens and astral beings he didn't know who to talk to about it.

"The only people, who would listen to me, were my friends," he said. "I started to talk to them about all these crazy topics. It was the only thing I wanted to discuss with them."

Jason soon realized these topics made his friends uncomfortable. They also started to look at him as if he was crazy.

"I just had all these things bottled up inside of me. I had to tell the people closest to me," Jason said.

Unfortunately, Jason could see that after a while his friends started to distance themselves from him.

"When I look back now I wonder why I ever opened myself up and exposed this type of craziness," Jason said.

But to make his paranoia worse, one night he received a chilling text message on his cell phone. There wasn't a number for this contact. There wasn't even a number at all. It was five strange symbols that showed up on his call display.

The message then read.

"We are watching you and listening to you. You better stop talking about us. There will be consequences."

Jason was absolutely freaked out. He deleted the message immediately.

"This really messed with my head," he said. "After that message I stopped talking crazy to my friends and just tried to be normal Jason again."

Jason hoped this message was just a prank pulled by one of his friends. But how did they get those strange symbols to show up on his phone?

Forbidden Knowledge

Today, nobody has ever admitted to him that they sent him this alarming text.

Jason often had a difficult time keeping these topics bottled inside of him. One night his father noticed he was distressed about something.

"Unable to hold it in anymore I burst out in tears and emotion," Jason said.

Jason told him what had been happening to him and how he was able to have out of body experiences.

"I also told him about the beings," Jason said. "He was stunned. He tried to calm me down. But he really didn't say too much to me."

But his father begged him to see a psychiatrist.

"I flatly refused and was actually quite hurt and insulted by this suggestion," Jason said. "But looking back I see how from his perspective why he wanted this for me."

A few days later Jason was back at his father's house and was using his computer when he noticed his father had bookmarked many pages dealing with schizophrenia.

"I knew then that I couldn't share these experiences again with people who didn't have a solid background in this subject," Jason said.

"It really made me think of how Experiencers are treated in this society. I can only imagine an Experiencer sharing their story with their parents and the next thing they know they're on heavy medication and told something is wrong with them or that the devil is influencing them."

How fearful are we of seeing outside our narrow view of reality?

"Maybe this is exactly the programming that was put into place by beings with agendas to keep us in this false reality," Jason said.

Never question authority.

Never think for yourself.

Never go against the powers in control.

"We have to be kept in line and obedient in order for our society to travel down a predetermined path chosen for us by an unseen hand," Jason said.

"The Healing Begins"

DRIVEN TO HEALERS

Ever since Jason received the message "you need to heal yourself" from the beings he found himself driven to seek healing and teachings from many alternative healers, shamans and gurus.

"If there was a special healer coming into town I would book a healing with them," Jason said. "I would experience many different forms of energy and spiritual healing from many different types of healers.

"These were eye-opening experiences. I sensed and felt what they were doing and how they would be doing it. What shocked me was what I started to experience with some of these healers.

"Instead of them healing me they were actually dumping their karma and heavy energies on me. I felt like a sponge. It was as if I was going to them so that I could clear them."

Jason often left these sessions feeling terribly sick and filled with heavy energies and entities.

"I would go home to meditate and do Qigong," Jason said.

He had many questions.

Why was he being sent to these so-called masters?

Why was he paying them large sums of money and taking on their garbage?

"The beings working with me explained that I needed to know how healing worked and what healing actually was," Jason said. "It was like I was being shown behind the scenes of how these healers operated."

The beings told him that he wouldn't be able to heal anyone unless he healed himself first.

"This was the lesson," Jason said. "These healers did not do their own work. This is the teaching. You are the filter of creative light consciousness. You move this energy through your mental, emotional, spiritual and physical bodies.

"Then this energy is projected outward to the universe or to the would-be recipient of this energy. If you are blocked or carry any heavy energies, thought forms, karma, or entities they can then be transferred to anyone open to receive your energies.

"Many people just say their energies are good because they are focused on love and light or they are working with an ascended master. But love, light or any being cannot hide what they hold deep within them. In fact, it will just amplify what you are trying to suppress."

So how can you heal someone when you still have work to do on yourself?

"There are channels of energy, which flow through you all the time," Jason explained.

What if these channels are small?

What if there are points on these channels that are blocked?

How will that affect the flow and nature of your energy and your health?

"We need to clean these pathways so that light can flow through without constriction," Jason explained. "These channels fill your vessel with life giving energies from the nature around you."

Picture yourself as a vessel, which carries light energies of source creation.

What if you had a mirror that could show you this vessel and what you're carrying within it?

Would you be happy with the results?

"Most people walking this planet look as if their vessel has a layer of clay formed around it and this vessel is filled with a mixture closely resembling mud," Jason said. "Not a very pretty picture and not what people would like to hear or admit."

Consider this visual example. Take a bottle of coke and a bottle of water.

Which one do you think holds more light?

"This is the healing journey," Jason explained. "How do we transform the darkness we carry into light? How do we become clear like the bottle of water?"

It's only through healing that we can open ourselves up to higher energies and beings.

"You have to be in the right resonance and energy structure to connect and channel these higher energies," he explained. "These higher beings can only channel through you if your energy bodies are strong enough to hold their consciousness fields.

"We also have to be very aware of what type of energy we are connected to or channeling. There are many psychics and channelers connected to very low beings in the astral realms. These beings connect to these channelers telepathically through their mental bodies.

"Remember there is a lot of deception out there and the information being provided is filtered through their perception of reality. This reality is the reality of what we carry. We see the world through our wounds."

Several channelers recently have come forward revealing they have been deceived and that they're deeply sorry for the messages they brought forward.

"They discovered they were under mind control experiments and the messages they were receiving was disinformation designed to fit a narrative and agenda," Jason said. "These types of events have ruined peoples lives and credibility.

"As we go on the healing journey we slowly release these sick and stagnated energies deep within us. As we do this we start to replace and replenish ourselves with pure energies from source. This process starts building and strengthening all your bodies.

"The clearer you become the more you allow light consciousness to flow through you in greater quality and quantity. This is a building process that changes the nature of your consciousness at its deepest level."

Forbidden Knowledge

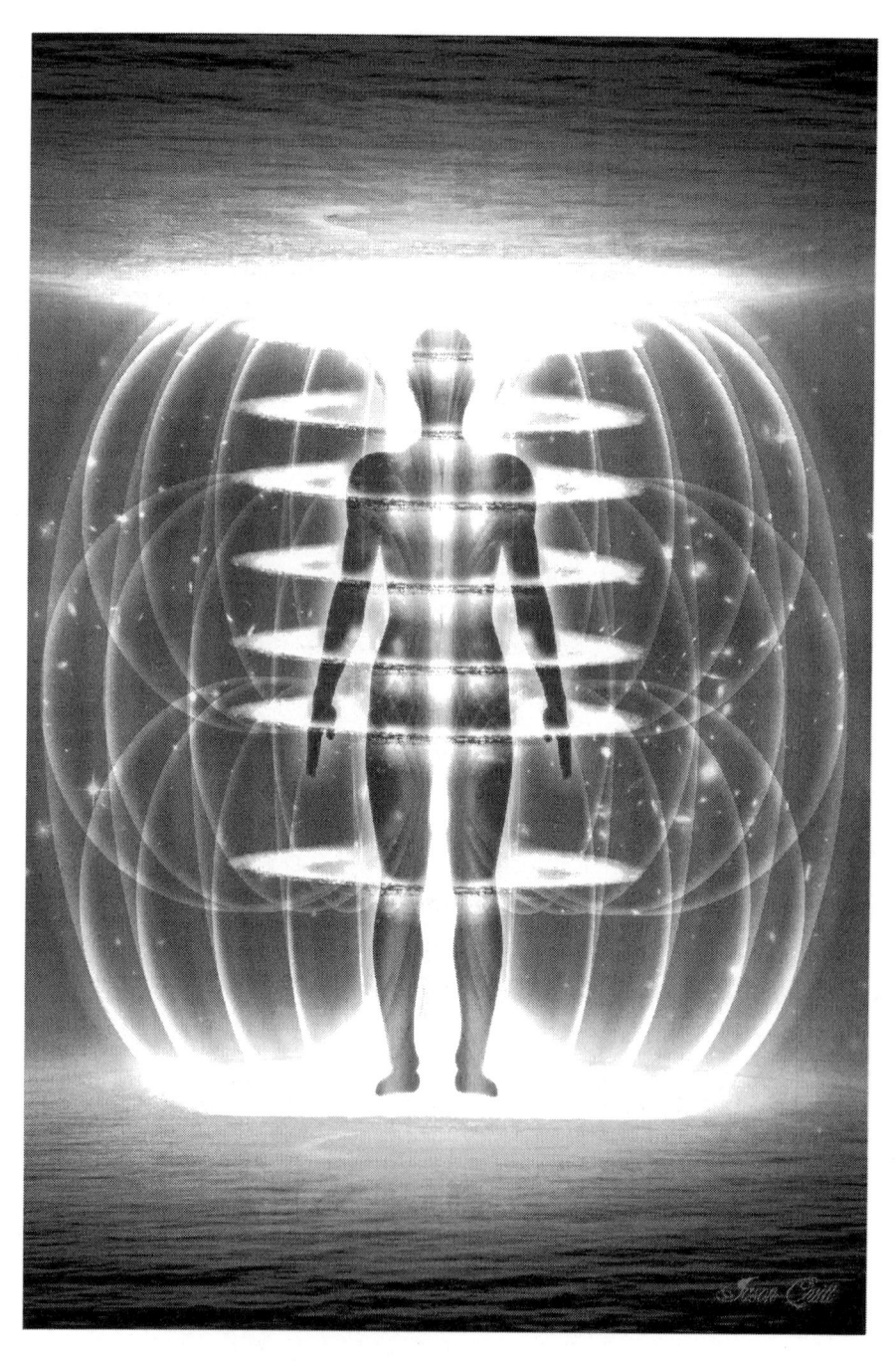

Jason Quitt's original artwork of the energy bodies.

Jason Quitt's original artwork of the chakra systems.

Forbidden Knowledge

"What you seek is seeking you."

- Rumi

Chapter 6
"Meeting Thoth"

It wasn't long before Jason knew he was absolutely destined for a life he couldn't have possibly imagined.

He was healing his body through unorthodox measures and having the most incredible out of body time traveling experiences with beings he still hadn't clearly seen.

What came next was truly life changing.

Jason decided to attend the annual health show in Toronto. As he walked down the aisles he came upon a booth where a secret Russian stone called Shungite was being sold.

These stones are said to be at least 2 billion years old and are alleged to contain very powerful antioxidant properties. The energies within this ancient stone are said to absorb and eliminate anything that presents a health hazard to human life.

"There was a picture at this booth of an Egyptian Pharaoh standing and holding rods in his hands," Jason said. "This drew my attention right in."

Marz, the owner of this booth, handed a set of these rods to Jason and he held them in his hands just like the Pharaoh in the picture.

"When I grabbed them I instantly felt a surge of energy circulating through my body," Jason said. "I knew the feeling well. It was the same feeling I have when I do Qigong."

Jason bought the rods and began using them at home. Once again his life took another dramatic turn. By now his health had improved remarkably since being consumed by the energy martial arts.

Jason practiced daily with the rods.

"When I held them I would get severe pain in my body in different places," Jason said. "I would then move my arms in various positions. When my arms ended up in the correct position I'd feel the energy travel to where the pain was.

"I would hold that position. The pain would increase but eventually it would feel as if the energy was pushing my pain right out of my body."

Jason woke every morning with a different pain and used the rods and did Qigong.

"I was actually doing my own healing," Jason said. "Just like the beings told me I had to do."

One night, a new being came to him.

It was an Egyptian Pharaoh.

"I was transported to an Egyptian temple and this Pharaoh stood in front of me and demonstrated various postures and different ways of holding my arms and hands," Jason said. "I copied his posture and when I did it would feel as if something would open above my head and warm Sun-like energy would suddenly flow throughout my entire body.

"This energy was so powerful that it felt as if everything in my body was vibrating intensely. When I woke up back in my bed I would still be holding my arms in the same position. I could still feel the currents of energy running through my body."

Jason was transported almost every night to a temple. Each time various Egyptian Pharaohs placed him in different postures.

"I basically copied what they were doing," Jason said. "Whatever they did, I did. There was no verbal communication. It was just postures."

For those who happen to own Egyptian paintings or artwork you

"Meeting Thoth"

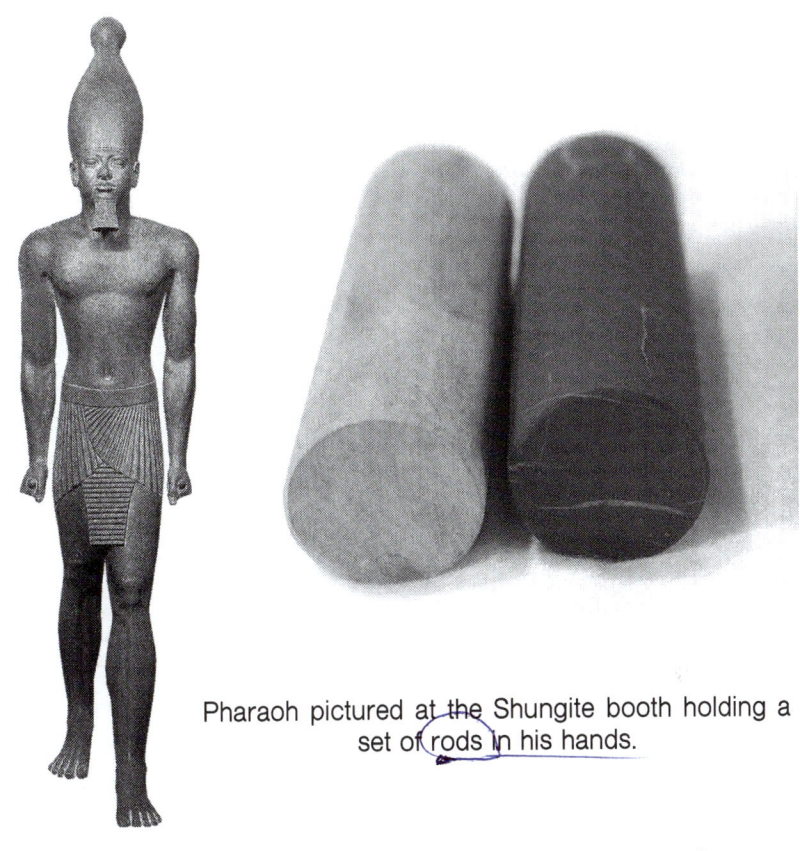

Pharaoh pictured at the Shungite booth holding a set of rods in his hands.

will notice the figures often seem to be standing or posed in a specific way with their hands and arms also held in a precise manner.

Jason was taught hundreds of different Egyptian energy poses during these night time experiences.

"It was almost as if I was being trained and awakened for my true potential," he said. "Their poses were straight out of the paintings I'd seen."

Jason began documenting all of the poses he learned.

"I went to libraries and took out Egyptian books and scanned all of the different postures," he said.

He compiled everything he could and took what he had to Saundra and explained what had been happening to him.

"She would channel the meanings of the postures and help me put them in the correct order," Jason said. "I practiced these postures day and night to familiarize myself to these new energies."

57

Forbidden Knowledge

This new practice also started to overtake Jason's Qigong practice.

"I felt the Egyptian postures had a much greater affect on me," he explained. "I literally felt my body's energetic system changing the more I practiced."

One night during one of his temple experiences he was introduced to Thoth. Jason was about 25 at the time.

According to mainstream historians and archaeologists on ancient Egyptian culture and religion, Thoth was considered to be the God of writing and knowledge. Ancient Egyptians believed he gave them the gift of hieroglyphic writing. He was also connected to the moon.

In drawings, Thoth is depicted as having a body of a man but a head of a bird.

Egyptian God Thoth.

But when Jason encountered him he resembled an old man. He was in physical form and wore a robe.

Despite this appearance Jason knew it was Thoth.

Thoth proceeded to take Jason to a temple during his astral time traveling experiences.

"His voice was so deep. It almost reverberated off the walls of the temple," Jason said. "He took me down a corridor. As he led me he talked but it was more like he was praying."

During this initial experience Jason found himself walking down a long hallway lit with candles. Although he can't be certain, he could very well have been walking along a corridor inside one of

"Meeting Thoth"

Jason's vision of Osiris with a bulls head in a sarcophagus.

the pyramids.

Ancient Egyptian records suggest Thoth played many vital and prominent roles in Egyptian mythology such as maintaining the universe, and being one of the two deities (the other being "Ma'at") who stood on either side of "Solar deity" Ra's boat. In later history, Thoth became heavily associated with the arbitration of godly disputes, the arts of magic, the system of writing, the development of science, and the judgment of the dead.

During one of Jason's experiences, Thoth led him into a chamber and they stood in front of an open sarcophagus.

Jason immediately knew whom he was staring at.

It was Osiris.

He had a human body but the head of a bull.

"But for some reason his legs had been cut off at the knees," Jason said.

History suggests the ancient Egyptians considered Osiris to be one of their major deities. He was the god of the after life and the underworld and judge of the dead. He was also considered the god of resurrection and regeneration.

Although he was sometimes depicted with a bull head most of the time he was drawn as a green-skinned or black-skinned man with a Pharaoh's beard, partially mummy-wrapped at his legs and wearing a distinctive crown with two large ostrich feathers on either side.

The Kings of Egypt were associated with Osiris in death and as Osiris rose from the dead they would also rise with him and inherit eternal life through a process of imitative magic.

Osiris was also depicted as a green-skinned or black-skinned man with a beard.

Jason was in awe of Osiris.

He also felt a strong connection to him. It was as if his energy was resonating with Osiris.

According to ancient text and the earliest records, Osiris was slain by an evil King known as Set. But Egyptians believed Osiris' power was so great that he was able to resurrect. This belief led initially to Pharaohs and those who could afford it to undergo mummification upon death so they could have eternal life.

Thoth prayed and removed jewelry from Osiris and placed it on Jason. Thoth wasn't a spirit. He was physically present during all of Jason's temple experiences.

"It seemed like a kind of initiation," Jason said. "I felt extremely special and privileged. A very sacred and ancient feeling overtook me. It was like I was being reconnected with something I had lost.

"Meeting Thoth"

Like I was a Pharaoh retracing his steps through this initiation."

Another journey felt like a graduation ceremony. In this journey Thoth handed him a brass cylinder and told him to open it.

"When I opened this cylinder an incredibly powerful and beautiful sound came out." Jason said. "It sounded like millions of people were chanting all at once. That's the only way I can describe it.

"The sound was so powerful. It felt as if at that moment every atom in my body had been cracked open to allow this sound in."

When Jason woke from this journey he was overcome with emotion.

"I sat up in bed and balled my eyes out," he said. "It was as if my body had been shattered by the experience. But these were tears of joy, tears of letting go of past wounds so that I could step into my future."

The next evening Thoth took him to a building that resembled a storing house.

"He handed me various scrolls and I was told I had been re-activated again as a Pharaoh and that I now carried all of the energies and history of Egypt," Jason said.

The phrase "re-activated" was interesting. It implied that Jason had once been a Pharaoh.

Using this new-found knowledge, Jason not only continued to heal himself but by 2007 was teaching Egyptian posturing classes. He also wrote a book called "Egyptian Postures of Power - Ancient Qigong System"

"I was given the clear message that what I had learned was very important and it was vital to share with anyone who wanted to obtain this knowledge," Jason said. "It was as if I became the vessel to activate these energies to mankind through the ancient practice of the Egyptian postures."

Jason received the following message when he was compiling the Egyptian Postures book.

"We have seen the planet you call Earth go through many stages in her development. Some would say that she is tottering upon disaster but we upon the other elemental planes know it is part of the evolution necessary for the expanding life forms to continue

Forbidden Knowledge

Jason demonstrating one of hundreds of the Egyptian postures.

on their spiritual journey of becoming. There are some children of Earth who have reincarnated here, and now act as messengers of the light to help lead those out of the darkness."

What this all means – and what Jason has been told is that he is one such evolved soul whose history began not on Earth but on another star system.

He has had many incarnations in Lemuria, Atlantis, and also in Egypt where he led the mystery schools of the Pharaohs.

Only those of royal bloodlines were trained in these schools.

Saundra and Jason - cousins in this lifetime - were brother and sister in ancient Egypt. Together, they taught and healed in the Egyptian School of the Eternal Life Force. They have recognized their commitment to this world and have remembered the Egyptian Postures of Power Qigong.

"These ancient techniques are well suited for our modern times," Jason said. "Egyptian Power Qigong assists in physical healing, psychic

"Meeting Thoth"

Jason demonstrating Egyptian postures on a beach in Florida.

retuning, and many ways to connect your life force to the supreme cosmic level of energy so you may fulfill your highest destiny paths."

For those reading this book, the idea that ancient Egyptian postures can benefit our wellbeing might seem difficult to understand.

But Jason hopes the following will provide some clarity to the concept.

"We live in an open energy system where we are constantly receiving, transmitting, connecting and communicating with our inner and outer worlds through our chakras, channels, and energetic bodies," Jason explained. "Everything that we are and everything that we hold, either positive or negative, is transmitted out into the universe, and like a great mirror, the energies of the universe are transmitted back.

"When we are walking in our highest state our energies are connected and aligned in perfect harmony with the natural flows of the universe. Being in this alignment strengthens, heals, transforms, and expands our consciousness to new levels. These natural flows of energy regulate and synchronize all our internal clocks and body functions.

"When we are not connected and aligned to the natural flows of energy, our energies start to weaken and we turn to other sources of energy to fulfill our needs through attachments, addictions, and obsessions. These do not follow the natural rhythms of energy needed to maintain health and vitality."

Over time these energies manifest as all types of symptoms and disease.

"Our bodies are literally big antennas of oscillating frequencies," Jason said. "The way we think, our belief systems, and our lifestyles affect what frequencies we put out into the universe. Unfortunately today most of our energetic systems are affected and even shut down just by living in this modern world consciousness.

"This is because the world we live in today is based on economy, capitalism, resources, and fundamentalist religion. These go against the natural flows of energy which then leads to destruction and chaos. These energies are reflected into our energy fields because it is of our own creation.

"We also carry with us all the memories and energies from all our past and future lives within our energetic systems. Depending on how much we carry negatively and positively, it affects our connection to these universal forces. By healing ourselves, we move closer to the natural order and balance of energies.

"We have forgotten that we are a microcosm of the macrocosm. Our bodies are specifically designed with sacred geometry and mathematical ratios that are reflected in nature."

Jason said the geometry of our bodies is very important for us to understand.

"When our bodies enter into a posture or mudra we are shifting and connecting ourselves to specific energy systems through the laws of resonance," Jason explained. "With all the Earth changes that are happening, it is very important for us to integrate these changes within us so we may stay grounded and balanced, no matter what is going on in our lives."

"Meeting Thoth"

Think of each posture as a unique vibration that creates an energetic field around the body.

"When done in a specific order you are consciously building unique energetic structures around your body," Jason said. "These vibrations are like a harmonic code sending music out into the cosmos.

"I believe we are here in this life to experience our purpose and live out our karma so we may evolve and ascend into higher planes of existence. When one holds onto past experiences, thought forms, traumas, emotions, etc, they unknowingly weigh down and cause havoc on current life situations and future life paths."

The ancient Egyptians believed when you died your spirit would be brought to the throne of the gods to be judged.

"This was done by weighing the heart of the deceased on a scale with the feather of truth," he said. "If your heart was heavier then the feather you were sent back to the world to try again. If your heart was equal the feather you were given a choice to ascend to become one of the gods or go back into the world as a pharaoh of the gods.

"This belief is very important to an evolving spirit. Its purpose was to teach that what you carry in your heart determines your life path. If you carry fear, anger, guilt, hate, etc, you would not ascend. Only a pure heart that carries truth and love will be on the right path.

"By practicing these postures, we are consciously moving and releasing lifetimes of heavy and stagnant energies that are holding us in negative patterns. The more we practice the more we shift and refine our energies so we may move into higher realms of experience."

But these postures are not just Egyptian. In fact, they date back further than our history.

"The history goes back through many eons, dimensions and star systems," Jason said." These postures were brought to our early civilization originally from the Pleiades and were used in Atlantis when things started to move out of balance."

The Pleiades is a star cluster is the constellation Taurus and among the nearest star clusters to Earth located about 500 light

Forbidden Knowledge

The Pleiades star system.

years from our planet. There is evidence this star cluster was known to virtually all of the ancient cultures, including the Mayans, the Aztecs, ancient Chinese and Japanese, Native American and Canadians and of course, the ancient Egyptians.

According to ancient alien theorists and some UFOlogists, the star system is also the home of an extraterrestrial species known as the Pleiadians.

Jason agrees with the ancient alien theory that mankind wasn't the product of natural evolution but was created as a result of the genetic manipulation of the then native Earth hominids with DNA of extraterrestrial origins.

Jason said the postures were channeled to us by the original star ancestors that brought mankind to earth.

"The purpose of the postures was to change the vibration of human and planetary consciousness to prevent future catastrophes,"

"Meeting Thoth"

Jason said. "Since the human race is once again heading down this path, these postures have been brought back to help those who practice to escape the negative influences and shift of the environment around them.

"Through individual practice these postures have the power to teach the secrets of ascension. The postures have been reformulated for the human nervous system. This is because each civilization has been slightly modified. The ones that are ready to receive these energies will be easily drawn to these frequencies."

Jason believes that this practice is a great gift to Earth and humanity. It is one of the top reasons he is back in this life time.

"I feel it's my mission to re-establish and teach this lost knowledge so that we can heal ourselves, our environment and our past which will enable us to create a new future," he said.

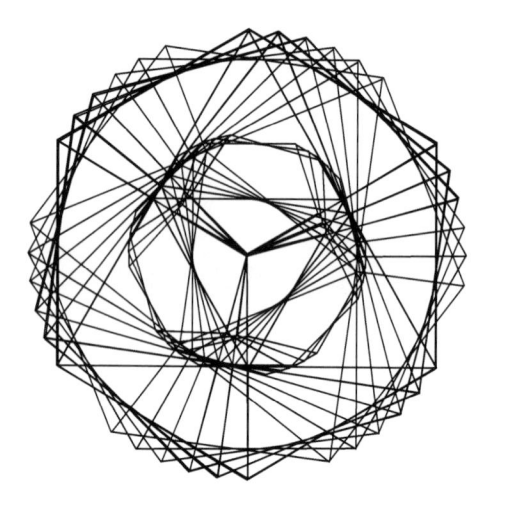

"The infinite vibratory levels, the dimensions of interconnectedness are without end. There is nothing independent. All beings and things are residents in your awareness."

- Alex Grey

Chapter 7
"The Spiders Web"

In August 2006 Jason was awoken one night by a very strong voice.
"Do you want to know your past lives?"
Needless to say he was startled.
"No," Jason replied.
He took a few breaths to calm down.
Then he opened his eyes.
Standing in the far corner of his bedroom was a hooded being. This was a different being than the "cloaked" ones he had previously encountered.
He immediately changed his answer.
"Yes, I would like to know my past lives," he blurted out, still amazed by what he was seeing.
This being then slowly walked towards him.
It appeared to be between 4 to 5 feet tall. Jason never saw any of its facial features or its body because he wore a long robe with a hood, possibly dark brown in color. The communication frequency of this being was extremely high.
"It was like a sharp ringing in my ears," Jason said. "I asked them why they wore a robe and their answer was quite interesting.
"They said their energies were so strong that if they removed

their garments at my level of consciousness that I would be instantly vaporized by their brilliance."

With each step the being took towards him Jason felt his vibration intensify.

This being then walked to the wall behind his bed and began writing vigorously on it.

"I could hear the writing as if he was literally scratching it into the wall," Jason said. "He then sat on the bed and asked me to repeat a mantra. He made me repeat it multiple times until I memorized it and got it right.

"Then he started to speak."

This is the message he gave to him.

"The writing that was left on the wall is called an "ectotrain." It was put there temporarily but will be available longer than time. It can be transferred to another location at any time. It is connected to the etheric 7 of parallel universes, which acts as a gateway to all realms.

"It can be accessed through meditation time, also through dream-time. It can also be accessed before bedtime by putting one's hands on the surface and meditate with a secret mantra, then take your hands gently and put them on your third eye, that so the energy will be made accessible during dream-time. This writing was a gift to you. It is a link between two worlds."

Jason was then given another incredible message.

He was told the "entity" known as "Jason" had reincarnated in this world many times. Most times he has not lived till maturity because other beings have stopped him from living in many life times.

In one lifetime back in China he was swept away by a river. In another lifetime he was killed in battle with a sword. That lifetime the entity was a hot headed young man and his energy was not used properly. It was used to fight wars, and not to heal.

Jason later recalled some of these past lives.

"The Spiders Web"

During a past life in Japan, he was a powerful master swordsman, who worked for a Shogun.

"I led many into battle to conquer territories," he said. "I carried a very long blade and was a master in the martial arts.

"I remember one of these battles. It was like right out of the movies. There was a solider charging his horse right at me on the battlefield. Without fear I started to run towards him with my blade held back behind me.

"Right when I got in striking distance I swung my sword around my body upwards slicing the horse's head off at its mid neck. As the solider started to fly forward I jumped in the air and followed the sword through him. In one movement I had taken down the horse and the rider.

"When this memory came back to me all I could think was what a bad ass I used to be. But it was just another lifetime that I had misused my gifts to fight wars."

In this life the entity (Jason) has learned from these past experiences and now shuns away from violence and negative energies.

In Jason's current life he has been told to always know that he is surrounded and connected to the source at all times.

Not only should he feel connected to the source by the aligning of the charkas but also connected to an ethereal web of light that

Robed being that revealed this information to Jason.

links all the other worlds together.

The being told him that his comrades and families wait for him there. He would also be able to access them through his meditations and dream time.

Messages would come to him to show him the path at hand that he must achieve.

The being then provided another message.

"Eons and eons before time began many lands many universes were drawn together by the "Spiderweb". This Spiderweb was a way for many civilizations many universes to connect and communicate with one another. Unfortunately these threads have been severed deliberately by those who would discover the connection and want to take control of different worlds themselves."

According to this hooded being, these threads were deliberately severed by beings in order to take control of different worlds.

"This is the biggest conspiracy, not just for mankind but the entire universe." Jason said. "Forget whether the government knows about aliens. We have known that for over 50 years."

According to Jason, the creators of this "Great Spider Web" were known only as the "Ancient Builders." They are extremely ancient and are not even part of our current time line.

"It is believed these beings ascended many eons ago," Jason said. "They were extremely powerful and very technologically advanced beyond our comprehension. Their presence was felt through the whole universe. No other species challenged them."

"But now that they are gone the infrastructure they created has now been taken over on many systems."

"Imagine if every planet throughout the universe is connected to each other and there is a communication among all of the civilizations on these planets."

"Then imagine there is a force that comes along and discovers this connection," Jason said. "And this force says, wait a minute, we are at an advanced level that allows us to sever these connections.

"The Spiders Web"

And now we can control entire solar systems.

"That's what happened. Our solar system and many others have been hijacked by these beings. All of these worlds have been cut off from this connection."

The infrastructure of the great "Spiders Web" is etheric in nature. It is a system of portals connected by a grid system that spans time, space and dimension. Through these grids one can travel to all reaches of space, visit other worlds and beings, and even travel through time. Just think of the advanced race of beings that could establish such a system.

Hopi Spider Woman

There are many myths and legends about this great spider's web found in ancient cultures around the world.

Here are some examples.

The Tewa and Hopi have a legend of the Spider Woman, who was sent to Earth by the Great Sun spirit to lead the then pre-humans out of darkness and to another world.

In the creation myths of the Yoruba people of Nigeria and Benin, the gods who lived in the sky would come down and play by descending spider webs that draped from the sky like lacy bridges.

The Maori of New Zealand tell the story of Tawhaki in which his grandmother teaches him that the only way to reach the upper world is by climbing the spider's web that hangs from the sky.

The story is the same in Africa where Anansi, the spider god, learned how to climb the great spider web of the sky to connect heaven and earth.

The Polynesians speak about the ancient spider that used a tridacna shell to form heaven and earth. (It is interesting to note that the tridacna shell is still used today in Christianity in baptism because they are thought to be the symbol of birth.)

The Lakota Indians have a myth of the trickster spider god Iktomi, who spins his own web of mischief from land to land. He is known as the god of new technologies and new languages, with the power to trick gods and mortals alike. It is said that he uses his web to control people like puppets. Many Lakota's consider Iktomi to be the god of the Europeans, who seem to readily follow in his bizarre behavior and self-entrapping tricks.

Lakota Indian spider god Iktomi.

Also the Egyptian teaching of the "Net" puts it all together. In mystical teachings they taught that the uninitiated souls of mankind were bound in a great net unable to move freely. It is only when one is initiated into the higher teachings of the net one can be freed from this bondage and travel the great web freely to any world on the spiritual planes.

So who are the beings responsible for this take over?

According to what the hooded being told Jason, they are known as the Reptilians.

"I was told the Reptilians actually consist of many different ET groups spanning many star systems," Jason explained. "These groups of beings might look vastly different from one another but they are all connected through reptilian genetics back in their evolutionary line.

"In fact, human beings also have this genetic ancestry deep

"The Spiders Web"

within them."

The Reptilians are found on planets throughout the universe.

"But they are way ahead of humanity in terms of technology," Jason said. "They existed long before humankind even developed."

Because of this take over many higher beings from other dimensions and star systems have decided to incarnate here in this time line to heal and reconnect this planet with these universal grids.

"These beings are known as the hybrids of mankind," Jason explained. "Many of them are starting to feel the "reactivations" coming to them from the other realms when they reach a certain age of maturity. This reactivation will start to cause them great satisfactions and dissatisfactions in the Earth bound planes. They will start to look for things to be done and they feel the need to connect with others of their kind to help them in the great path."

When Saundra initially channeled Jason over lunch she told him that he was one of these beings "at war with the Reptilians."

At the time he had no idea what she was talking about.

But he would soon find out.

"The being told me that I was one of a select group of higher dimensional beings chosen to incarnate here on Earth in order to shift the consciousness of the planet," Jason said. "The children born with these gifts become targets of the Reptilians."

"The Reptilians can feel them and know who and where they are. They know these children are incarnated here to expose them and work against them by shifting the consciousness of the beings we come in contact with."

"But many of these children are located and killed before they reach maturity. I have had many previous lives on Earth and I never reached maturity during most of those lives."

As indicated earlier, in some of his lives where he managed to reach maturity, he misused his power.

"My powers were misused to fight many wars," he said.

One night during another meeting with these hooded beings, a male and female arrived. They were roughly his age.

"The female sent a telepathic image into my mind," Jason said.

"She showed me a map of the Earth. I could see lights in different locations all over the world, some brighter than others.

"These lights were where all the higher beings chosen to incarnate here were located on Earth. There were hundreds of them scattered all over the world, but less then a handful had truly mastered their powers."

The male then worked on Jason's energetic field to help free up his energy further.

When they left, Jason realized he wasn't alone. There were others just like him.

"We are here to show humanity how to free itself," Jason said. "To take our sovereignty back and learn the truth about whom we are.

Jason had his latest encounter with a group of Reptilian beings in June 2015. It occurred in a dream-like state where the communication was telepathic.

Essentially, in these communications Jason will be sleeping and dreaming but then he senses a presence. This presence will then "kick" him out of his dream state and thrust him into another state of consciousness that is similar to a dream but actually takes place outside his physical body in an astral plane of existence.

"It's almost like a dream take over," Jason explained. "Suddenly my consciousness will be in this state but my physical body remains in a sleeping state. I still feel as if I'm totally there and present but the experience is being done within my mind.

"You know you're having this experience and you know it's not a dream. When it's over, you wake up."

This encounter occurred just two days before he was scheduled to be one of the 24 guest speakers at the Alien Cosmic Expo in Brantford, Ontario.

The encounter was completely different from what he could have expected. Three Reptilians presented themselves to him in his mind through dream state.

The being, who appeared to be the leader of this group, looked humanoid in appearance.

"He was big and muscular but with green scales and reptilian

"The Spiders Web"

Reptilian beings that visited Jason.

eyes," Jason said.

"The other two looked more dinosaur-like than humanoid. They were very big and muscular but they had a tail. They were almost dragon-like in appearance."

Jason asked several questions of his strange visitors.

Who were they?

The leader replied that his race was known by many names.

"It provided names such as Reptoids, Saurians, Reptilians, Dinoids, Sirians, Raptors and several others I can't recall," Jason said.

Where were they from?

The leader replied Sagittarius.

"I'm guessing he was referring to the constellation," Jason said.

Why had they come to see him?

The leader said that they knew that he had been searching for Akhenaten.

Indeed, at the time of this encounter Jason had been researching this enigmatic pharaoh, who was formerly known as Amenhotep IV. According to some ancient alien theorists, he changed his name in 1347 BC after seeing a UFO in the sky and having a communication with its occupants that instructed him to build a new capital of Egypt. A month later he changed his name.

So why was Jason so interested in Akhenaten?

All will be revealed later in this book.

Suffice to say, ancient Egyptian historians and archaeologists believe Akhenaten was a pharaoh from the 18th dynasty of Egypt. He ruled for 17 years and then died sometime between 1336 BC and 1334 BC. He was known for abandoning traditional Egyptian practices of worshiping many gods and goddesses and ordained that his people worship only the sun god Aten.

Akhenaten was known as the "heretic Pharaoh." But after his death, Egypt not only returned to its former religious practices but Akhenaten's name and existence was basically stricken from all records.

In 1907, a mummy was located in a tomb in a dig led by Edward R. Aryton. Many believed that it was the remains of this unusual pharaoh.

"The Spiders Web"

DNA analysis determined the man buried in the tomb was the father of King Tutankhamen but confirmation that the mummy was Akhenaten remains buried in controversy.

"The leader told me that Akhenaten's remains were actually located back in the 1920s but they have remained hidden in Italy," Jason said. "My best guess is that he was referring to Rome and the Vatican."

For Jason, it had been a very strange visitation.

"For one thing, I never had the sense of any hostility towards me even though I was supposed to be at war with them," he said. "There was no ill intent. It was simply a meeting in order to pass some information to me."

During this encounter the leader told Jason that his race is not even part of our current time line.

"They were from another time line, another space altogether," Jason said.

Essentially, this means they originally came from another universe, which is completely separate from our time line.

Statue of Akhenaton.

"I sensed this being's race was much older than we could even fathom." Jason said.

Just like with humanity, there are good and bad human beings so we need to have this same understanding with regards to extraterrestrials.

"They are not all the same and they each have different motives," Jason said.

According to what Jason has been told, there are two main

groups of Reptilians. One group is highly evolved spiritually and are here to help advance and shift those who are ready. The other Reptilians represent a group of beings with immense power, control and influence over many star systems.

"They believe they have the right to do this because they have been around longer then any of us," Jason was told. "They also believe that they are our ancestors. In fact, many of our ancestors believed they were gods.

"So you can see why they would assert their dominance over different worlds with this type of belief system."

However, not all Reptilians believe in their right to dominate other worlds and civilizations.

According to what Jason has been told, some Reptilians such as the group that visited him and other Reptilian-like species absolutely believe that some of them are being influenced and controlled by some other artificial consciousness and dark force.

"In fact, this AI force is something humanity is getting close to in our time," Jason said.

Interestingly, in early 2016, companies such as Google, Microsoft, Facebook and IBM just to name a few were actively working on AI technology that would soon change the way people used computers and even their mobile devices. Companies have also suggested it won't be too far down the road before AI chips can be inserted in humans to create a sort of "Smart" human.

"Many of us would prefer to steer away from this future," Jason said. "It's called Trans-humanism- merging machines and AI with flesh and blood humans.

"I believe this will be a disaster for mankind just like it has been on many other star systems that I have visited."

In early 2015, Jason time traveled to the year 2700 where humanity was controlled by a common AI presence.

"This system was implemented in everything and everyone," Jason said. "When you walked into a building you could communicate with the building through this AI. It was directly interfaced into your biological system so that you had direct connection with

"The Spiders Web"

it at all times.

It was like having telepathy and being connected to the Internet at the same time all in your mind."

Jason explained that this time line took place after a historical war between two alien species over the control of Earth. He has no idea which aliens but if he were to guess he would suggest the war was between the Reptilians and an Insectoid species.

"After the war it was decided that there would be no government or ruling class and that everything would be controlled by this AI consciousness," Jason said. "When I first woke up from this journey I was really excited by this future. It was so high tech and amazing.

"Then this creeping feeling came over me when I thought about this AI. I started to get the impression that this might not be the best idea for the future of mankind. Fortunately, we have the ability to change our future."

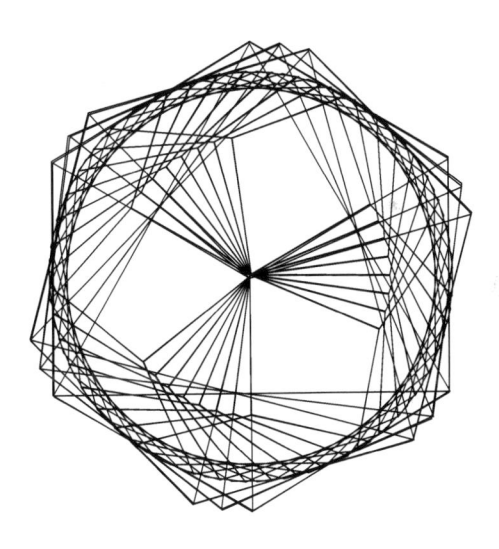

Forbidden Knowledge

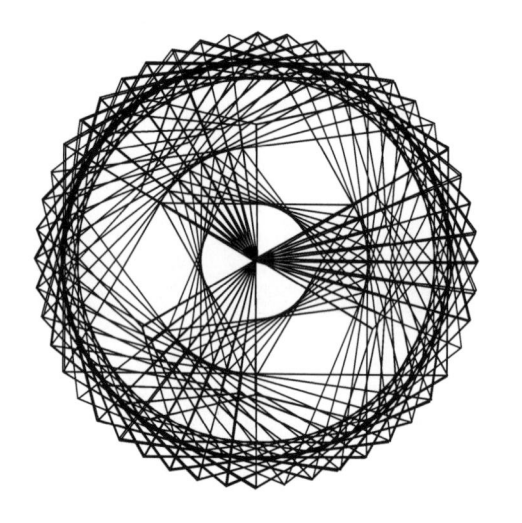

"No one saves us but ourselves.
No one can and no one may.
We ourselves must walk the path."

- Buddha

Chapter 8
"The Shaman Factor"

In 2006, Saundra invited Jason to attend an event with Algonquin Shaman Peter Bernard, who was speaking at her friend's house.

Bernard is from the Algonquins of Pilwakanagan First Nations of Golden Lake, Ontario. Essentially, he believes anyone or anything can heal and that humanity can use the mind and dreams to help heal.

The topics discussed that night during the private teaching resonated on many levels with Jason. Bernard ended his talk by announcing that he would be starting a Shamanism school called "The 8th Fire" to teach his Algonquin Shamanic lineage to anyone interested.

"I didn't even hesitate and signed up for the course with Saundra and her husband Neil," Jason said. "I felt a strong connection to Native Canadian heritage and the truths they have struggled to keep alive. They say when the student is ready the teachers will appear. Well at this point in my life many influential teachers suddenly started to appear on my path."

Jason enjoyed the classes he took at The 8th Fire School of Algonquin Shamanism. But in these early days he could never have imagined how important Peter Barnard would one day be to him, in-

Forbidden Knowledge

cluding how he would eventually save his life nearly a decade later.

The first thing Peter said to the group was, 'before we go forward in this class I will have to kill each and every one of you. Your greatest fear is death so we must overcome that before we get to any teachings.'

"This made me laugh but it was the truth." Jason said. "How could we move forward in anything when we have many patterns and fears preventing us from having our full experience? There were about 30 students in this class and we were all from different walks of life. We were all there to change something in our lives, to learn, and to experience. What an opportunity."

Algonquin Shaman Peter Bernard

During the second day of class Jason learned basic healing techniques using pendulums for chakra healing work.

A woman from the class approached him and asked if his name was Jason.

"I said yes. She felt relieved to find me," Jason explained.

She told him that her "guides" had told her that she needed find "Jason."

They proceeded to work on one another. When they were done their healing work many people surrounded her and asked her questions. This woman was Nora Anderson, a well-known local healer known as "Nora Walks In Spirit"

From the city of Mississauga, Ontario located just west of Toronto, she has been channeling beings of light for nearly 20 years.

Her prophetic visions began in 1987 but her life changed dramatically in 1992 when she was about to have surgery to remove a stomach tumor. The night before her surgery a white light suddenly filled

"The Shaman Factor"

her bedroom. When she tried to speak she started talking in a strange language.

After recovering from surgery she went to a Catholic church in downtown Toronto to talk to somebody about the mysterious occurrence. She was approached by a woman wearing a long white robe with long white hair. A gold cross dangled from a chain around her neck. Nora told her what had happened. The woman explained that she (Nora) had been blessed and gifted with the speaking of the "Fire of the Tongues."

Algonquin Shaman
Nora WALKSINSPIRIT

When Nora told her she didn't understand the words she had spoken, the woman in white asked her to open her mouth. When she did the woman touched her (Nora) tongue with her finger and told her that she was "being gifted" with the "Gift of Interpretation."

Nora was then told to speak. When she did, she spoke in this strange language again except this time she understood everything.

She returned to the church the following day to talk with the woman but she was told no such woman had ever been in the church.

By 2002 Nora began healing others with her energy and by 2008 had begun to travel the world, visiting such sacred sites a Machu Picchu, Sedona, Easter Island, Stonehenge, Mt. Shasta and Egypt to name just a few.

Jason didn't know it at the time but he and Nora would become close friends and that she would play crucial roles in his life.

Overwhelmed with the crowd that had gathered around Nora, Jason quietly started to walk away from the scene.

"As I was walking away I suddenly felt someone kick me full

Forbidden Knowledge

strength in my butt," Jason said. "I flew a foot forward and I turned around but nobody was behind me."

What had just occurred?

When Nora was finished talking to all the people Jason approached her again and explained what had just happened.

Nora started to channel.

"Spirit says that we need to continue to work together in this class," Nora told Jason. "But not just in the class. We need to work together outside the class too. They want us to get together right away."

So they started to work with each other every week.

"I would do healing work on her and she would do healing work on me," he said. "Spirit informed us that our energies were very balanced with one another and that we should only focus on healing each other before we also heal others."

A close friendship developed between them.

"We also became each other's support group," Jason said. "If something happened to us that we could not explain we could meditate on it and find the explanation. If one of us was sick or being energetically affected by other forces, the other one would fix the situation."

The following month they were sitting in class in a circle when Jason suddenly felt something fly across the room and strike him on the side of his arm.

"It felt like a dart and when it hit me the sensation was like someone had dropped a hot ember on my skin," Jason said. "It was quite painful. I instantly turned to Nora and told her what had happened."

Nora looked at him and said, "You just got hit by a dart."

She then calmly picked it off of him with her fingers and threw it on the floor.

"The pain instantly stopped," Jason said. "I was amazed."

What had just happened?

Nora explained this was someone's jealously being directed at him.

It was at that moment this new ability opened for him.

"I could feel these things flying from person to person. Things were being sent unconsciously from other people's thought forms," he said. "When this new ability opened up it took me awhile to figure out how to take these 'darts' off of me when I would be hit. But after awhile I got the hang of it and was able to just pull them off as soon as I was hit."

Jason soon discovered that in order to protect him from these darts he needed to strengthen the shield around his body.

"I did this through Qigong," Jason explained. "The stronger I got energetically the less these things would bother me. Soon I didn't experience them at all because they were no longer able to penetrate my energetic shielding."

Around this time another unique ability also opened up for Jason.

"When I had conversations with people I started to see these etheric strands of light shoot into their heads," Jason said. "It looked like a bright spark was at the end of these strands of light. Different colored orbs and sparks also appeared around the person as they were talking.

"I was witnessing thought forms of intelligence shooting into their minds while they were speaking. When I saw an orb or spark appear beside them it was a higher being connecting with them. This became a common occurrence for me to witness."

One day Peter Bernard asked him to stand in front of the class for a demonstration.

"He asked the class to try to tune into my energy to see what they could pick up from me," he said. "Once the class got their impressions he went around the class and everyone had to say out loud to me what they saw, experienced or felt. The things the students were saying about me were completely outrageous and humorous."

After everyone was done Peter informed the class that they were not reading Jason. They were actually reading themselves and that they needed to work on these things within themselves.

"He went on to explain that we are all a filter; that we see the world through the wounds we carry," Jason said. "Until we heal ourselves of our wounds we will continue to see the world with distorted eyes. This was a truly profound statement."

MEETING SWAMIJI

In July 2006, Jason and his mother were invited by his mother's friend Francine to attend a Puja led by a high spiritual master named Sri Sri Sri Ganapati Sachchidananda Swamiji.

A Puja is a prayer ritual performed by Hindus to host, honor and worship one or more deities or to spiritually celebrate an event. Sometimes it honors or celebrates the presence of special guest(s) or their memories after they pass away.

Jason didn't know anything about the man, who would become his next teacher. He also didn't know anything about this guru's Indian culture or his spiritual practices.

Francine, however, insisted that he and his mother absolutely needed to attend. So they went to the temple located in Mississauga, Ontario.

At the time Jason had no idea Sri Swamiji was known throughout the world and had been conducting tours to spread spirituality through concerts providing healing benefits.

Sri Swamiji would later establish three different feats that ended up in the Guinness Book of Records.

More than 200,000 people in Tenali, Andhra Pradesh (India) on Jan. 31. 2015, chanted the sacred Hindu verse Hanuman Chalisa 27 times each at this global peace event. The previous record had been 128,918 participants

The largest music therapy session at a single location involved 1,824 participants following his instructions for more than two hours at the Sydney Opera House on April 6, 2015.

Also, the longest chanting marathon was achieved by more than 500 participants for 24 continuous hours in Frisco, Texas from July 31 to Aug. 1, 2015

When Jason, his mother and Francine arrived everyone was already inside was singing ancient Sanskrit songs led by Sri Swamiji. They found a place to sit and listened to the music.

"But I really felt out of place," Jason said. "I felt as if I didn't belong there."

"The Shaman Factor"

Sri Sri Sri Ganapati Sachchidananda Swamiji

After the ceremony a beautiful spread of vegetarian food was prepared everybody. Suddenly, people started coming up to them and introduced themselves. Jason began to feel at ease. Everybody was so friendly to them.

But Jason never felt anything special from his first experience with Sri Swamiji, the songs or the ceremony. He simply enjoyed the experience, the music, the people and the food.

About a year later Francine again contacted them. Swamiji had returned. So they attended another ceremony.

Swamiji had yet to arrive by the time Jason, his mother and Francine entered the banquet hall. But as Jason stood inside the hall he suddenly felt something.

"It felt like waves of heat were flowing through the room," Jason said. "Each wave progressively got stronger and stronger. This had a profound affect on me. I couldn't control it.

"Suddenly I felt huge emotion start to bubble up through me and I started to release energy. I could not believe the power that I felt running through my body. And this all happened before Swamiji had entered the building."

Jason later learned that Swamiji always sends his energy to clear the space before he enters any location.

During the ceremony Swamiji placed black ash on their foreheads and talked about opening the spiritual eye, healing and the power of music.

That evening Jason experienced another incredible event.

"As I was falling asleep I was startled by the sounds of blood curdling screams coming from my mother's room," Jason explained. "It sounded like she was being murdered."

Jason jumped out of bed and ran to her room and opened the door. His mother was just sitting in bed, screaming and looking forward.

Jason calmed her down. She explained something had awoken her and when she opened her eyes there was a man standing at the foot of her bed.

"This man was just staring at her and smiling," Jason explained. "This was so real that it only faded away when I burst into the room.

"Till this day she won't put ash on her third eye (spiritual eye on forehead) because she's afraid she will see something like that again."

Jason told his mother that if it ever happened again that she should try to remain calm and not be afraid. Instead, he encouraged to ask questions such as, "Who are you" and "why have you come to see me?"

In 2009, Swamiji came again and this time Jason took Nora and their mutual friend Kevin to the Puja. Once again Jason had an experience.

"As Swamiji played and sang the ancient mantras the sounds felt as if they were like laser beams shooting into the room," Jason said. "They struck me and it felt as if these lasers were doing surgery on me.

"I felt them moving through my body. I also sensed things were being placed in my body. It was like the music was doing the healing work and the initiations all at the same time.

"This was a magical experience."

Swamiji broke off some rose petals at the end of this Puja and gave them to Jason, Francine, Nora and Kevin. They were then told to eat the rose petal.

Several months later Jason found himself transported to Swami-

"The Shaman Factor"

ji's Ashram in the astral realm.

"I remember it being a big celebration," Jason said. "We were all dancing and singing these ancient mantras."

Swamiji walked up to him and hugged him.

"It felt like I had graduated from his school," Jason explained. "He looked me right in the eyes with a big smile and said that he was no longer my guru."

Jason woke from this experience both happy and sad.

"I didn't understand what he meant," Jason said. "I felt like he had left me and that he no longer wanted to be my guru."

Confused with the experience, Jason met Nora and Kevin for lunch and told them about his experience.

"Nora just looked at me, smiled and started to channel," Jason said.

She explained that Swamiji had taught him everything that he could and that he (Jason) was now his own guru.

"Nora said that I needed to let him go but that his energies would always be with me when I needed them," Jason said. "This message brought great peace to my heart knowing that whatever I needed from these experiences I had integrated.

"This would allow new experience and new teachers to come into my life."

THE GHOST CAT

Very early in Jason's awakening a spirit animal appeared to him.

"I started to have very realistic dreams where I could sense I was being watched from outside my bedroom window," Jason said. "I didn't have a good feeling. In fact, it was quite frightening."

These dreams occurred every night until Jason had the courage to look outside his window.

"Waiting for me outside my window was a ferocious white lion," Jason said. "It was growling and scratching the glass, trying franticly to get inside the room."

Jason also sensed the lion was stalking around his house.

In the dream he ran around his house to make sure all the windows were shut and all the doors were locked.

"This lion frightened me so much that I would wake up in a cold sweat with my heart pounding," Jason said. "This dream just kept happening and I would just replay the same events.

"Then for some reason I decided enough was enough, it was time to change this dream."

This time he calmly walked to the front door of the house and opened the door.

"I then lay on the floor, remained very still and played dead," Jason said. "This massive beast slowly walked into the house

White Lioness with cubs that appeared to Jason as his Totem.

and stood over my body. Then it brought its nose down to me and sniffed my face."

Suddenly, Jason realized that standing directly behind the beast were three small white lion cubs.

"I realized then that this lion was a mother," he said. "The lioness then turned around and walked back outside."

Jason awoke from this dream feeling a sense of relief. He had also changed the outcome of the dream. He was also no longer afraid of this lion.

"A couple weeks later I decided to attend one of Nora's gatherings in a park where people would come to hear her channel and do healing," Jason said. "As I walked through the park one of her students looked at me and said, "You have very beautiful lions around you."

Jason was flabbergasted.

"This stopped me dead in my tracks," he said. "I asked the woman if she could describe them to me."

The woman told him that he had a "great big white lion with

"The Shaman Factor"

her cubs" was around him and that she was "very fierce and protective" of her cubs.

"Right then I received conformation from a complete stranger that what I had experienced was real," Jason said. "This is what Native Canadians and Americans would call my totem or spirit animal.

"I was blessed to have them. I would later have experiences where I felt these cubs jump on my bed and snuggle up next to me while I was sleeping.

"This felt incredibly real. I felt the bed move when they jumped onto it. I also felt them jump off of the bed when I woke. But my room was empty and my door was shut. I called them my ghost cats."

THE MADI EXPERIENCE

In April 2007 a unique healer was brought to Toronto by Jason's friends Kathy and Dennis to run a workshop called White Lotus Healing - Psychic Surgery.

Jason had attended their lecture a week before at a Toronto health fair and it fascinated him.

Dr. Madi Nolan, the healer, claimed to be a reincarnated Tibetan Lama and that she had been training her entire life in the spiritual arts.

"She had to have been in her 70s at the time and her stories were completely out of this world," Jason recalled.

Her Tibetan name was Lama Rigzden Chodon Rinpoche and during this Canadian tour she shared her secret self empowerment and knowledge from the part of Tibet known as Shangri La.

Born in the U.S., she claimed

Dr. Madi Nolan

to have entered the world with memories and talents from her previous lives as Lama Rinpoche, also known as a Tulku.

A Tulku is considered to be a reincarnation of a Buddhist master, who, out of his or her compassion for the suffering of sentient beings, has vowed to be reborn to help all beings attain enlightenment.

She claimed to have started speaking Tibetan at two even though she grew up in an English-speaking American family.

At four, she was able to remember her past lives as a Tibetan, and at five, was taken to a Tibetan refuge city in northern India. She was ordained as a Lama and a doctor of Tibetan medicine by 18.

At the health fair that Jason attended she discussed past lives, dimensional beings, magic and manifestation. She even told stories of her training as a child and how her grandfather was a member of the Great White Brotherhood and taught her how to walk through walls and disappear.

"Her stories were so far out – white brotherhood – crazy stuff but it really fascinated me," Jason recalled.

The Great White Brotherhood dates back to Sumer around 6000 B.C. but it rose to prominence in ancient Egypt under the leadership of the god figure Thoth. Essentially, it created a belief system that supernatural beings of great power were spreading their spiritual teaching and powers, including walking through walls, through selected humans.

The term "white" refers to the use of "white" magic not "black" magic and has nothing to do with race.

Jason attended her workshop essentially so he could hear more of her stories. The workshop was mostly about manifestation. This was after the popular book and movie "The Secret" came out so many people were interested in this topic.

Nearly 200 people attended and because the topic was manifestation each day they would have a raffle draw to see who would win a prize. People wrote their names on a small piece of paper and dropped it in the raffle box.

You guessed it. Jason won the first night. But his luck was just beginning. He also won the second night and by the third night

"The Shaman Factor"

Madi looked at him and said, "Jason, you stay out of this."

Incredibly, Jason's name was pulled out again.

"She took the paper with my name on it and threw it onto the floor and pulled out another name," Jason said. "To me this was pretty hilarious winning each time." What were the odds of that happening?

Impossible?

"I'm sure there is a message to that and some type of ability I have but it hasn't helped me win any lottery," Jason said.

Shortly after the workshop many people on the Internet started to post messages about Madi, accusing her of being a fraud and not to trust her.

How could such a sweet lady have such anger thrown at her?

Jason didn't think much about it and went on with his life.

But he would have a remarkable experience about a year later.

One night he was awoken in the middle of the night.

Madi was standing in his bedroom.

Of course he was startled.

"Madi? What are you doing here?"

She walked up to him, sat on his bed and told him that she had something for him.

"I sat up and she put her hands behind my head and brought me forward," Jason said. "She then blew air into my mouth. It felt like suddenly my energy had expanded out like a huge air balloon.

"She then stood up and walked right through the wall and disappeared."

When he met his friend Kathy again he asked her about his strange experience.

What did Madi do to him?

Kathy explained that Madi had transferred sacred information into him and had given him the gift of public speaking.

A fraud?

No way.

Jason hadn't been dreaming. He was absolutely totally awake when it was happening. He was now convinced more than ever that Madi was a true master.

Forbidden Knowledge

"I knew right then and there she was the real deal," he said.

Interestingly, Madi seemed to vanish from the face of the Earth soon after this encounter. Jason has never been able to locate her.

Now being given the gift of public speaking was very crucial to Jason's development. Jason stuttered terribly throughout most of his life. The thought of standing up in front of a crowd – and actually speaking – well, that was never a possibility.

But after the experience with Madi his stuttering disappeared and his confidence built.

In school he hated reading mostly because he was dyslexic. But now he found himself addicted to books. Everything from ancient history to philosophy now interested him.

"I could literally pick up a book and read it in a day," he said. "I could also almost remember every line from the book I was reading."

Chapter 9
"Where Did He Go?"

As Jason practiced his Egyptian Postures one night something extraordinary occurred.

Midway through these Qigong movements it felt as if out of nowhere he felt and heard a sudden explosion.

"It started in my stomach and shot out through my entire body," Jason said. "Not only did I feel this explosion, which shook me to the core, but it also sounded like an explosion."

What had he just experienced?

Jason immediately phoned Saundra.

Could she channel for him?

Could she find out what had just happened?

He never expected her reply.

"They said that you have shifted your energy to an entirely other level," she explained to him. "You have completely moved your energies out of the lower dimensions."

Could she be correct?

Jason didn't feel much different, but he definitely had experienced something unique.

The next morning his brother Lorne knocked on this bedroom door.

Lorne urgently needed to tell him something.

"Something very strange happened to me last night," his brother told him.

Lorne described how many different beings woke him up.

"Apparently, they were looking for me," Jason said.

These beings essentially interrogated his brother.

"They told him that I had vanished and they needed to know where I had gone," Jason said.

Lorne said one of the beings even threatened him and shone an orange light out of his forehead to try to make him tell them.

"Being the tough guy my brother is he told them to fuck off and leave him alone," Jason said. "Then my brother said he sent a blue light out of his third eye and that freaked them out and they left."

Jason found his brother's experience both amazing and funny.

But this story directly connected to what Saundra had told him the night before about his life energies no longer living in the lower dimensions.

Could both events just be a coincidence?

Was Saundra right? Did his energy really shift out those lower dimensions?

"According to the beings that accosted my brother I had simply disappeared and they were desperately trying to locate me," Jason said. "I was invisible to those dimensions now. I had shifted my consciousness."

Jason experienced the same explosion about a year later.

He was working at the health show in Toronto and it was a very slow day.

"I was sitting in my booth alone and I was just thinking about how to pass the time," Jason recalled. "Next to me was a poster with the image of Sekhmet, the Egyptian Lion Goddess sitting and holding a posture."

In ancient Egyptian mythology, Sekhmet was considered to be a fierce hunter and that her breath created the desert. She was seen as the protector of the "Pharaoh" and led them in warfare. She was also known as the daughter of an earlier sun god Ra.

"So I thought, I would do a meditation and sit like Sekhmet,"

"Where Did He Go?"

Jason said. "While in this meditation for some reason I decided to put my tongue on the roof of my mouth.

"When I did that I could feel energy charging and start to rise from my stomach up to my neck. When I would take my tongue off the energy would simply drop down through my body and out my feet. I thought "wow, this is a cool new experience."

So Jason started to play.

"I would build the energy up and then drop it back out through my feet," he said. "Then I decided I would build this energy up and not take my tongue off the roof of my mouth.

"I started to build and build until I felt a sudden explosion burst out through my entire body. I jumped up out of my chair in shock and decided "ok no more playing around with that stuff."

What made this event comical was that a random stranger walked by my booth, stopped and looked around. Then looked at me in shock and asked, "What happened here?"

Jason just shook his head pretending he didn't know what the man meant. Truth be told, Jason had no idea what the man saw.

Sekmet, the Egyptian Lion Goddess

What had his energy done to the environment when he did this?

"I think I completely shifted the energies of the environment I was in," Jason said. "I think I cleared the space and brought in higher dimensional frequencies.

"When we work with the energies of the mind, body and spirit with Qigong we change the nature of our being. We awaken our energy bodies and allow them to connect to the universal streams of light.

"This change is a gradual process but it has profound implications. It's as if we are starting to build a muscle we never realized we had and when this muscle is strong enough it takes on a life of its own. As we strengthen the energy within and around us we start to expand out into our environment touching many dimensions at once. The energies of this environment can then be brought within us to feed and strengthen every cell in the body."

One summer Jason decided to cleanse by fasting. He knew fasting produced multiple health benefits and was recommended to try something called the master cleanse.

"This is the lemonade with maple syrup and cayenne pepper fast," he explained. "The regiment was to drink six to eight glasses of this mixture a day with lots of water in between. Then in the morning you have to drink warm water with sea salt. This was to flush the body every morning.

"After the third day all my hunger pains went away. Instead I felt euphoric. I continued my Qigong practice while on the fast. I experienced the best sleeps of my life while not eating food."

Also, his dreams became very vivid and felt as if they lasted for hours.

"I would wake up with 100 percent memories of every detail of my dreams," Jason said. "This is very difficult to do under normal circumstances."

Jason fasted for more than a week. He started to become much more aware of everything around him.

"As I was walking down a street I became hyper sensitive to the environment around me," Jason said. "Every time I looked at something it felt as if I suddenly connected to it by some type of magnetic attraction.

"My energy would also suddenly connect when I walked by trees. Once connected, I felt the energy flow through my entire body from each tree. It was as if I was feeding off the energies of the

"Where Did He Go?"

environment.

"The more I fed the more euphoric I felt. I guess because I had weaned myself off of food another mechanism started to kick in and I was deriving energy from another source. "

While Jason experience euphoria around natural environments, the exact opposite occurred when he was in artificial space such as a shopping mall or store.

"When I went into a store I would literally feel as if the life force was being pulled out of me," Jason explained. "I would instantly feel sick and even stranger my eyes would instantly turn blood red and it would as if sand was in them."

By day 14 Jason decided enough was enough and slowly weaned himself back onto food.

"I tried to do three-day fasts every couple of months just to keep my body moving properly," he said. "It's amazing what our body can teach us when you put it through the right situations."

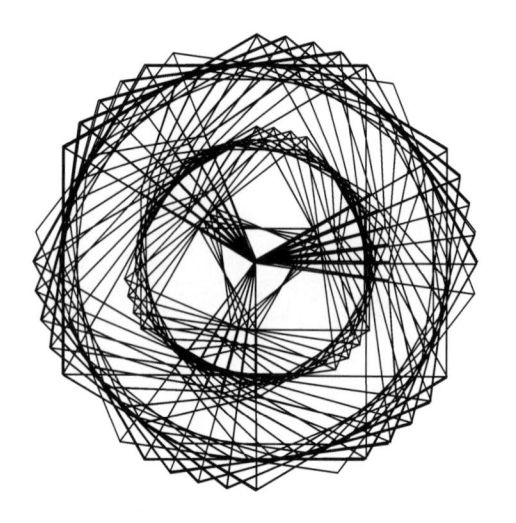

"You are in prison. If you wish to get out of prison, the first thing you must do is realize that you are in prison. If you think you are free, you can't escape."

- G.I. Gurdjieff

Chapter 10
"We Are Not The Voice In Our Minds"

In 2007, around the time Dr. Madi Nolan came to Toronto, Jason's friends Kathy Wilson and Dennis Barnett were running a company called Healing Nexus.

Both were master dowsers and held classes on this and other topics. Both were and remain incredibly gifted psychics.

One night Jason and Dennis were at Kathy's house with a couple of other people when Dennis pulled him aside and told him something strange.

"What if I told you that the voices and visions in your mind are not yours?"

Jason was obviously perplexed.

What did he mean?

Dennis then explained further.

"You know when you're trying to go to sleep and your mind just keeps going and going? What if you found out those thoughts are not even your own thoughts?"

Jason just stared at him with a look of confusion.

What was his friend telling him?

But Jason knew that if his friend felt a need to tell him this strange concept then he had good reason to be telling it.

Dennis continued.

"When your mind starts to wonder or run wild or a strange thought just suddenly pops in your head, I want you to just stop, take out your pendulum and say - 'You are not my thought form. I ask you to leave now.'"

Jason was still quite confused. But took what Dennis was telling him very seriously.

"So I did what I was told and every time a strange thought popped into my mind I would ask it to leave," Jason said. "I treated these thought forms as foreign intruders.

"If my mind ran wild and kept me up at night I would state assertively, "You are not my thought forms. Leave now!"

Jason did this for several months until something clicked.

"I literally felt something in my brain click and then there was silence," Jason said. "My mind was silent. It was like there was nothing between my ears except wind.

"I believe this is the Buddha mind. This is the state of Zen when there are no ripples in the pond. It's a very surreal feeling of deep peace.

"In this state you have a very real sense of the here and now. You become present in every breath you take. It's my understanding this is the state most who meditate are always searching for."

Several months later Dennis' words took on an entirely new meaning for Jason.

One night while having a normal dream, he suddenly heard his own voice in his head say something very disturbing.

"Jason, you're dying of cancer. You only have a couple more years left."

He immediately felt depressed.

"I thought 'oh no, I'm dying, that's so sad,'" Jason said.

But then he remembered what Dennis had taught him.

"Wait a second. My thought forms are not mine," he said out loud. "At that moment I popped myself out of my body. What I saw was a truly amazing sight."

A being was lying on the bed beside him and speaking into his ear.

Jason immediately grabbed the being by the arm and angrily

"We Are Not The Voice In Our Minds"

shouted at it.

"Who are you?"

The being was completely surprised. It had been caught. It desperately tried to get away from him but Jason held on to it with a tight grip.

Jason asked again, "Who are you?"

The being spoke but it sounded just like random gibberish.

Jason then asked another question.

"Are you a being of the light?"

The being then stopped struggling and looked back at Jason and calmly said, "No I am not."

Jason had heard enough.

"Get out of here," he shouted at the being. "You are never allowed to connect with me again."

And it left.

So what did this being look like?

That's the real disturbing part.

"What was really scary about this experience was that the being was beautiful," Jason said. "It was like an angel, glowing white light with sparks around it.

"If this being presented itself like this to someone who didn't know better, they would probably drop to their knees in prayer, blessing it like a god or angel."

And then an even scarier thought occurred to him.

What if he had taken the words inside his head to heart?

What if he truly believed he was dying?

Would he have actually manifested what was implanted?

"At that moment I fully understood Dennis's teaching," Jason said.

But Jason soon discovered that what he now knew went much further beyond than anything he could have ever imagined.

"This experience opened me up to an incredibly dark world," Jason said.

This is one of the reasons why Jason decided to share his experiences in this book.

"Most people never think about these things or believe these things exist," he said. "That's why I don't tell stories about rainbows

105

Forbidden Knowledge

and unicorns. They have to be a little scary because everything we experience always starts from a level of fear and then turns into anger. These emotions are our survival mechanisms.

"The only love and light you have is your own love and light. It's at the core of who we are.

"At the highest source of love is compassion and forgiveness but to get there we have to go through all those other emotions and have balance. We have to learn how to navigate fear and anger."

Jason recalled watching the movie Matrix and the scene where Morpheus tells Neo the truth about reality.

"He then shows Neo a battery and says, this is what we are, an unlimited source of energy for them," Jason said.

"Although this was just a line from a movie the truth is that from what I have been told, that line is very close to the real truth of the world we live in.

"Human beings are food for some astral beings. The energy we create here feeds other dimensions. These beings actually feed off our thought forms and our emotions."

When Jason discovered this to be true it was the start of what would become a fight for his life on many levels.

"These beings want us to remain asleep so when one wakes up there is a cascade effect that happens on many levels," Jason explained. "These beings try to prevent this from happening at all costs."

According to Jason, these energy-feeding beings are astral beings from the 4th and 5th dimensions.

"They are not our dead ancestors," Jason said. "They are not fallen angels or demons even though they can take these forms.

"They are very conscious beings in their own category with their own agenda. And that agenda is to keep the human energy buffet going."

So how does it all work?

A thought is initially implanted into your mind.

"You might think it's your thought form but it isn't," Jason said. "This thought form connects you to energy outside of you.

"Let's call them morphogenic fields. These are like clouds of collective consciousness. This thought then stimulates you to feel an

"We Are Not The Voice In Our Minds"

emotion. Let's say fear. Once you go into resonance with the energy of fear you open yourself up to allow these beings to extract energy out of you."

There are many ways this is done.

"For example, let's take a very extreme example. Let's say you have experienced a terrorist attack and survive," Jason said. "This trauma is programmed into your energetic body like a blueprint. It has the memory of this event and also the emotions relating to it.

"Because this trauma is now part of your energetic system these beings at any time can stimulate this program to extract energy from you."

But this doesn't just have to be done individually.

"This type of programming can be done on a mass level," Jason said. "For example, take 9/11. The entire world was collectively traumatized when we watched that horrific event live on TV over and over again."

Who were we feeding this energy too?

"Because this is purposely done in such a way it's obvious to see once you understand its design," Jason said.

Have you ever witnessed a person go from being completely normal and nice to having instant rage and anger?

"We even have an expression for this," Jason said. "Somebody pushed their buttons. When someone's button is pushed the energetic structure of that trauma is brought forward and their emotions are unleashed. This again opens them up for energy transfer."

The energy used the most against us is fear, anger, hate and lust.

"These energies weaken us and open us up to these beings," Jason said. "A symptom of this is constantly feeling drained and lethargic. The only energies that combat this type of manipulation are love, joy and humor."

So how do we stop this energy vampirism?

"It's quite simple," Jason said. "You have to heal yourself. These beings can only manipulate you through the wounds you carry. If you let go and heal those traumas these beings have nothing to grab on to.

"We also call this Karma. We continue to incarnate here to work out our Karma or else we are perpetually stuck here.

Forbidden Knowledge

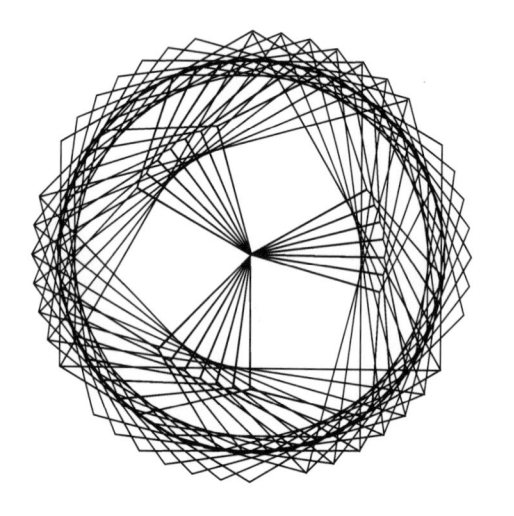

"You are only as strong as your deepest darkest wound."

- Peter Bernard

Chapter 11
"Astral Teachings"

Waking up to this new world for Jason was like being thrown into a vast ocean and then trying to learn how to swim.

But it was all part of his necessary training.

"I would discover later that many beings were going to test me," Jason said. "These beings had been sent by higher beings so I could learn how to navigate these worlds."

What Jason experienced tested him on every level of his psyche, both emotional and physical.

"Looking back at these experiences I now see them with new eyes," Jason said. "I know that even the most awful and horrific experiences were actually a great blessing, a great teaching for me.

"I would never have progressed or learned what I needed to learn without having these experiences.

Jason eventually viewed the dark beings with a new perspective.

"I didn't fear them anymore. They were my greatest teachers," Jason said. "What people don't understand about the spiritual path is that when you take a step forward you have to equally take a step back.

"All things are in balance throughout the universe and you must respect both sides because from another perspective both sides make the one whole. You can't have one without the other. This is

Forbidden Knowledge

The Nightmare - Oil painting by Henry Fuseli 1781. This painting shows an entity siting on a woman while she sleeps.

the dance of the yin and yang symbol."

The following are some of the experiences that Jason endured.

BEING CRUSHED

Jason would suddenly feel something had climbed into bed with him when he was sleeping.

"The astral being actually climbed on top of me," Jason said. "It felt as if I was being crushed. My body felt as if it was frozen, something like being in sleep paralysis."

What did this being looked like?

"All I could see was an outline of what resembled a human,"

"Astral Teachings"

Jason said.

But he couldn't make out any features.

"It was almost like a shadow with mass," Jason said.

He experienced this same event hundreds of times.

"Many people have had similar experiences," Jason said. "It's even found historically in books and artwork. It's like something comes into your room while you're sleeping and sits on your chest. You feel like your being crushed and it's very difficult to breathe."

Jason tried everything to stop these events from happening. He even called out in prayer to any angel or some other being to help him.

"But this only made things worse," he said. "I had to find another way to end these experiences.

"Eventually I just stopped freaking out when it happened. I remained calm as possible. I focused on my heart and felt love for this being. And when I did the experience suddenly ended."

POSSESSION THWARTED

Another being tried to possess Jason.

"This one tried to get inside my body not crush me," Jason said. "This was the most horrible feeling you can imagine

"It was like trying to fight something from overtaking your body."

This experience began the same way as the ones with other astral beings. Jason would be asleep and then suddenly felt a presence climb into his bed.

"But this time the being tried to push me out of my body," Jason explained. "As the being pushed I felt its energy entering my body. I knew I had to fight like hell to push this being out."

The strategy worked but it was more difficult each time.

"No amount of praying or calling out higher beings helped me," he said. "In fact, the more I did, the weaker I became. It became a fight for my life to stay in control of my body.

"I was extremely afraid of what would happen if this being actually managed to push me out."

Forbidden Knowledge

Would it take over his body?
Would he be lost in the astral plane forever?
Fortunately, Jason never had to find out.
"This had been a test for my mind," he said. "I couldn't loose this fight. I had to be stronger then it. My mind had to know that I was stronger and that this thing could not enter."
One of the most powerful experiences Jason had occurred one night when a very dark being appeared.
"I sensed it had entered my bedroom and everything became black and heavy," Jason said. "Instantly I was paralyzed.
"This being's energy then moved over my body. It was the worst feeling ever. It felt like a Mac truck had just driven over top of me.
"It felt as if my body was being crushed. I couldn't breathe. It felt as if my heart was about to stop. The pain was like nothing I had ever experienced before."
Jason thought his life was over.
"I remember thinking "well, I had a good life, I'm ready," Jason recalled.
But then he remembered what Peter Bernard had taught him.
"That within our heart is a fire. This is the fire of creation. This is our essence," Jason said.
So he thought, "Ok, I'm going to die, I'm just going to go back to the flame in my heart and go back to the fire of creation."
When he did that something totally unexpected happened next.
"Instantly I experienced this fire in my heart explode outward," he said. "This explosion was the most intense event I have ever experienced. Fire exploded out of every part of my body in all directions and expanded to the farthest reaches of space.
"Instantly that dark being was vaporized. My consciousness became this fire and my awareness expanded with this fire to what seemed like the ends of the universe.
"At that moment I knew what it felt like to be a god. I know that's a weird thing to say, but it's the only way I can describe this feeling. It was as if I was this creative force. I was fire.
"The power that ran through me could not be explained. It

could only be felt. I was touching every part of the universe at once feeling the all presence."

Then suddenly the fire was pulled back into Jason's physical body. He woke with his body shaking and his heart pounding. He had so many questions.

Who are we really?

What power lays dormant within us?

Undoubtedly this experience changed Jason. He no longer feared any being.

"I felt as if I had faced the most extreme being and had won," Jason said.

NOSFERATU?

Jason was tested every couple of months.

In one test, Jason felt as if he was being viciously pulled out of his body through his throat.

"This being was huge. It stood about 8 feet tall," Jason said.

Incredibly, the being looked very familiar.

In fact, it looked remarkably like the Nosferatu character from the classic black and white silent vampire movie of the 1922.

"It was bald with big Reptilian eyes and had large pointed ears and huge fangs," Jason said. "This being lifted me up by the neck and held me up against my wall.

"It snarled and hissed about an inch from my face."

Had this frightening experience happened to him a couple years earlier, Jason admits he probably would have "shit" his pants.

But Jason was now a different person.

In fact, instead of being frightened, he laughed at the horrible being.

"The first thing that came to my mind was – hey, look at his cute ears," Jason said. "I picked my hands up and played with his ears.

"I then said to him "look at how cute you are" and made baby faces at him.

"I know this sounds crazy but that's exactly what I did."

Almost instantly, the experience ended.

Forbidden Knowledge

Nosferatu type being with reptilian features who attacked Jason.

"Astral Teachings"

"It was as if it vanished once I decided not to express fear but love," Jason said.

As a result of that experience Jason realized these dark beings only had access to you if you allowed them to dominate you.

"When you feel fear you basically open your door and let the vampire in," he said. "The more I struggled with these beings and the more fear I felt, the more intense the experience became.

"It was as if fear pulled them closer to me. But if you changed your energy and went into a love mode for these beings they simply ran.

"But this cannot be faked. It really has to be genuine heart felt love towards these beings."

Jason also learned that when people felt fear during an experience, this emotion actually came from the being itself, not from the person.

"If you carry fear within you they can then access this and add their fear inside of you," Jason said. "So they can manipulate your fear against you and that gives them more access to you."

Jason also learned these dark beings could change their form.

"They can come to you as someone you know," he said. "You have to really learn how to discern who these beings are."

NOT HIS MOTHER

In one such experience Jason was sleeping on a couch in the den at his mother's home when in an astral state his mother walked up to him.

"She started to talk to me but something didn't seem right," Jason said. "For some reason something in my mind told me to do something that I had never done before.

"I created a MerKaBa in front of my heart chakra."

MerKaBa is a divine light vehicle allegedly used by ascended masters to connect with and reach those in tune with higher realms.

"This MerKaBa was red in color," Jason said. "I started to spin this geometry and when it was at a good speed with my mind I expanded it to encompass the entire room.

115

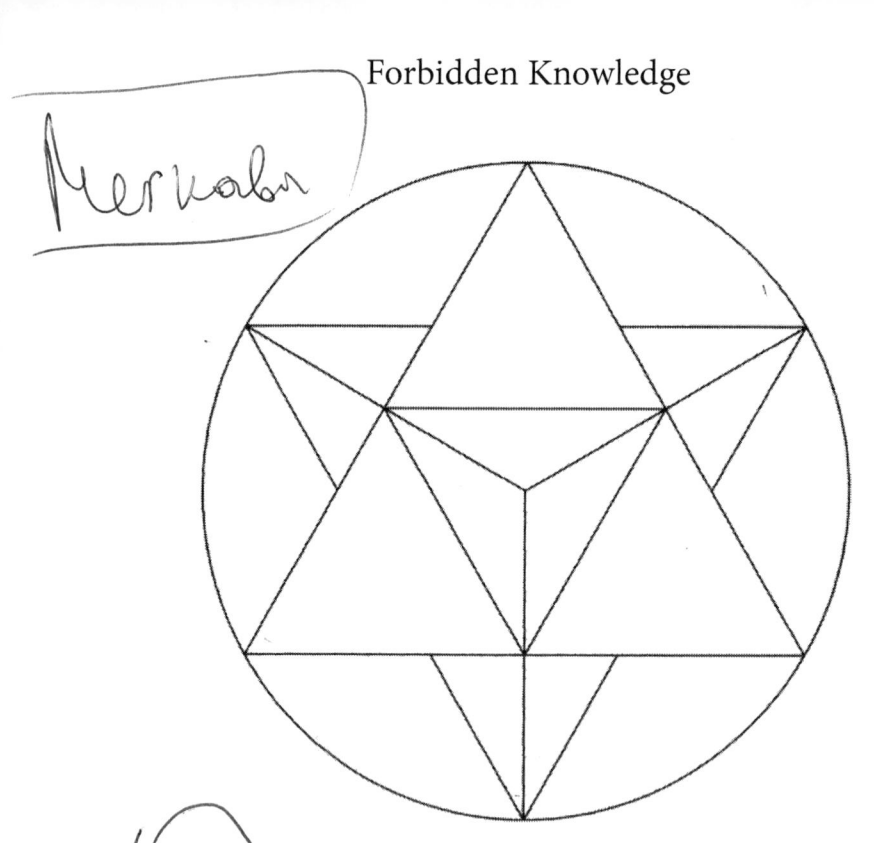

The MerKaBa is an ancient symbol with the geometry of a star tetrahedron.

"As it expanded and passed through my mother, instantly its disguise was taken away. Its voice changed from my mother's voice to a man's voice and then I saw that it was some astral being taking my mother's form.

"When it realized that it was caught I took the MerKaBa and put it around his body. Then I said goodbye and shot him out into the universe to be healed."

How did he know how to do that?

Jason has no idea.

"It was like something just clicked and I remembered something that I had possibly learned in one of my past lives," Jason said.

CONVERSATION WITH AN ENTITY

A gifted psychic healer once told Jason that whenever he entered the room she could hear the entities within people scream for their lives.

He soon understood why.

"I began to sense them not only in the room but in the people they were connected too," Jason said. "For some reason I had the ability to remove these beings with little to no fight.

"When I saw clients for healing I removed these entities from their energetic fields and they would feel much better. But this was short lived within them. They often came back to see me with the same entity attached to them."

One time Jason received a message directly from one of these entities. It would change the way he looked at these beings forever.

"I asked this entity why it was causing issues for this person," Jason explained. "The entity responded that it would continue to make this person's life a living hell because she refused to let go of it."

Essentially, until the person learned how to let go, this entity would continue to take over her life.

What did this really mean?

"This person was unconsciously or consciously holding on to a lower energy," Jason said. "This could be an addiction, obsession, emotion, thought form, karma, or trauma. Whatever the case, this energy was linked to the energy of that entity.

"This entity would freely leave only when this person let that energy go and heal. Before this I never thought people could possess entities. I thought it was the other way around.

"But in this case it was this person's energy which entrapped this being within her. This is why you have to treat every being with respect and all on the same level. You never know which being will be your next teacher."

THE RIGHT THING TO DO

Jason found himself being placed in situations where he needed to figure out what had to be done in order for the experience to end.

In one such test, Jason found himself in the body of a WWII pilot.

Forbidden Knowledge

Suddenly the plane would be hit by enemy fire and started falling out of the sky. The plane started to nose dive into a building.

"I started to panic," Jason said. "It didn't seem like a dream. It was too real I hit the building and died."

Everything went black but then he heard a voice, "You failed, try again."

Suddenly, he would be back inside the same plane and the exact same scenario would happen again.

"I started to panic again but this I tried to steer the plane out of the path of the building but it was no use," Jason said. "I died again."

Once more there was nothing but blackness and the voice, "You failed, try again."

This time while involved in the exact same scenario he tried to find the ejection seat release button, but it was no use.

He died again and heard the same voice in the blackness. "You failed, try again."

This continued multiple times but it always ended with the same results.

He always died.

Fed up with this repeating scenario, the next time Jason simply wrapped his hands behind his head and relaxed.

"I just enjoyed the moment," he said. "I was calm. I looked around me at every detail of this environment without any fear whatsoever. I didn't even care that I was heading for this building and to my death."

Jason hit the building and died again but surprisingly, this time the voice told him that he had passed the test.

"I'm not sure what the message of this test was but I think it had to do with fighting with your fate," Jason said. "If you know 100 percent that you are going to die, why fight, why struggle, just enjoy the view and be at peace.

"I also think it has to do with the idea of dying in peace. I think that is very important. If we die in fear or anger I believe these emotions follow you into the afterlife."

118

WITNESSING THE MATRIX

Another time Jason was dreaming that he was on a beach, watching the waves come ashore. It was extremely peaceful.

Suddenly he woke and was back in his bed. But he quickly realized he wasn't in his own bedroom.

"I sat up in my bed fully awake and realized that I was still on this beach," Jason said.

He was confused.

Was he still dreaming?

Something told him to look to his left and when he did he saw a portal open about six feet from him.

"This looked like a black wormhole," he said. "This portal started to suck this vision of the beach away to reveal my bedroom behind it.

"This was an amazing thing to witness."

Jason absolutely believes he was wide awake when he witnessed the portal suck away the environment of the beach.

Was he being shown the matrix of reality?

Did he exist in something similar to the holodeck of Star Trek?

Jason began to question what reality actually is.

What if we are living in somebody else's dream?

Do we really know for sure what our reality is?

Forbidden Knowledge

Machu Picchu archaeological site in Peru.

Chapter 12
"The Peru Experience"

In May 2009, Jason traveled to Peru to experience the sites and mysticism of the South American country.

He was one of several students from the 8the Fire School on this three-week journey of discovery. The trip was organized by a woman named Sher, a local medicine woman and a shiatsu therapist.

The itinerary involved meeting shamans and participating in several sacred ceremonies along with visiting some of the country's notable ancient sites.

"Peru had always been one of the top places in the world that I wanted to visit," Jason said. "I was so psyched to be going."

Nora also went on the trip. Intuitively, they knew they had to watch each other's back.

The trip was organized by Incan Tours and the group traveled to various sites by shuttle bus operated by some of the country's top tourist guides. But they also were accompanied by a spiritual guide, who knew the legends and mysteries connected with each of the sites they visited.

Jason felt at home in Peru. Even the altitude didn't bother him. Altitude sickness is one of the most common illnesses that affects tourist in countries such as Peru. It can often take up to three days

Moray archaeological site in Peru.

for a person to adapt to the decrease in oxygen.

Places such as Machu Picchu are more than 8,000 feet above sea level while Lake Titicaca is more than 12,000 feet. By comparison, Los Angeles is 5,000 feet above sea level while Toronto is just 300 feet above sea level.

"I had no trouble breathing the beautiful mountain air around me," he said. "I knew this would be where I would discover the power of the ancient sites."

Indeed, Jason's energy was activated when he entered each of the ancient sites and temples.

"These sites are still active and still hold a tremendous amount of power," Jason said. "There are many power spots in Peru. When I would step on these spots it would feel as if I was falling into the earth up to my knees.

"Suddenly I would feel an electric current start to flow up my body. This feels very similar to pins and needles just more intense. If I

"The Peru Experience"

stayed too long on one spot it would overtake my body and my spirit would suddenly pop out of my body and I'd have an experience.

"This happened multiple times in multiple places in Peru. I have never had this experience anywhere else."

At Moray, an archaeological site about 31 miles northwest of Cuzco on an 11,500-foot plateau just west of the village of Maras Jason experienced the most powerful of forces. The site contains Inca ruins mostly consisting of enormous terraced circular spirals or depressions, the largest nearly 100 feet deep.

The Inca civilization existed in what is present day Peru, Chile and Ecuador in the early 13th century and created the largest empire in pre-Columbian America. Its capital was located in Cusco, Peru.

But less than 100 years later the Inca Empire was decimated by Spanish conquistadors. Moray is just one of several ancient Inca ruins still in existence in the highlands of South America.

"We were allowed to go right down into the bottom bowl of this structure," he said. "I felt my energy change with every step down a terrace. I proceeded to go right into the center of the bottom the bowl. Once there I laid down on my back and closed my eyes in meditation.

"I felt the energies of the Earth slowly taking over my body. It started at the hands and then moved through my arms, feet and legs. It felt like an intense electrical feeling. It was very powerful as it started to enter my torso."

Jason never expected such intensity. In fact, he became frightened.

"I had never experienced anything like this before," Jason said. "I had to fight this energy to regain movement of my limbs so that I could snap out of the experience and sit up.

"The only way I can describe what was going on was that the Earth's energies were merging with my body. This was putting my body in paralysis so that my spirit could leave and travel."

Jason also felt incredible energy forces at a nearby circular stone temple. Its foundation is the only surviving remnant of the temple.

"We were instructed to walk into this temple and start to walk around in a spiral until we reached the center," Jason said. "The moment I reached the center of this temple my body shut off and I was instantly shot out of my body. It was an amazing yet sudden and scary experience.

"I had to jump out of the center before I would be plunged into unknown times and dimensions."

Jason believes these sacred sites are portals to other worlds and dimensions.

"It's very easy to shed your meat suit in these environments," Jason said.

Jason also participated in an ancient Ayahuasca ceremony.

"I couldn't turn this experience down," he said.

The ceremony was conducted near the foothills of Machu Picchu considered one of the most beautiful and impressive ancient Inca ruins in the world. Known as the "Lost City of the Incas," it was re-discovered in 1911 by American historian Hiram Bingham after it lay hidden for centuries more than 9,000 feet above sea level above the Urabamba Valley. Until then, this ancient ruin was largely unknown to the outside world. Now, it's one of Peru's most sought after tourist destinations. Many archaeologists believe it was built as an estate for Inca Emperor Pachacut.

Jason prepared himself for this ceremony by fasting on only liquids and chewing large amounts of coca leaf for three days before consumption.

Ayahuasca is an ancient tea that can be made from about 40 different plants. This is the shaman's strongest medicine and it's used to purge the body, mind and spirit of heavy energies and toxins.

Interestingly, many people who have consumed the plant as part of this ceremony have reported having alien encounters.

Well-known author and researcher Graham Hancock theorizes that when this psychedelic brew is consumed it opens up the human mind to an altered state of consciousness allowing the interaction with beings from other dimensions.

Interestingly, DMT, a naturally-produced substance in our pineal gland, is also an active ingredient in Ayahuasca,

An illuminating study of the effects of DMT was done by Dr.

"The Peru Experience"

Rick Strassman at the University of New Mexico between 1990-1995. His pioneering study was the first legally-sanctioned analysis using psychedelic drugs on human test subjects in the U.S. in more than 20 years.

Some 60 volunteers were given the drug. None of them knew each other. They also weren't allowed to talk or compare notes afterwards.

He wrote about the research in his book "DMT: The Spirit Molecule."

The results of his study were startling.

Nearly half of his subjects found themselves in a different reality with various beings, including alien entities. One of the most predominant alien species was a Mantid insectoid. Others saw Reptilians and plant-like stick beings. The test subjects also saw clowns, reptiles, bees, spiders and stick people.

These volunteers interacted with the beings. Some said these strange entities had also been waiting for them. Some reported undergoing experiments. Others received knowledge. Some test subjects had sexual experiences with the beings. Some were told of future events.

It would seem fairly straightforward – and logical – that Dr. Strassman's groundbreaking research indicated that DMT caused hallucinations.

But why did so many see aliens?

Dr. Strassman had another answer.

What if they didn't have hallucinations?

What if DMT somehow opened a gateway to another dimension where these entities lived?

His conclusion isn't that outlandish considering how some UFO researchers and Experiencers – and of course Jason - have suggested that many alien species live and operate in the fourth or higher dimensions.

"These beings are able to enter our world, which exists in the third dimension, when they need to for whatever reason," Jason said.

What if DMT actually does open a doorway?

What if alien encounters aren't hallucinations but actually other dimensional experiences with other worldly beings?

Dr. Strassman speculated that under certain circumstances the human brain might increase its levels of DMT and make it easier for the so-called alien abduction experience to occur. He also theorized that the aliens might also be able to manipulate the DMT levels in the human brain in order to make journeys to other worlds possible or alternatively for other worldly beings to cross over into our world.

It certainly is something to think about.

During their ceremony Jason drank the brew, which almost had the taste and consistency of cough syrup.

"About 10 minutes after my body started to throw up," Jason said. "What I threw up perplexed me. It was a large amount of what looked like dark burgundy thick liquid. This was strange because I only drank about a shot glass size of Ayahuasca and had been fasting for days."

Jason Quitt in Machu Picchu, Peru.

"The Peru Experience"

So what was this liquid leaving his body?

"We were then instructed to lie down on the ground to allow the Earth's energy to flow through us," he said. "Our spines had to be touching the ground for this ceremony to work properly."

As he lay on the forest floor Jason stared up at the night sky and the full Moon overhead.

"It was so bright it felt as if there was a spot light shining down on me. The light of the Moon was a majestic silvery purple color.

"When I closed my eyes all I could see was bright white light sparkling within my body. It was almost blinding. I felt the Earth's energies flow through my body again.

"I could clearly see in this state how we are connected to the Earth. In fact, the Earth and our bodies felt as if they were one and the same organism. In this state I could let go and travel the spirit world. It was incredibly easy to do. But it was difficult to maintain presence. I had to get up periodically and walk around just to main-

Jason and Nora WALKSINSPIRIT with Incan Medicine man in Peru.

tain the here and now."

After many hours of being in this state it was over, or so Jason thought.

"Ayahuasca is very power medicine," he explained. "I felt it moving through every part of my body as if it was searching out problems within me and then correcting them.

"Needless to say, it's a good thing I had access to a washroom. I remained close to that washroom for two days afterwards. I lost 20 pounds of waste and toxins. So this type of ceremony is not for the faint of heart."

Jason said the ceremony essentially purged every cell in his body and mind.

"I felt as if I had let go of many things on many levels," he said. "Thankfully I had Nora by my side the entire time watching over me."

Jason and his group went next to Lake Titicaca to spend a couple days out on the islands. Many in the group had trouble breathing because of the extremely high altitude.

Once at the islands they were greeted by a family that had lived there for their entire lives. Torvidio, likely in his late 60s, instructed Jason's group in his native tongue to throw all of their bags on a large tarp because they would have a long and hard hike up to the top of this island.

"He then closed the tarp, threw it over his back like Santa Claus and walked up the entire island," Jason said. "This was a very hard hike even for me. It just shows you the difference between us and them."

They stayed that night with Torvidio and his wife at their house at the top of the island.

"This was not a first class hotel. We basically slept on a bed made of straw with no electricity, toilets or running water," Jason said. "This was real living.

"When the Sun goes down it's time to go to sleep. It was amazing at night there. The sky was so clear and the stars were so bright that it felt as if you were in outer space."

But Jason didn't have a peaceful night's sleep.

"The Peru Experience"

He was awoken by spirits of the land's ancestors.

"Hundreds of them packed into my room and even outside my room," Jason said. "They projected images in my mind of their life and death on this island. It was overwhelming. They all wanted to share their story with me."

Jason needed to get some much needed rest so he asked the spirits to please allow him to sleep. He promised the spirits that he would conduct a healing ceremony for them the following morning if he would be left in peace.

Jason with Torvidio and his wife, Lake Titicaca, Peru.

Almost immediately his room became clear and silent.

For Jason, this wasn't the first time that spirits had come to him. In fact, it occurs quite often.

"Most of the time I'm not prepared for these encounters," he said.

Jason described one such incident when he was spending the night at his then fiancé's place.

"I felt something touch my arm while I was sleeping," he said. "I opened my eyes to see a little girl standing in front of me and her face was all ripped up and bloody."

Jason was still half asleep and the appearance of the child startled him.

He screamed "get away from me."

Then something else came into his consciousness. The spirit of this girl needed his help.

"At that moment I felt like a total jerk," he said. "How could I act this way in front of a little girl? So I calmed down and opened my eyes and looked right at her with a warm heart and said, "Hey sweetheart. I will help you now. I'm calling your angels."

Suddenly, the room filled with light and she was taken by her angels to be healed, Jason said.

"Being human in physical form is an incredible gift," Jason said. "We do not realize the true power and nature of who we are. We can bring such healing to this world and others if we were to wake up and know our truth."

Jason had a very good sleep that night in Peru and in the morning he shared his experience with Nora. "She then received a message indicating there was a special place on the island where they needed to go to conduct the healing ceremony for the island's ancestral spirits.

Mantis type being that appeared to Nora WALKSINSPIRT

"We asked the older man (who spoke no English) that we needed to do a ceremony," Jason explained. "He then guided us on a hike to the other side of the island and to a stone that was just lying on the ground.

"As if he knew exactly what we were doing he started to take flowers and place them on this stone. The three of us then stood around this stone and did the ceremony for the ancestors of the island."

The man smiled when they were finished and Jason and Nora then followed him back.

"Even with no language between us he knew exactly what we wanted and where to take us," Jason said. "These people have something very special."

A Mantis-like being visited Nora the next night.

"The Peru Experience"

"She tried to sleep but had trouble breathing because of the high altitude," Jason said. "She started to panic and thought she was going to die on the island from lack of oxygen."

But almost as soon as that thought entered her mind, she saw a presence step out of the shadows.

It was a Mantis-like being.

Her fear immediately subsided. In fact, she felt overwhelming love from the Insectoid being.

The fact that Nora felt overwhelming love from the Mantis being isn't unusual. In fact, it would have been very unusual had she felt anything but love. Nearly every Experiencer who encounters a Mantid has this same feeling of overwhelming love.

In Bob Mitchell's recently published book "What if? Close Encounters of the Unusual Kind," several Experiences have Mantid encounters, including one scenario that raised the possibility that the reason they experience this incredible attraction is because they were also a Mantid being in a previous life and had a past life connection to the being.

Indeed, this reincarnation theory directly links to what Jason has been told. That we are all connected to a higher source and our consciousness takes many forms and shapes throughout our never-ending existence.

Jason took a picture of a sacred island in Peru that the locals say was the landing site for the spaceships of the ancient gods.

Forbidden Knowledge

The Mantis approached her face and breathed air into her mouth. Nora told Jason about her experience the next morning.

"She felt her entire lungs and body open up and she was able to breathe again," Jason said. "She then asked this being what it was."

According to what Nora told Jason, the Mantis revealed that its species was called the "EYLS," which essentially stood for "Elevating your levels and elevating your lineages."

"The being explained how they have been assisting humanity in shifting and raising their consciousness," Jason said.

"It seems that when a person comes in contact with one of the EYLS it means they are ready to shift into a higher level of consciousness and they are there to assist in this process," Jason said.

"Nora told me this being was connected to Torvidio's higher self and wanted to work with us. When we tuned into this being we felt nothing but love and gratitude for the work we had done with the spirits of the island."

Near the end of the Peru trip Jason and his group travelled to the famous sacred doorway of Amaru Muru near Lake Titicaca. Inca legends suggest life on Earth was created by Viracocha, believed to be the supreme God of the Incas. He was the God, who created all other Inca gods and also created the Earth, the Sun and all living things.

Interestingly, ancient texts suggest Viracocha actually created mankind after a failed attempt to populate the world with a race of giants. Legends suggest Viracocha didn't like what the giants had become and destroyed them with a great flood.

In Amaru Mura there is a carved opening in the rock face that is known as the Amaru Muru's portal. This doorway-shaped niche is located in an area known as the Valley of the Spirits. Local legends tell stories of people disappearing through the doorway and that it was used in the past by beings as a so-called star gate.

"As our bus drove towards this site I got a strange feeling that it would not be safe for me to go near this site," Jason said.

But something else caught his attention as they drove into the site.

"I saw another hidden doorway on a different wall," Jason said.

"The Peru Experience"

The Amaru Mura "portal" is believed by some to have once been used as a stargate to other worlds and dimensions.

"So when everyone got out of the bus I walked in the other direction to see the other doorway.

"As I was walking towards this new doorway I passed another structure. It looked to me like a seat was carved out of this rock outcropping. I sat down on the seat and took in the scenery."

Within seconds Jason felt something strange happening to him although he didn't know why he felt peculiar.

On the way back to the hotel Nora looked at him and sternly asked "What did you do?"

So Jason explained about sitting down on the seat.

Nora told him that he had picked up a very dark spirit when he sat on that "throne". Through channeling she determined that a very ancient alien entity had attached itself to him and this spirit had a great thirst for blood.

"This being apparently had ruled there and I had somehow connected with this energy when I sat on its seat," Jason said. "I asked Nora if she could help me remove this entity but there was nothing she could do."

When Jason fell asleep that night he was visited by the spirit of his Algonquin Shaman friend Peter Bernard.

"I guess I really was in trouble for picking up this entity," Jason said. "Peter held me down and took out a snake and forced it to bite me on my arm.

"I felt the venom flow through my body. Later I woke up in a cold sweat. I'm guessing he needed to use his snake medicine to purge this entity out of my body."

It took Jason about a week to heal and fully release the malevolent energy that he had picked up.

"Fortunately for me I have a close team of shamans and healers watching my back," Jason said. "But every experience teaches me new things."

LORD MELCHIZEDEK

Jason was never really drawn to the new age movement or the information of the ascended masters.

But he is absolutely certain they exist because of a couple of experiences.

His first powerful one happened after Nora gave him an energy healing after they returned from Peru. She told him afterwards that Lord Melchizedek would finish the healing later that night in his dreams.

Lord Melchizedek is an ascended master who shows himself through our dreams and meditations. Ascended Masters are beings who have become self-realized and serve humanity as a being who has raised their vibration to a sustained frequency of light. They can come and go at will from the Earth without being part of the birth/death cycle.

Lord Melchizedek is believed to oversee humanity's consciousness and his energy strives to bring higher wisdom to humanity through the arts and sciences, education and technology.

"I never really gave it too much thought but that night I was dreaming and the dream was very dark and cryptic," Jason said. "It was like being in a horror movie.

"I heard strange sounds and voices around me. Then as if it couldn't have gotten worse I started to feel things moving in my

"The Peru Experience"

Ascended Master Lord Melchizedek   Ascended Master El Morya

body and under my skin.

"It became very painful. Then, all at once as if the flood gates had opened, hundreds of insects burst out of every part of my body.

"They came out of my skin. Swarms came out of my mouth and nose."

Jason awoke from this horrific experience still seeing the insects leaving his body. But the experience wasn't quite over.

He looked to the side of his bed.

An ancient being stood there.

"My guess was this was Lord Melchizedek finishing the healing work just as Nora prophesied," Jason said.

During another out of body journey he was taken to Master El Morya, an ascended being, who represents the godly attributes of courage, certainty, power, forthrightness, self-reliance, dependability, faith and initiative.

Jason's still not certain how this all was arranged or why it was arranged.

"All I remember was someone took me there because they wanted us to meet," Jason said. "He wanted to experience my energy so I connected to him. I put my hand up and projected my energy.

"He just looked at me and smiled. That was the entire memory I have of this event. What really drew me to this master was his turban. It had many beautiful gemstones. I could not take my eyes away from."

Another time he was once again transported to the pyramids of Egypt. Upon his arrival he saw a lengthy line of people trying to ender the pyramid.

"Then I remembered this was not where I was being called to," Jason said. "I was shown the location of a secret entrance into the pyramid."

He walked around the pyramid until he discovered a doorway that led down below the pyramid.

"As I entered this secret room I found that the room was filled with many ascended masters, gods and goddesses," Jason said. "There were various Hindu gods, Buddha. Even Jesus was there," Jason said. "It looked as if they were preparing for a meeting."

Jason was ushered into the room. It resembled an extravagant Bedouin tent with rich carpets, drapery, pillows and tables. He selected a place and sat down."

"That's all I recall," Jason said. "My journey ended. I have no idea what I did in the room or what else happened.

"This is the frustrating part of being an Experiencer. It's almost as if you are allowed to keep a sliver of the experience but when you return most of it is gone and you can't recall the rest."

This is exactly the sense Experiencers often feel following an alien abduction encounter. Most only are allowed to remember fragments of their entire encounter and often their experiences end with total blackness or darkness.

Chapter 13
"All Roads Lead To Tesla"

A series of synchronistic events lined up for Jason when he met a man named Bob Connolly in November 2013 at the Toronto Health Show.

Jason's company "The Crystal Sun" was one of the show's exhibitors and Connolly approached him on the final day of the event.

He wanted to know the meaning behind the name of Jason's company.

"He was very interested in the significance of the name – The Crystal Sun – so we started talking about crystals, radios and the power of the Sun," Jason said. "He was interested in the practice of sun gazing and wanted to know if I had ever heard of it."

Jason's company and its website – www.thecrystalsun.com – were created so he could share his information to anybody interested in these topics.

Connolly wanted to hear more and asked Jason to meet him for lunch. They met a few weeks later in Toronto and it was at this meeting that Connolly revealed he was a Canadian film producer, who was responsible for "Timeless Places," one of the first alien-related documentary shows on television.

The show aired on Vision TV in the early 1990s and would travel to the world's most mystical places examining archaeological wonders from Egyptian pyramids to the strange sculptures on Easter Island.

During lunch they discussed many different topics, including the dangers of EMF, and Nicola Tesla's lost technologies and healing devices.

"It was a very enlightening conversation," Jason said.

Connolly explained that for the past four years he had been traveling the world and working on a new documentary project entitled "The Healing Field."

"The film was an ongoing project documenting alternative methods of healing throughout the world," Jason said. "He intended to get into Tesla and his lost technologies."

Jason and Connolly had numerous meetings and telephone conversations over the next couple of months.

"At this time Bob was already starting to plan his next adventure. This time he would be traveling to locations all over the United States to document footage of sound healing and light therapy," Jason said. "He asked me if I wanted to join him as his assistant and camera man."

Jason didn't have to think twice. They spent April and May 2014 traveling on this documentary journey.

Their first stop was FDA (Food and Drug Administration) headquarters in Washington, D.C. to get an establishing shot of the FDA sign. At least that was their intention.

But they discovered the FDA had moved its headquarters out of Washington to what is officially a former site of a navy laboratory in nearby Silver Springs, Maryland that was once known as the White Oak Naval Surface Warfare Center. It is now known as the Federal Research Center at White Oak.

The FDA is a federal agency of the U.S. Department of Health and Human Services. It's responsible for protecting and promoting public health through regulation and supervision of food safety, tobacco products, dietary supplements, prescription medicine, over the counter pharmaceutical medications, vaccines, blood transfusions, medical devices, electromagnetic radiation emitting devices, cosmetics, animal food and veterinary products.

It seemed strange that a government-regulated drug and food agency would have its headquarters on a former military base, especially one still guarded.

"As we pulled up at their new location before we could even get the camera on the tripod we were surrounded by military police," Jason said. "They demanded to know why we were there and what we were doing.

"It turns out they had the authority to shoot anybody who enters their property without authorization. This surprised us because as far as we could tell there were no signs indicating this or warning us."

Once they realized they were Canadians they let them leave.

"But they basically told us not to come back," Jason said.

Again this left us with some questions.

Why would the FDA be under such militarized conditions?

Why did they move their headquarters to a former naval base?

"This certainly fueled our conspiracy theory minds," Jason said.

Their next stop Asheville, North Carolina and Moogfest, a music, art and technological festival held annually. They had arranged to meet August Worley, one of the country's top engineers in analog synthesis.

Worley was also one of the earlier pioneers of the Moog Voyager Synthesizer (one of the top synths in the world) and worked side by side with the legendary Bob Moog.

"Worley left the synthesizer world to create a unique instrument," Jason said. "It's a pyramid that uses a Tesla coil and crystals to create pure analogue vibrations similar to an electric singing bowl"

For Jason, this was the highlight of his trip.

"I have always been a synth guy and while growing up I always wanted a Moog synth," Jason said. "Now, I was hanging out with one of the people responsible for that instrument."

Jason was also excited to experience his new and magical instrument - the "Pyradym."

But something even more magical happened soon after Jason and Connolly arrived at Worley's home and waited for him to finish giving a Pyradym sound healing session to a client.

Forbidden Knowledge

August Worley with his instrument the Pyradym.

Essentially, the Pyradym is an electrically-powered device that synergistically uses sound and color therapy for pain relief and emotional and physical balancing.

"As we waited we heard these amazing sounds reverberating through the walls," Jason said. "These sounds put both of us to sleep even though we were sitting upright in his chairs.

"We could not believe that we just passed out. It was like nothing we had ever experienced before. It put us in such a deep state of relaxation and healing that it just knocked us both out."

From there they went to Florida to visit Cape Canaveral and NASA to get shots of the rockets and anything to do with space.

"Being at NASA was like being at an amusement park," Jason said.

They attended a lecture given by Charlie Walker, the first commercial astronaut in space, but nothing of real interest happened while they were there.

While in Florida they visited Jeff Behary, who runs the Turn of the Century Electrotherapy Museum in Pompano, Beach, Florida. The museum houses a collection of hundreds of amazing electrotherapy devices invented by Tesla from the early 1900s.

"We had the chance to play with some of the devices that were still in working condition sending lightning bolts and creating ozone," Jason said.

Afterwards they drove to St. Petersburg on the Gulf side of Florida to attend the International Conference of Light and Vision held by a group of optometrists interested in the healing power of light known as Syntonics that has been in clinical use for more than 70 years.

"This involves shining a light into your eyes in various color spectrums to give specific healing results," Jason said, "All of these optometrists use light and color as their main healing tool."

Light has been used as a medical treatment since ancient times. The ancient Egyptians used gems to filter light and the ancient Greeks built solarium cities in mountains to harness ultra violet light for healing purposes.

"Incredibly, this was their 82nd annual conference," Jason said. "After so many years of using these methods to heal they have documented thousands of cases of healing using the power of light and color."

This healing therapy also touches on the color healing of the work of the late Dinshah Ghadial in the early 1920s and 30s.

"Dinshah was thrown in jail and his laboratory burned to the ground just because he was healing people by using the power of light and color," Jason said. "He believed the body could fend off disease by systematically exposing it to colored light."

Topics such as the healing power of the Sun and Sun gazing were among those discussed at the conference.

"Sun gazing is a very ancient practice dating back to Egypt where they would look directly into the Sun during sunrise and sunset to produce a powerful healing effect," Jason said.

From there they headed to Green Bank, West Virginia. It's a place where people claiming to suffer from electro-sensitivity escape

Forbidden Knowledge

Jason sungazing with protective glasses at the Syntonics conference in Florida.

to so they can live normal lives.

The National Radio Observatory is also located there.

This small hamlet about four hours west of Washington, D.C. is an extremely unusual community.

"There is a complete and total ban on electromagnetic radiation in the community," Jason said. "There are no cell phones, Wi-Fi, radio or even TV within a 13,000 square mile range of the area that borders the states of West Virginia, Virginia and Maryland.

"Many people, who suffer from this type of electromagnetic pollution, seek refuge in locations like these. You are not even allowed to have a microwave oven in your house because the Robert C Byrd Green Bank Telescope is also located in the hamlet and microwave signals could interfere with its transmission."

It's the world's largest fully steerable radio telescope with a dish

"All Roads Lead To Tesla"

so huge that the locals have dubbed it the "Great Big Thing or GBT.

Astronomers use this telescope to detect and study objects in space that give off very little light but emit radio waves such as pulsars, gas clouds and distant galaxies. But the GBT is so sensitive that any device that generates electromagnetic radiation can interfere with the data it collects from deep space. So since 1950, by federal law, residents can't have devices most of the world uses every day.

"You definitely notice a difference being in an energetically clean environment like this," Jason explained.

No matter where they went, conversations inevitably turned to the work of Tesla.

"This really was the theme to every place we went to and it was obvious that we needed to learn more about this famous inventor," Jason said.

Jason had no idea that fate or synchronicity was already on his side. When they returned from their trip, Connolly was contacted by Tesla Magazine. They were looking for a new team to help produce its next issue.

"Bob and I decided this would be a good chance to work on a new project together and soon I found myself working as the new creative director of Tesla Magazine," Jason said. "Bob even set up a Tesla Exposition at the Ontario Science Centre where he showcased the latest Tesla technologies and played parts of the film he had previously produced on the topic."

The connection to Tesla Magazine exposed Jason to information and people he would likely never have known.

"I became obsessed with the work of Tesla and was amazed at just how little has ever been made public about this infamous inventor," Jason said.

But this obsession would eventually lead Jason to hidden truths and put him directly on a path to danger.

Fig. 2

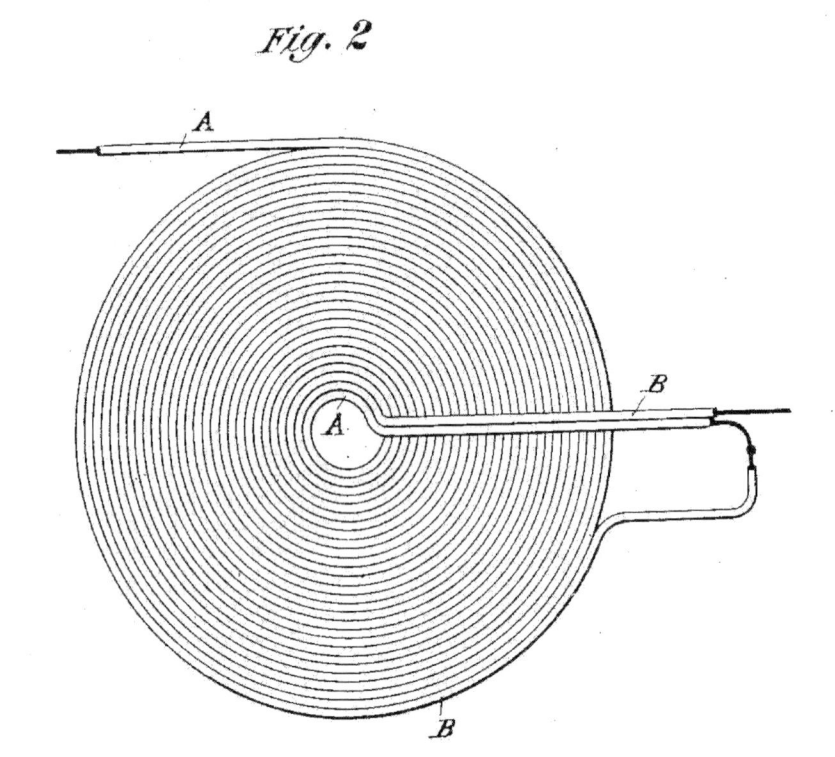

The feeling is constantly growing on me that I had been the first to hear the greeting of one planet to another.

- Nikola Tesla

Chapter 14
"Tesla's Hidden Medical Devices"

While most are familiar with Nicola Tesla's involvement with electricity very little is known publicly about his obsession with medicine and the remarkable inventions he created to help keep people healthy.

In 1903 when the electrical current wars were raging, Thomas Edison was pushing for DC (direct current) as the way to power the future while Tesla insisted AC (alternating current) was the way to go.

"AC eventually won this war because electrical transmissions could be sent many miles through wires without losing strength while DC did," Jason said. "Tesla demonstrated this by lighting up the city of Hamilton, Ontario and Buffalo, NY using the hydro station at Niagara Falls. A statute of Tesla at this location commemorates this historical event."

But Edison mounted a formidable campaign against AC.

He insisted AC, which used much higher voltages than DC, was simply too dangerous to be used in homes. He conducted a media campaign designed to instill fear into the public by saying that AC was very dangerous and could kill very easily. He even made propaganda videos, which played before the movies in all of the Edison theaters across the U.S.

"In fact, in an effort to showcase the dangers of AC and discredit Tesla, Edison held public demonstrations where he actually electrocuted animals such as dogs, cats, horses, and even an elephant in front of an audience," Jason said. "You can still watch an elephant named "Topsy" being electrocuted on YouTube."

To provide an even more convincing demonstration of the dangers of AC, Edison used it in 1899 to kill convicted murderer William Kemmler by using an AC-powered electric chair.

"Tesla naturally was horrified about the electrocution of these animals," Jason said. "He knew he needed to show the world that AC was safe.

"He not only maintained AC was safe but also insisted that it could be used as a health cure of the future. He promised he would one day provide devices that everybody could use for healing purposes.

"Tesla was very passionate about healing."

In 1896, Tesla took out a patent for his first ozone device and in 1910 he formed the Tesla Ozone Company. He personally funded this project with $400,000 of his own money, an equivalent of about $11 million in today's currency.

"So this was a huge investment at the time," Jason said. "It also shows just how much he believed in the healing power of ozone."

Ozone in this case was created by the sparks formed by high frequency currents produced by Tesla's coil designs. While experimenting with high voltage currents Tesla noticed that his laboratory became filled with this strong smelling gas.

Tesla Ozone generator - 1896.

"Tesla's Hidden Medical Devices"

Tesla working in his laboratory surrounded by high frequency bolts of electricity which is filling the space with ozone gas.

The UV light from the bolts of electricity converted the oxygen in the air to ozone gas. Tesla also noticed that this ozone gas killed the bacteria and mold in his laboratory.

But there was another effect.

"While Tesla and his staff worked in the laboratory they were being exposed to large amounts of high frequency currents and ozone gas," Jason said. "He realized their physical and mental health were benefiting from this exposure."

This led to some very interesting experiments in Stockholm Sweden and New York in 1912.

Tesla designed and hid high powered coils inside the walls of public schools. For six months his machines blasted high frequency voltage into the air electrifying the children in these classrooms.

"These children were essentially bathed in millions of volts of electricity day in and out," Jason said. "The test was designed to see if these students experienced any physical and mental changes compared to those not receiving the electricity blast."

Forbidden Knowledge

Today, it is highly unlikely that Tesla would have ever been given permission to conduct such an experiment on a group of unsuspecting children.

But it was a different time back then and Tesla insisted the experiment was simply the equivalent of exposing the children to the Sun. He also insisted light from a light bulb was many times more harmful than the type of therapy being used on the students.

The New York Times even published a piece on Tesla's experiments in its edition of Aug. 18, 1912.

"Tesla believed this type of electro therapy would one day replace all pharmaceutical drugs for neurological and digestive disorders," Jason said. "He also believed this was the cure for many aliments."

Was he right?

The results of the student experiment were eye opening to say the least.

The children exposed to this type of therapy grew an average of 2 1/2 inches taller than the controlled group and were physically stronger. Their class intelligence increased from an average of 75 per cent to 92 and 15 out of 50 students even scored 100 on all their tests.

"These students also appeared more active than the other students and didn't show any signs of fatigue," Jason said. "Also, their health improved and they didn't get sick as much as the students, who didn't receive the electrical charges.

"Tesla was so passionate about this work that he wanted every person to have access to these healing benefits."

He also created a device called the 'Violet Ray' - a hand held unit that generated the same healing benefits of his high frequency current and ozone. He gave this patent out free of charge to any company that agreed to produce these machines so the public could access this technology with ease.

"They were even selling them in Sear's Catalogue," Jason said. "Tesla thought every home should have on of his devices.

"He knew the health-healing potential of the device but he also was strongly against the pharmaceutical industry because he believed his device and therapy would replace numerous and poten-

"Tesla's Hidden Medical Devices"

tially-dangerous drugs.

"Surprisingly, doctors making house calls at this time in history often brought a violet ray with them to treat their patients.

"Even the most famous psychic in the world, Edgar Casey, mentioned the Tesla violet ray as the cure for various medical issues in more the 900 separate channels."

But Tesla was also interested in other healing technology using his coils. He created several different pulsed magnetic field devices. He believed electromagnetic fields produced by his coils strengthened and revitalized the human energy system.

There is a famous picture of Tesla in the New York Recorder in 1896 healing Charles Broadway Rouss with one of his PEMF devices. Rouss was one of New York's most famous store keepers

BROADWAY ROUSS RECEIVING TREATMENT FROM NICOLA TESLA.

at the time. Unfortunately he went blind. Against the advice of his doctors he offered $1 million to anyone who could cure his blindness and Tesla tried to do so with one of his devices.

"Today some companies are still using this same technology in their healing devices," Jason said. "Some are even FDA and Health Canada approved.

"Tesla discovered the healing power of magnetism, electricity and the secrets of ozone."

These technologies became very popular and homes across America had them in their medicine cabinets in Tesla's day.

"Some doctors even started to prescribe these inventions and used them as their go to device in their private practice," Jason said. "Electro medicine was exploding."

Unfortunately, the pharmaceutical industry had other plans and the financial means and political influence to kill Tesla's medical cures.

In fact, an all out war was waged.

"The industry needed to do something to stop the spread of Tesla Medicine," Jason said.

In 1910, the Carnegie Foundation and the Rockefeller Group sponsored the infamous Flexner Report, which shut down any medical school teaching subjects outside of mainstream pharmacology.

"The edict was so powerful that only a few medical schools survived such as John Hopkins and McGill and a handful of others connected with these groups," Jason said. "They were the only schools that could legally license doctors.

"Doctors who used any method besides pharmacology were threatened with a loss of their medical license. This is essentially how today's doctors lost their freedom to prescribe alternative therapies."

To further discredit Tesla's medicine and his devices, the medical establishment started to describe the devices as "Quack Devices."

"This term stuck," Jason said. "It became synonymous with discrediting any practitioner or device that used methods outside of mainstream pharmacology. If a doctor was caught using these devices or promoting them they were threatened with the loss of their medical license and labeled a Quack Doctor."

"Tesla's Hidden Medical Devices"

By the 1930s all of these devices were subsequently banned by the FDA. Today very few people have ever heard of them.

"This is an amazing history that has been swept under the rug by the medical profession," Jason said. "But we need this information and devices now more than ever."

Most of these devices can be easily purchased and used for personal use. Companies such as Centurion Systems even hold Health Canada approval for their Tesla coil healing devices.

Would it surprise you to learn that the veterinarian industry today uses Tesla's pulsed electromagnetic devices?

Jason was invited to Wellington Florida in 2014 by the owner of Centurion Systems to show how Tesla technology was being used in the horse industry.

He was given a tour of some of the most prestigious show horse stables in America. The horses, used for racing and show jumping, ranged in value from $1 million to $5 million.

"Having a horse of such value is quite the insurance risk," Jason said. "If they injured or break a bone, or get sick you could be out millions of dollars. So this is not an option.

"Many of these stables are using the Centurion Tesla devices exclusively on their horses. These devices are helping them recover from their rigorous activities."

At some race tracks, horses that break a leg are still euthanized. In fact, it wasn't too long ago that horses with broken legs were put out of their misery by a bullet, sometimes right on the track in front of spectators.

"Euthanizing of horses still happens but there is now an alternative choice. Instead they wrap a Tesla coil around the break and within a couple of weeks the bone is completely healed and they can race again."

Impossible?

Or is it just something the public is simply kept in the dark about?

"Even NASA holds patents in these types of technologies to heal astronauts from the damaging effects of muscle and skeletal atrophy," Jason said.

Forbidden Knowledge

What makes this technology so amazing?

"It turns out that this type of technology is based off of the Earth's magnetic field," Jason said. "Tesla figured out that all biological life is intimately connected to the Earth's magnetic field. He discovered that our health is determined by the strength of our connection to this magnetic field.

"By stimulating the body with these fields we can generate a healing effect. This is the secret of Tesla technology. Tesla just focused and reproduced natural Earth phenomenon using his advanced coils."

Tesla used magnetism and electricity to stimulate healing at the deepest level of our being.

"This was virtually free and extremely effective," Jason said. "Tesla knew this would replace the use of pharmaceutical drugs because it had no side effects."

Let's examine football injuries.

"Broken collar bones are very common," Jason said. "It's also very painful and can take a long time to heal.

"But it's possible for players to recover from this injury and play football very quickly after being injured."

How is this possible?

"It turns out that the sports medicine practitioners know about these technologies from the veterinarians," Jason said "And these technologies are being used behind the scenes."

Doesn't it seem odd how these devices are legal to be used on animals but not on humans?

"Something is terribly wrong here," Jason said.

Did you know these devices are also available in the hospitals?

Would it surprise you to learn it's not the first approached used?

"If you badly break a bone they will first put you in a cast. If the cast does not heal you then they will operate and put pins in your bone," Jason said. "If this does not heal then they will wrap one of these devices on the bone and within a couple of weeks your bone is healed."

But why not use the technology first?

"Tesla's Hidden Medical Devices"

"Well they can't make money if they did it this way," Jason said. "It's just the simple truth. In fact these devices have also been found to be extremely effective in dealing with mental illness.

"Psychologists can only prescribe this type of therapy after two drugs have failed after a six month period. Something is wrong with this picture."

But the most important discovery made by Tesla was ozone.

"It turns out that nothing is immune to the power of ozone," Jason said. "In fact, UV robots are used to enter rooms with patients infected with Ebola.

"The UV shines on every surface of the room creating ozone. This kills the virus and sterilizes the space so that it can be used again.

"Ozone is 500 times a more powerful disinfectant than bleach. It's harmless and turns back into pure oxygen within five minutes. No superbug in the world can survive being exposed to ozone.

"This is the biggest conspiracy of the medical establishment. We have been taught that nothing is immune to the viruses and superbugs that plague our lives. We are told that we are in constant need of vaccinations to keep us safe.

"It turns out that ozone is the medical miracle we have been looking for. That's why Tesla put all his money into the Tesla Ozone Company in 1910. This is one of the most suppressed knowledge to date."

When the Ebola outbreak took place in 2014 a Canadian group set up a medical tent in Sierra Leone to treat victims of this horrible disease.

"They administered the ozone by direct intravenous of the gas, rectal infusion and through ozonized water," Jason said. "This treatment was given to four critically ill patients who tested positive for the virus.

"Within two to four days all of the patients made a full recovery. This group was subsequently visited by the US Army. They were informed this was not a licensed therapy and that they would have to leave Sierra Leone immediately or be arrested.

"You can see why this information is so threatening to medical mafia."

Forbidden Knowledge

But one of the easiest ways to receive ozone therapy is also free.

Did you know that your eyes are the only place in your body where UV light can enter your bloodstream?

"When the UV hits your blood it creates ozone, which is then spread through your circulatory system to kill all viruses, mold and bacteria," Jason explained.

"This is done by Sun gazing. When you let the light of the Sun enter your eyes you are allowing UV to create ozone in your blood. This was also well known throughout ancient cultures."

Now this doesn't mean you should stare at the Sun without sunglasses for long periods of time.

"This is done the safest within the first 20 minutes of sunrise and sunset," Jason explained. "There are so many capillaries in your eyes that 40 percent of your blood's volume passes through your eyes every 20 minutes.

"The Sun is one of the most powerful healers we have."

Interestingly, chem-trails effectively reflect UV radiation from the Sun back into space.

"But we need UV for our immune systems," Jason said. "It is the only wavelength of light that can naturally produce vitamin D within our bodies."

Have you ever noticed how everything we have has a coating of UV protection on it?

It's in every pair of glasses.

It's in windows.

Why are we being completely shielded from this wavelength of light?

Tesla realized that UV was one of the many secrets to the healing power of sun gazing.

"We need at least 15 minutes every day of full Sun exposure to allow the production of Vitamin D in our bodies," Jason said. "Long-term Sun exposure is harmful. That's why the times around sunrise and sunset are the safest. These are the times when light entering our eyes is harmless. But it's also the time when sunlight has the most benefit to us."

"Tesla's Hidden Medical Devices"

Skin cancer is also found in people who are UV light deficient.

"We are taught to fear the Sun when it's the Sun that is our greatest connection to source and healing," Jason said.

"In fact, medical statistics indicate that the lowest rate of skin cancer occurs the closer you are to the Equator. It's the chemicals in lotions and lack of proper light that are the main cause of health problems.

"It's also the excessive build up of toxins in the body. Our skin is one of our largest organs. It excretes toxins from our body. Sun exposure can damage areas of the skin where toxins have built up."

Now you might wonder that if ozone kills everything then why would it not also damage the cells in our bodies?

"Humans have something that other organisms do not," Jason said. "It is called SODs (superoxide dismutase). This enzyme is found within all our cells. It is this enzyme that makes us immune to the harmful effects of ozone.

"If we have a cell that is damaged or cancerous then the ozone will kill that cell and leave the other healthy cells alone.

Even Otto Warburg, one of the world's top biochemist and sole recipient of the Nobel Prize in Physiology in 1931, publicly stated in many papers that no virus or cancer can survive in an oxygen rich environment.

Warbug said "Cancer above all other diseases has countless secondary causes. But even for cancer, there is only one prime cause. The prime cause of cancer

Otto Warburg in his laboratory.

155

is the replacement of the respiration of oxygen in normal body cells by a fermentation of sugar.

"All normal cells have an absolute requirement for oxygen, but cancer cells can live without oxygen - a rule without exception. Deprive a cell 35 per cent of its oxygen for 48 hours and it might become cancerous."

Why have we ignored more than 100 years of documented research in these subjects?

Why are these topics buried in obscurity?

What powers would this information threaten if publicly accepted?

"I believe this line of research made Tesla more of a threat to the establishment than even his goal of giving the world free energy," Jason said.

Chapter 15
"Pyramids And The Galactic War"

In May 2015, Jason was invited at the last minute to be the headline speaker at the Canadian Society of Dowsers Conference in London, Ontario, Canada. The original speaker had to bow out because of a family emergency.

What is dowsing?

Some call it pseudoscience. Others absolutely believe in it. Essentially, it's the process where a person uses a stick or a rod or an object held from a string to locate ground water, buried metals, oil, gemstones, grave site, etc. without using any scientific device.

According to the Canadian Society of Dowsers, the earliest recorded dowser was Emperor Yu of the Hsia Dynasty in China nearly 4,000 years ago. It has also been practiced by Native Canadians and Americans as well as those living in Ancient Egypt and throughout the Roman Empire.

Internationally-renown psychic Uri Geller is a notable dowser.

At that time Jason had been working on a research project involving the lost technology of Nikola Tesla and the connection between this brilliant inventor, and the pyramids of Egypt.

"This research connected many dots for me between the hidden energy source of the Egyptian pyramids and Tesla's Wardenclyffe tower," Jason said.

The Wardenclyffe Tower, also known as the Tesla Tower, was a wireless transmission station designed and built by Tesla in Shoreham, (Long Island) New York in 1901.

Tesla believed this tower would be able to send unlimited wireless electricity transmissions anywhere in the world for free. But financial difficulties forced him to abandon the project and it never became operational.

"I believe Tesla stumbled – or was provided information about the ancient grid system of the planet by an enlightened species," Jason said. "This information, if made public, would have changed the world.

"This was the same technology that was used to power the pyramids."

While working on his research many past life memories resurfaced for Jason. It was information people have been searching for answers to for their entire lives.

How the ancient pyramids of Egypt or pyramids found throughout the world were built and what was their purpose has been one of the questions of the ages.

Mainstream scientists, archaeologist and historians have repeatedly voiced their views based on what they have learned while earning their degrees and reading and listening to other mainstream experts who obtained their information the same way.

Ancient alien theorists and enlightened scholars have rejected such views and have provided other educated opinions based on reason and common sense – and in some cases such as Jason, first-hand knowledge.

Indeed, Jason has been provided with some of the answers to one of history's most interesting and puzzling questions.

"I have been told the true purpose of the pyramids and why – and how they were built," Jason said.

Of course, what Jason knows absolutely goes against everything that we have been taught or that mainstream experts believe and have repeated.

Based on Jason's knowledge – the following is true.

"Pyramids And The Galactic War"

Pyramids were not built by thousands of slaves hauling massive and very heavy stone slabs across the desert – a construction time table that would have taken more than a lifetime to complete.

"It's my understanding that many of the very ancient pyramids were actually constructed in the 4th Dimension and then for all intents and purposes, placed on specific locations around the Earth," Jason said. "When something of such magnitude suddenly appeared, it's very easy to understand how the indigenous population would view the builders as Gods."

They were also not built solely as burial chambers for the pharaohs.

Modern research has revealed that pyramids are virtually scattered all over the planet.

"Some of these structures are hidden by mainstream archeology because it just doesn't fit into their belief system of history," Jason said. "Many of these pyramids are dated to well before the last ice age."

Most mainstream scientists believe the last ice age ended about 12,000 years ago. In fact, it's believed there might have been at least five different ice ages or periods since Earth was believed formed some 4.8 billion years ago.

"Many mainstream scientists, scholars, historians, you name it rarely if ever mention the fact that pyramids existed on the Earth well before the last Ice Age," Jason said. "It's as if they have chosen to either, look the other way and won't even consider the possibility or they simply tell you someone else built these structures after the last ice age.

"But either way, these structures exist and so do many other ancient sites on the ocean floor just waiting to be found and acknowledged.

"In a world that believes history began 6,000 years ago, the acknowledgment that a highly advanced global civilization existed thousands of years before our known recorded history would completely destroy the mainstream story."

Jason would love to be able to recount minute by minute all of his past lives. Unfortunately, he can't.

"Most of these memories are just pieces with no context and

Forbidden Knowledge

might be a little far out for anybody hearing this information for the first time," Jason said.

But this is the history Jason has been told from his past life experiences and astral world travels.

There was once a great war spanning many star systems.

"Just like most wars, this was about control, power and resources," Jason said. "The Reptilians, a highly advanced group of beings, started using force to colonize many planets.

"They used these conquered worlds for strategic bases, their natural resources and even enslaved the indigenous populations."

One of their strong holds in our solar system was a planet located between the orbit of Mars and Jupiter.

"In the ancient Sumerian texts this planet is referred to as Marduk although today we know this planet a Nibiru," Jason said. "Marduk (Nibiru) entered our solar system during its 3,600 year orbit and collided with a smaller planet known as Tiamat."

The late Zecharia Sitchin, a well-known author and ancient alien theorist, surmised that an advanced alien race known as the Anunnaki came from Marduk (Nibiru) and provided the Sumerians with their knowledge of science and religion. In fact, Sitchin believed all ancient mythologies came from the Anunnaki interaction with Earth.

Now, not every ancient alien theorist believes Sitchin was dead on. In fact, some have suggested he mistakenly interpreted the tablets or deliberately ignored things contained in them that didn't fit his narrative.

In Jason's view, Sitchin's theories have a ring of truth although the Anunnaki arrived on Earth long after this Great War – and were not the first alien species to provide advanced knowledge to humans.

"The Reptilian dominance had become a great concern for a more benevolent, peaceful and enlightened group of species," Jason said.

According to what Jason has been told – and experienced in his past lives – other star beings (such as the Pleiadians, Acturians and other star nations) knew that if they did not intervene and stop the spread of this takeover by The Reptilians that it would eventually cause chaos across the galaxy.

"Pyramids And The Galactic War"

"They decided the best way to weaken the Reptilians was the complete annihilation of this planet," Jason said.

A weapon of immense power was then used to destroy the planet.

"This destruction created the asteroid belt we see today," Jason said. "But the destruction was so great that it also caused massive destruction and environmental changes to nearby planets.

"We can see this ancient destruction today on Mars and on Earth."

Could this be the cause of the perplexing K-T boundary found in our fossil records?

Based on his knowledge, Jason believes this was the mass extinction event that took place on Earth around 65 million years ago that ended the reign of the dinosaurs.

It unleashed the massive six-mile wide asteroid that struck the Yucatan peninsula in Mexico, leaving the 12-mile deep and 124-mile wide Chicxulub crater, wiping out more than 80 per cent of the Earth's species, including the dinosaurs.

"This event still has not been conclusively explained but it left a one inch black sedimentary deposit in the fossil records found around the world," Jason said. "This was a massive planet changing event.

"I'm convinced this event caused the mass extinction of life on this planet. It also turned Earth into a water world."

Jason believes this is likely where at least some of the stories of the Great Flood came from – and were passed down by ancient cultures.

Despite the Bible's interpretation of the Great Flood there is more than enough archaeological evidence to suggest long before Noah built his ark similar Great Flood stories existed about 4,400 years ago in ancient civilizations of Mesopotamia and Sumeria. In fact, the Sumerian Epic of Gilgamesh has a flood story that dates back nearly 5,000 to 7,000 years.

Similar Great Flood stories are found in numerous ancient cultures around the world, including the destruction of Atlantis.

"All we know from the fossil records was that this event was the most extreme event that has ever occurred on our planet," Jason said.

According to what he has been told, this destruction caused many unforeseen complications.

Forbidden Knowledge

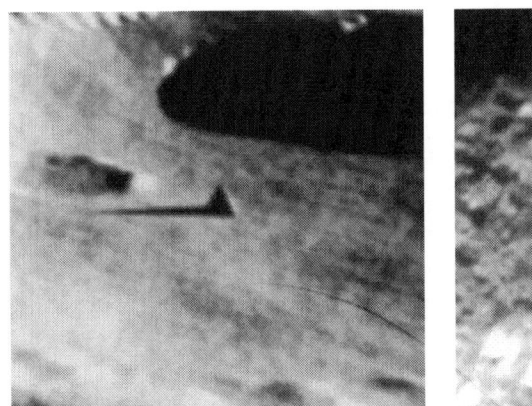

Pyramids photographed on the surface of the Moon.

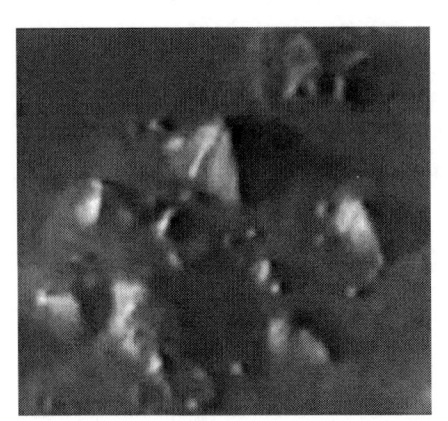

Pyramids photographed on the surface of Mars.

"Besides destruction on nearby planets, this disaster also caused the orbits of our solar system to be thrown out of balance," Jason said. "You see, all stars are bound together by a great force.

"When one star system has experienced a trauma other star systems feel its effects."

"The star beings responsible for these unintended catastrophic events agreed that it was also their duty to fix what they had caused," Jason explained.

"They did this by building pyramids on the Earth, the Moon, Mercury, Mars and Jupiter," Jason said. "Pyramids are very sacred structures that have many purposes.

"Pyramids And The Galactic War"

"These structures were placed on very specific points on these planets. This was done to correct wobble of all of these planets, which in turn would correct their orbits."

It works much like a counter weight on a wheel.

"If your car's wheel is not aligned it will start to wobble," he said. "This problem is corrected by placing a very tiny weight on a specific point on the wheel. This corrects its alignment and fixes the wobble."

"But the pyramids also had other functions that remain virtually unknown," Jason said.

STAR GATES

"They acted as star gates, which allowed beings from other star systems to travel back and forth," Jason said. "This was done using specialized machinery located in the pyramid structure. It was similar technology to a Tesla coil but it used very rare metals and other worldly technology.

"This allowed these star beings access to these planets. The pyramids also controlled the environment of a planet. Using this specialized technology like the Tesla tower it would manipulate the ionosphere.

"We still use this technology today under the name HAARP. But the original technology in the pyramids has since been taken off planet."

It was also revealed to Jason why mapping of the stars was so important to many ancient cultures and societies on Earth.

"We find stone circles and structures all over the world that are specifically designed to align with either specific stars or the Sun at important times of the year," Jason said. "Like the solstice or equinoxes."

Why were they so obsessed with these alignments?

Was it just to develop calendars so they would know when the festivals were? When to sow and when to reap the crops?

"While this is true, there was also far more to it then that," Jason said.

"They were obsessed with knowing their position in the solar system," Jason said. "This was done to monitor the position of the Earth relative to markers in the sky.

Forbidden Knowledge

"The ancient people knew about the wobble of the Earth and its orbit. They could see if the Earth was out of alignment if their markers didn't line up. This would be a big problem. These star beings would then use the pyramids to correct this alignment so that the Earth and other planets could stay in their proper orbit."

According to Jason, there were many previous civilizations before our known recorded history and long before the Anunnaki arrived. Some of these civilizations were even highly advanced spiritually and technologically.

"There is much written of these lost cultures such as Lemuria and Atlantis," Jason said. "But the story is always the same.

"A civilization grows advanced and powerful, they develop high technology, philosophy and spirituality. They make contact with other star nations and share information, technology and resources. They learn how to travel using the Earth's grid system and the pyramids or by building ships and other star gates.

"Then power and greed take over. Wars become the answer and they destroy themselves. This is the pattern that happened in both Lemuria and Atlantis.

"There are always survivors and record keepers that start new civilizations after their self inflicted or other worldly cataclysms. This is what happened with Egyptian, Sumerian and other post Atlantean civilizations.

"These cultures just didn't pop up over night highly advanced. They were already advanced. They were the survivors. Some of them were not even human, but different star beings, who had remained on Earth from these past epochs."

Many of these star beings are still with us here today. We're just not allowed to know that information.

"Many still remain underground in the Earth," Jason said. "Many others are working side by side with black budget and above top secret, unacknowledged military and governmental factions.

"In fact many UFO sightings, cattle mutilations and even abductions are exclusively orchestrated by one or more of these factions. True information is hard to come by and there is deception and disinformation at every turn."

It might interest readers to know that when Jason and Bob began co-writing this book in September 2015. Both of them were completely shocked but not entirely surprised when they watched the return of television's X-Files in January 2016. The essential theme dealt with some of the many truths revealed in this book.

"This is what I worry about with the entire disclosure movement," Jason said. "If the government or the Vatican admits they have known and been in contact with ET visitors for all these years it would give these agencies even more power because they would be the ones controlling the information and new alien technologies. This scenario would be a complete disaster."

Jason is also very concerned about the possibility of a false flag operation – such as a fake alien invasion – being perpetrated on humankind.

"This would bring the world leaders together to create a one world totalitarian government to fight this fake enemy," Jason said.

"Sounds far out? You should listen to President Reagan's speech at the UN Assembly 1974. And if this is not a serious concern then why the push for massive amounts of space based weaponry already positioned around our planet."

What are they preparing for?

Also, why do most Hollywood movies portray aliens as hostel invaders?

"Is this vision of aliens being programmed into us so that we will fear them," Jason asked.

While researching Tesla and his connection to the pyramids Jason was inexplicably drawn to the stories of the infamous Pharaoh Akhenaten.

"I wanted to share the story of what happens to you when you try to change the paradigm," Jason said. "Tesla tried and so did Akhenaten."

So Jason decided this would be the theme of his keynote address at the Canadian Society of Dowsers.

He could never have imagined the dangerous territory he was about to enter.

Forbidden Knowledge

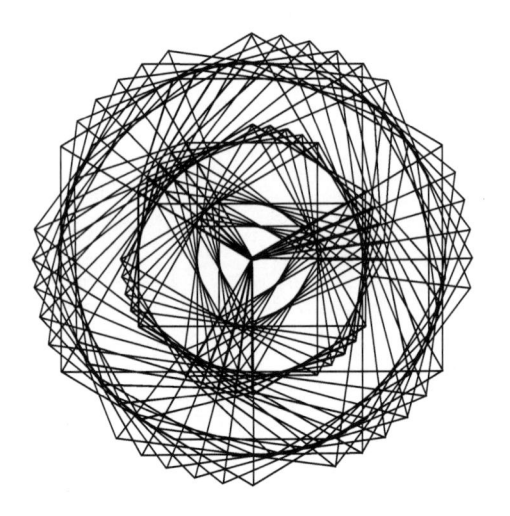

"The desire that guides me in all I do is the desire to harness the forces of nature to the service of mankind."

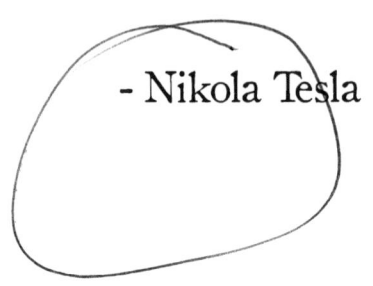

- Nikola Tesla

Chapter 16
"Tesla's Hidden Technologies, Government Secrets & Alien Treaties"

What if you learned an inventor created technologies that would provide humanity with unlimited free clean energy anywhere in the world?

What if you discovered this same person also discovered the way to increase the quality of agriculture without the use of any chemicals?

What if you found out there was such a thing as anti-gravity, a way to end all wars and to cure humanity's illnesses and diseases?

Don't you think the world would be a better place?

"Such a person did exist and he devised the means to provide all of the above to mankind," Jason said.

"His name was Nikola Tesla and he was virtually erased from the history books.

"Tesla created all these gifts for humanity before 1930."

This is how Jason began his talk at the Canadian dowsers gathering.

He went on to provide information connecting Tesla to Akhenaten.

Born in 1856 in what is now Croatia, Tesla came to America in 1884 and worked with Thomas Edison in creating the electric light bulb.

But Tesla believed wireless transmission of energy was possible. In 1900 he devised a way that a world-wide wireless communica-

Forbidden Knowledge

Nikola Tesla reading in front of a electromagnetic coil of his design.

tion system could be transmitted through large electrical towers, providing free electrical power throughout the world.

Imagine free electrical power.

No bills.

Unlimited free power for everybody on the planet.

Tesla initially had financial support for his grandiose project from well-known financier J.P Morgan. But investors had doubts

"Tesla's Hidden Technologies, Government Secrets & Alien Treaties"

Tesla's Wardenclyffe Tower which was capable of sending wireless electricity around the world.

and funds were eventually withdrawn. Tesla declared bankruptcy and his tower on Long Island was eventually dismantled and sold for scrap to help pay off his debts.

He died on Jan. 7, 1943 in New York at 86.

One of his alleged inventions was a weapon that he believed would end all wars. He described it as a "peace ray" – a laser-beam device that could create a stream of particles of immense power that was capable of destroying a fleet of 10,000 airplanes from nearly 200 miles away.

If every major country had one of these "peace rays," then all wars would essentially end because no country would be able to defeat another.

Newspapers, however, in 1934 changed its name to a "death ray."

As far as anybody knows, Tesla never actually built one or even a proto-type.

But insiders today suggest governments later created such a weapon. In fact, conspiracy theorists suggest "black opt" operations have successfully – and secretly produced several of Tesla's inventions, including a death ray and time travel jump pods.

So have governments really developed such capabilities?

169

Forbidden Knowledge

President Dwight Eisenhower's great grand daughter, Laura Eisenhower says yes.

In fact, she made startling claims during a jaw-dropping address in 2014 at the 22nd World Symposium on UFOs and Related Phenomena, Extraterrestrials and World Politics in the Republic of San Marino. Her entire presentations can be read at www.CosmicGaiaSophia.com

In recent years Laura has publicly revealed numerous claims, including that an alien invasion has already taken place but our governments have never told us about it.

But here is one of the first things she said in Italy.

"There has been a massive cover up in regards to ET contact with our governments and there has been much secrecy in regards to those who have been either abducted or contacted - this is because an invasion has already taken place and they don't want us to know this.

"This invasion has infiltrated every sector of our society, in disguise to most, but blatantly obvious to others."

Laura also claimed that she was recruited by government agents in 2006 for a mission to an existing Mars colony. This colony was set up under secret treaties and is known as "Alternative 3".

She also claimed the world was being run by a Shadow Government with ET technology from treaties that were signed before her great grandfather even became President of the United States.

In fact, she claimed the U.S. in 1934 under President Franklin Roosevelt made a treaty with one of the Grey-alien species agreeing to trade animals and humans in exchange for high-tech knowledge. The Government also allowed this alien species to build underground bases without interference.

This agreement was known as the "Grenada Treaty and in return for advanced technology, the U.S. allowed the Greys to freely abduct humans for their ongoing genetics program. This treaty was allegedly signed after the U.S. refused help from the Pleiadians, who insisted on military disarmament.

This might seem unbelievable to many people, especially those who refuse to believe the world they live in isn't what they think

"Tesla's Hidden Technologies, Government Secrets & Alien Treaties"

it is. The agreement provided the U.S. with technologies such as anti-gravity devices, free energy and medical advancements.

But according to Laura, after being rejected by the U.S. government, the Pleiadians signed a treaty with Adolf Hitler and the Nazis in return for promising not to attack Jewish people.

By 1941, the Pleiadians canceled their deal because Hitler reneged on his Jewish promise although the Nazis did develop space craft prototypes (Foo Fighters). The Greys were quick to make an agreement with Hitler.

Laura claims the alien treaties are re-worked every decade, including in 1954 when her great grandfather met the Pleiadians at Edwards Air Force base.

It was at this meeting that the Pleiadians warned Eisenhower against continuing agreements with the Greys. In return for providing technological and spiritual help, Eisenhower had to again agree to dismantle and destroy all nuclear weapons. He didn't.

Laura claimed she declined the offer to go to Mars. But she revealed to Congress that CIA-operated jump rooms (teleportation rooms) exist in the U.S. and similar rooms are also located in Russia and Great Britain. She has also been told that as many as 500,000 people currently live in off planet colonies.

So what are we to make of Laura Eisenhower?

Either she is completely delusional or her pedigree gives her incredible credibility.

Interestingly, in late 2014, the U.S. Navy conducted a very public demonstration of a laser beam weapon that set fire to an unmanned drone.

Now let's suppose for the moment that Tesla succeeded in creating many of his inventions but the elite powers running the world's finances and governments didn't allow him to provide these amazing gifts to humanity.

Laura Eisenhower's revelations would certainly change your view of reality but so would the fact that Tesla's inventions were also kept hidden.

"The truth is, for nearly 100 years these technologies have been

171

Forbidden Knowledge

available to free us all from economic slavery and ecological destruction," Jason said.

Tesla became a recluse and confined himself to a tiny hotel room in New York where he lived out the rest of his life in solitude because of the power struggle over the suppression of his inventions.

"It's estimated that more than 400 of his patents are still classified and under military control," Jason said. "And if this technology existed nearly 100 years ago, just imagine how far todays technologically would have evolved had Tesla's work not been kept secret."

In Jason's view, we would be light years ahead of what we believe technology is capable of today.

"The truth is, Laura Eisenhower is correct," Jason said. "We just haven't been allowed to know that we are.

"Needing to use gasoline as a fuel source is the biggest lie our society has been built on. We have had the capability of building anti-gravity engines since the 30s. We have had nuclear engines since the 50s.

"To think we use rockets to shoot people into outer space is laughable. This is why many have come forward, including those who have provided inside information to Laura Eisenhower about alleged secret space programs that have been going on since the 1940s."

The Foo Fighters have become the stuff of legends. Although the existence of these round glowing flying objects has always been debated, many Allied aircraft pilots saw them and reported them to their commanders but were told to remain quiet.

Laura Eisenhower told the Italian congress that "Foo Fighters" existed and were developed under an alien treaty. Officially, mainstream scientists suggested these weren't craft or even physical entities but electrostatic phenomena similar to St. Elmo's fire.

Really?

Many people, especially conspiracy theorists, suggest the moon landing of July 1969 was also hoax.

"This is the wrong question or assumption considering how Earth has had contact with other worldly beings and advanced space technology way before the infamous moon landing by the

"Tesla's Hidden Technologies, Government Secrets & Alien Treaties"

Americans even took place," Jason said.

"As Laura indicated, many insiders have come forward to tell of alleged secret exchange programs involving humans living on other planets before we even officially landed on the moon."

People such as Randy Cramer and Gary McKinnon have gone public about what they know.

In 2001, McKinnon, a British systems administrator, hacked into nearly 100 U.S. military and NASA computers looking for files about free energy. Instead, he claimed to have discovered files about a secret space program called "Solar Warden" and spreadsheets containing names of "non-terrestrial officers," and transfers between fleets.

Cramer's story is far more incredible. He claims he spent 17 years on Mars serving at a secret military base protecting breakaway human civilization colonies. He also claims two highly intelligent indigenous species, Reptoids and Insectoids, live on Mars. For the most part they existed in a truce with the Mars Defense Forces and Mars Colony Corporation until a fierce firefight that resulted in the deaths of more than a thousand humans after the group tried to retrieve an artifact from a cave belonging to the Reptoids.

Known as "Captain Kaye," he also claims he was recruited as a 17-year-old teenager and after serving with this special military group was returned to his bed, never aging a day but retaining his memories.

In email conversations with Cramer he confirmed he is currently working on a book about his experiences. In fact, Cramer now says he works for the United States Marine Corps Special Services and has been given permission to talk publicly about what happened to him.

"So do I believe the moon landing was a hoax? Let's put that in a different perspective," Jason said. "I believe the entire space program is a hoax designed to perpetuate the idea that we don't have the technology that we actually do have."

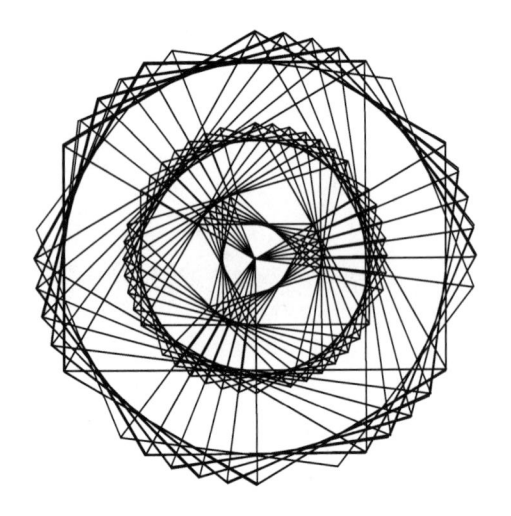

"Knowing yourself is the beginning of all wisdom"

- Aristotle

Chapter 17
"Attacked"

In May 2015, Jason decided to share his views about Tesla and his connection with ancient Egypt with the gathering at the Canadian Society of Dowsers.

So he did but then something very strange happened when he began to talk about where Ancient Egyptian Pharaoh Akhenaten fit in with the Tesla story and the truths that had been hidden from humanity.

Jason was showing pictures of the elongated skulls that have been discovered throughout the world and how Akhenaten and his family also had these strange skulls. He described how these beings with elongated skulls weren't human but a completely different race of beings.

Some have suggested they were star beings. Others believe they were another line of humanity. Others are convinced they were the Nephilim that the ancient texts refer to.

"These beings were from our untold prehistory dating far back to the times of Atlantis," Jason said.

Interestingly, both Jason and his wife Monika, have memories of their life in Atlantis.

"I remember working with the crystals underground," Jason

Forbidden Knowledge

Limestone carving depicting Akhenaten, Nefertiti and three of their daughters from 1350 BC. Image source: New World Encyclopedia. Notice the shape of their skulls.

said. "I was high priest in that life. These crystals were alive and could communicate telepathically.

"They forewarned about the destruction of Atlantis for many years. So we prepared colonies on various places on Earth. When the moment came when the island had to be evacuated the main method was in large boats."

But the elite Atlanteans escaped in spaceships. Jason recalls watching from the air as the destruction occurred.

"It was very tragic," he recalled. "The waves were too strong for these boats and many were sucked into the water."

Jason said the craft he was in held many of Atlantis' most important people and they carried the information and history of Atlantis.

This island was first described by Greek philosopher Plato, who said it was destroyed around 9400 BC.

"We went to our new home, which is located in modern day Egypt."

After the destruction of Atlantis many of these beings with elongated heads established new colonies of rule around the world, including Egypt and South America as the pyramid culture once again emerged from the ashes of Atlantis. You will find these elongated skulls around the world near ancient pyramid sites.

"Even infant elongated skulls have been discovered," Jason said. "This was not done as a deformation. They were born this way. Many ancient cultures did deform their skulls using archaic methods of head binding.

"But this was only done so that they could be closer to the gods. They were trying look like them."

"We are lucky to have artifacts from Akhenaten because he made the artists of the time depict him and his family as they actually were," Jason told the audience. "To draw a so called 'god' as they actually were was considered a huge crime at that time."

DARKNESS EMERGES

But as Jason started to delve deeper into this talk, Monika, his then fiancée, who is also very psychically gifted, noticed the room appeared to be filling with very dark beings.

"I could see her face change and knew something was wrong," Jason recalled. "She actually looked pissed not concerned. She seemed angry that I had gone into this topic and was almost signaling for me to stop."

But Jason didn't. He continued his presentation.

"As soon as my talk was over I started to get physically sick," Jason said. "Monika was furious. She had seen these beings enter the room to attack my energy."

But Jason wasn't concerned. He had been attacked before by dark forces and won.

However, this time was very different.

This time – a hit had been put on his life.

"I started to develop what looked like hives on my arm," Jason said. "It was like I had hundreds of tiny mosquito bites.

"The bites blistered and burnt like fire. The pain was intense."

Jason tried every remedy. He used oils, tinctures, salves, apple cider vinegar, even heavy duty medication. But nothing worked.

"In fact, each and every day after this event I just got sicker and sicker," he said. "Each day was worse than the last and the hives began to spread all over my body."

His face swelled like he had been punched silly by a boxer or that he had suffered some severe allergic reaction to something.

"I had cauliflower ears. My eyes were almost completely shut," Jason said. "It felt as if my life had been drained out of me.

"I could barley move or walk. I could also barely see. I was going blind because I lost about 70 per cent of my vision.

"I lost my appetite. In fact, I couldn't handle any solid foods. I just drank liquids,"

Jason had long given up on doctors but he had no choice. So he went to several different doctors to find out what was wrong with him.

"The first doctor ran every blood test he could think of but like many years before the results indicated there was nothing medically wrong with me," Jason said. "Both of us were speechless… Once again all the tests showed that I was healthier than the average person my age.

"My blood cell count was perfect. It showed that I wasn't fighting any virus or bacteria. An allergy test also came back negative. In fact, I wasn't allergic to anything. There were zero allergens in my body."

The doctor just stared at him and said, "This is a true mystery," Jason said.

There was no denying it. Jason had to face the only other conclusion.

"This was an energetic poisoning," he said. "I had crossed a line and I now somebody wanted me out of the picture."

Now, Jason had to figure out why.

"Monika couldn't even bare to look at me," Jason said. "It looked

"Attacked"

as though I was actually turning into a zombie. My skin started to open up and fall off and at this point my face had no similarities of the Jason she once knew."

The once happy couple had planned to get married in August but this health crisis put their wedding in doubt.

"I thought about taking pictures of myself in this state, but I couldn't even bring myself to do so," he said. "I was so upset that I did not want any memories of this event documented."

In hindsight he now wishes he did because it would be absolute proof that he was accurately describing what he was enduring.

There was nobody to turn to for help except to his psychic friends so he reached out to Kathy, Saundra and Nora.

"But even with their energy work I continued to get worse," Jason said.

A HORRIFIC PAST LIFE DEATH

It was at that point that Jason discovered what was happening. His past life memories started to resurface.

They were about the life and death of Akhenaten.

"Many people refer to Akhenaten as the heretic pharaoh because during his reign he denounced the worship of many gods and implement monotheism to all of Egypt," Jason said. "In its place he established the worship of Aten, the sun god, as the source of creation.

"This created a huge divide in his kingdom. Akhenaten grew up in the shadow of the priesthood and saw their deep corruption. At the time the priesthood held as much power as the pharaoh and his family. This was because money, power and greed had entered the priesthood.

"Imagine you grow up and your family line is connected to the worship of Sobek, the god of the Nile. Your entire life was devoted to this god and his temple led by many priests."

Sobek was an ancient Egyptian deity often represented in human form with a crocodile head. He was connected with Pharaonic power, fertility, and military and a protector of the Nile River.

Forbidden Knowledge

"The priests would ask your family for donations to the temple," Jason said. "When you grew up and events happened in your life you were obligated to also give donations to the temple.

"If you wanted a free pass to the afterlife then that would cost you even more. If you wanted a proper burial and mummification, well, that would cost you more.

"The temple and the priests of each temple to each god became increasingly wealthy. They even mummified your pets or offerings for a hefty price."

"Akhenaten knew well of this corruption and that if this were to continue it would threaten the Pharaonic rule," Jason said.

"This power and corruption reached every part of Egypt even to the point where wars and who would be pharaoh was decided by the priesthood," Jason said. "You can say this was the start of the secret societies."

"With this knowledge, Akhenaten shut them all down," Jason said.

"This had a huge impact on Egyptian life," he said. "It was like he purposely crashed the economy of Egypt just to re-establish a new system with new ideas and teachings that would help free his people from the economic slavery of the priesthood."

He started to teach about the healing powers of the sun and how the light from the sun was our closest link to the source.

"He even took the roofs off the temples so that Aten could shine in," Jason said. "He taught self realization and responsibly that you are the temple of Aten. That you can connect to the divine not through the priesthood but through your direct connection to the nature around and within you.

"The closest representation we have to this source in the physical world is the Sun. This enraged the priesthood. They started to plot against him and his family. It wasn't long until the old priesthood decided it was time to take him out."

Now, perhaps you wonder how Jason knows all of this history about a pharaoh, who was basically erased from recorded history?

He knows it because he has very vivid recalled memories from that lifetime.

"Attacked"

Statue of Akhenaten at the Cairo Museum, Egypt.

Jason, you see believes he is strongly connected to Akhenaten.

His wife Monika also has a strong connection to Nefertiti. Today, depictions of Nefertiti are among the most recognized works of art surviving from the ancient Egyptian civilization.

"Monika actually still remembers this to this day and she has a deep emotional connection to it," Jason said. "She remembers being sent out of Egypt with her children.

"She knew she would never see Akhenaten again and it ripped her to pieces. She hid from those sent to find and capture her. She's not sure if they ever found her."

According to ancient Egyptian scholars, Nefertiti vanished in 1335 BC. Scholars have also suggested the couple had six children, all daughters.

Her tomb has never been found.

"We all come from a source," Jason explained. "We can call this source God, light, the universe, nature or simply just creation.

Forbidden Knowledge

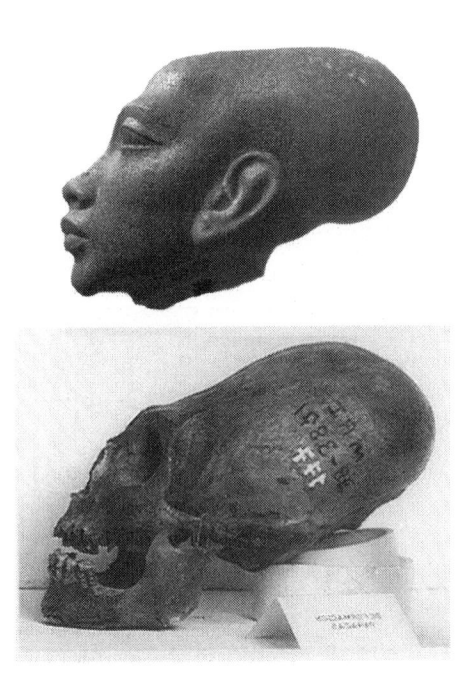

Bust of Nefertiti is believed to have been created in 1345 BC. Also pictured is a bust of Nefertiti's daughter. Notice how the scull is elongated just like the elongated skulls found all over the world.

"We all have a divine spark of creation within us and around us at all times. As this energy flows from its source it passes many fields of vibration.

"Each one of us has a unique vibration. This vibration is like music broadcasting out into the universe. We all have our own song. When we incarnate on a planet the vibration we carry starts to resonate with other frequencies of similar nature and experience. This will bring these beings together in one way or another. You can call them soul groups.

"The earth like all other planets is a living being. As we experience our lives on Mother Earth we are recording our lives within her electromagnetic field. This is referred to as the book of life and death.

"If my source energy is in resonance with the past life experiences of another person recorded on Earth then those memories and experiences can flow through me. That's not discounting the notion that we live past lives. It's just explaining it in a different way.

"In fact, we live multiple lives in multiple time lines on multiple locations through time and space all at the same time. So in this life I have chosen to access many past life memories in multiple time lines and locations. These are to bring forward these experiences, information and energy into my current life stream.

"We can call these types of experiences archetypes. One of the life streams very close to me throughout my entire life is Akhenaten and Osiris."

The priesthood knew that Akhenaten was a powerful master and that it would not be such an easy matter to capture and kill him.

"The priesthood made arrangements with what we would call dark shamans or sorcerers," Jason said. "Using their dark magic they were able to poison Akhenaten.

"They then placed him in a sarcophagus while he was still alive. The dark shamans then did a ceremony that placed many curses on him. They then filled the sarcophagus with hundreds of live scarab beetles and sealed the lid.

"This was an excruciating death, literally being eaten to death by hundreds of insects."

This is why Jason became so sick.

"These poisons, these dark shaman curses, and these scarabs were brought through the time lines and started to physically manifest through me," Jason said. "This is called a "reliving".

"I started to manifest Akhenaten's energy within my body in this time line. This is how he died then and this is how these dark sorcerers wanted me to die again,"

HELP ARRIVES

Without anyone else to turn too, Jason left a frantic message for Peter Bernard, his friend and Algonquin Shaman.

"Please help me, I don't know how many days I have left," was the message.

Forbidden Knowledge

The next day Peter returned his call and promised he would heal him that night. The healing took place and Jason woke up the next morning feeling much better.

"He called me back to confirm these stories with me," Jason said. "On how I was going through a reliving and that there were these dark shamans trying to end my life.

"He said it was a good thing I had called him when I did because I didn't have much time left. I was literally being eaten to death by invisible scarab beetles and that's actually exactly what I looked like.

"It looked like something was slowly eating me. Again Peter came to my rescue when no one else could. He said to me that it was like someone had put out a professional hit on me."

Almost instantly Jason felt better and his skin healed.

"It was like I was a snake," he said. "My skin started to peel off every inch of my body. I was born again."

So what is the connection between Tesla and Akhenaten?

"It's my belief that they both knew about the secret source of energy known as the Earth's grid," Jason said. "And that both suffered consequences for trying to change the power structures in place during their time period.

"For Akhenaten, it was the priesthood and for Tesla, it was the electrical companies owned by wealthy businessmen."

As indicated earlier, Jason believes Tesla re-discovered the ancient grid system that was used by ancient Egyptians.

"He learned how he could tune into frequencies using his electromagnetic coils, which could tap into and transmit wireless electricity throughout the Earth and the air," Jason said. "Tesla also learned the secret of the planet's ionosphere. He discovered the resonant frequency of the Earth and the ionosphere was 7.8 Hz.

"Using his towers he could alter this resonance. He also discovered the frequency of the ionosphere was the same resonance as that of the human mind. And if one could alter the ionosphere, then one could also alter the mind.

"I believe Tesla figured out just how dangerous this technology could be and he stopped any further research. Today, we have

"Attacked"

the same technology that Tesla thought was too dangerous. It's called HAARP."

Officially, HAARP (High Frequency Active Auroral Research Program) is an ionospheric research program funded by the U.S. Air Force, the U.S. Navy, the University of Alaska, and the Defense Advanced Research.

Also, officially, its purpose is to analyze the ionosphere and investigate the potential for developing ionospheric enhancement technology for radio communications and surveillance. The HAARP program operates out of a major sub-arctic facility, named the HAARP Research Station, on an Air Force-owned site in Alaska.

However, conspiracy theorists have a different take ranging from suggestions that governments are using the technology to manipulate the weather as a military weapon with the capability of triggering floods, earthquakes, tornadoes and causing droughts. Others have suggested it can and has been used to transmit radio waves as a mind control or manipulation weapon.

Jason insists there's no doubt whatever HAARP has been used for these purposes, the technology came from Tesla.

"Tesla was also a highly-gifted psychic," Jason said.

"He would be able to see his inventions in his mind so clearly that he could visualize how every part worked and fit together.

"If it worked in his visions then he would put it together in the physical world," Jason said.

Jason explained how Tesla also described being visited by metallic spheres that would enter his laboratory and observe him.

"He found these to be very distracting," Jason said. "He created technology to broadcast a field that would keep these spheres out of his laboratory."

What were these spheres?

"They sound like the same spheres people have witnessed creating crop circles," Jason said. "Perhaps ideas for all of his inventions were actually downloaded by a benevolent and advanced race of star beings into his mind for the benefit of humanity.

"Remember, Tesla was the first person to send – and receive –

the first radio signals."

Jason provided the following excerpt from one of Tesla's communications.

"I can never forget the first sensations I experienced when it dawned upon me that I had observed something possibly of incalculable consequences to mankind. I felt as though I were present at the birth of a new knowledge or the revelation of a great truth.

"My first observations positively terrified me as there was present in them something mysterious, not to say supernatural, and I was alone in my laboratory at night; but at that time the idea of these disturbances being intelligently controlled signals did not yet present itself to me.

"The changes I noted were taking place periodically and with such a clear suggestion of number and order that they were not traceable to any cause known to me. I was familiar, of course, with such electrical disturbances as are produced by the sun, Aurora Borealis, and earth currents, and I was as sure as I could be of any fact that these variations were due to none of these causes.

"The nature of my experiments precluded the possibility of the changes being produced by atmospheric disturbances, as has been rashly asserted by some. It was sometime afterward when the thought flashed upon my mind that the disturbances I had observed might be due to an intelligent control.

"Although I could not at the time decipher their meaning, it was impossible for me to think of them as having been entirely accidental. The feeling is constantly growing on me that I had been the first to hear the greeting of one planet to another. A purpose was behind these electrical signals."

- Nikola Tesla

"Attacked"

As indicated earlier in this book, during the time of Akhenaten, when the pyramids were active, it created a word-wide energy grid for power communication, travel, and controlling the weather.

"The main power source and control for the grid system was located in the Giza pyramid of Egypt," Jason said.

What was this great power source?

According to Jason, the power source was what is known today as the Arc of the Covenant.

"When Akhenaten saw how the priesthood was taking power he foresaw the end of Egyptian rule," Jason said. "He knew this power could not fall into the hands of the priesthood.

"Akhenaten ordered that the arc be taken out of Egypt and hidden so the priesthood could not use its power for themselves. He foresaw that if this technology fell into the wrong hands the world would be destroyed again.

"He then dismantled the pyramid removing its capstone and sending the other technologies off planet. This is where some believe the story of Moses came from; that Akhenaten was actually Moses taking the arc out of Egypt away from the corruption of the priesthood."

Was this the start of the biblical shift to monotheism?

"It's interesting to note that after Akhenaten, Egypt declined until there civilization crumbled," Jason said. "Many people think Tutankhamen was the son of Akhenaten, I believe that he was installed as the new ruler by the priesthood once Akhenaten was killed.

"This is why Tutankhamen is found in such a lavish setting in a casket of gold. This was the wealth and power Akhenaten warned about."

Forbidden Knowledge

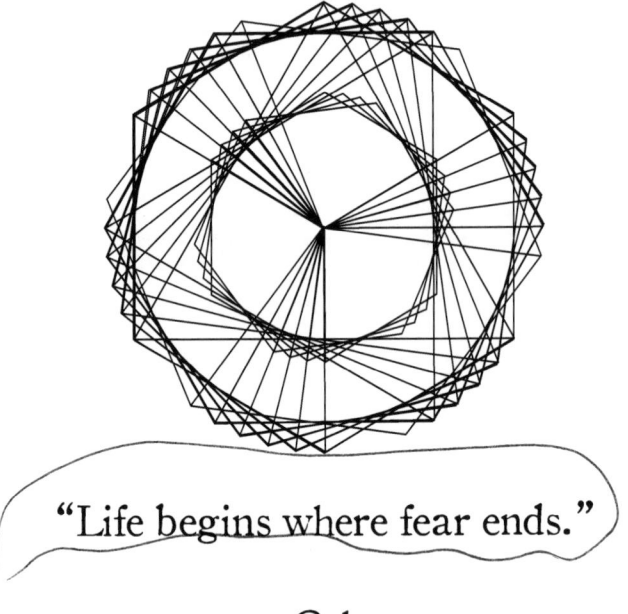

"Life begins where fear ends."

- Osho

Chapter 18
"The Ancient Serpent Gods"

One doesn't have to look far in ancient texts to find words such as Serpent Gods, Dragons and Flying Serpent throughout the world.

These are just some of the descriptive names given to the ancient gods.

Looking with today's eyes, we still scratch our heads.

Why did ancient cultures describe their deities this way?

What do the words in the ancient texts really mean?

Are we to take these names as literal descriptions or merely figures of speech?

In Jason's view, these were accurate descriptions of the real leaders – or what ancient culture described as gods – that created civilizations and controlled the indigenous populations.

They were beings who came from the stars.

And over time, theses Serpent or Dragon gods faded into the background – behind the curtain so to speak – and controlled human power and influence in secrecy.

"It is still happening today," Jason said based on what he believes is the case from the knowledge he has been given through his journeys and teachings from astral and dimensional beings.

"Stories of these Dragons that descended from heaven are found all over the word," Jason said. "They retell a story that some time in our past a group of beings descended on Earth and took residence on this planet.

"These beings then through genetic manipulation created mankind to become their workers, to toil in the fields, to feed them, to mine for resources and to build their temples.

"These so-called 'Dragon Gods' then created a lineage of rulers, kings, emperors along with cities, economy and even religion.

Anshar, the Sumerian god of the celestial world was believed to have been born of Serpents known as Lakhmu and Lakhamu and was the father of Anu.

"Anu was considered the Lord of Heaven," Jason said. "Anu's wife was Antu and their children were the Anunnaki."

Recorded history of this phase of human evolution suggest the first civilizations sprang up in what is known as Mesopotamia around 5,000 to 3000 BC around the Tigris-Euphrates rivers although archaeological evidence suggests small pockets of nomadic people existed as far back as 8000 BC.

Discovered in what today is essentially southern Iraq, the word "Ushumgal," in ancient Sumerian text was used to describe the "flying serpent' or 'dragon' and "The Great Serpent God of Heaven" as well as the Anunnaki god 'Enki," along with other major deities.

"According to ancient Sumerian text, some 600 of these Serpent Gods descended from heaven," Jason said. "There are many stories suggesting these god-like beings lived in the temples and only the high priests were allowed to interact with them.

"These priests were given strict instructions on how to interact with them as well as what kind of nourishment they needed. But this was mostly done behind closed doors.

"It was as if these beings wanted to shield themselves and their image from public view. In fact, ancient writings suggest it was considered a great crime to even talk about or depict what these Serpent Gods looked like.

"Many stories suggest these beings were hideous."

Is this why they ruled in secrecy behind the literal curtain?

"The Ancient Serpent Gods"

Oannes the half man, half fish god of Sumeria.

Recorded more than 2,500 years before the time of Moses, the ancient history of Sumer, Assyrian and Babylon mentions how their knowledge was provided by an half-man, half-fish amphibious being known as an "Oannes" from the lineage of the "Annedoti" or "Mursai," Jason said. "The word "Annedoti" means "repulsive" and the word "Mursai" roughly translated as "abomination."

"Ancient text suggests these beings taught the population how to build temples, how to farm, how to govern and create order and stability," Jason said. "But if the population discovered that Reptilian-looking beings were the ones giving the orders from the temples the people would likely have revolted and tried to overthrow them".

The existence and slaying of Dragons is also very common in

Forbidden Knowledge

Ryujin the Dragon God of Japan

the mythology and sacred texts of other ancient societies.

"In Egypt we have the story of Set killing the evil serpent called Apop," Jason said. "This story was revised in the 18th dynasty to the killing of the Hyksos, known as the Serpent King, who ruled ancient Palestine.

"There are countless stories from medieval times about knights slaying Dragons. The Mesoamerican deity 'Quetzalcoatl' translates to the Feathered Serpent. The Mayans believed their creator god 'Itzamna' descended from the sky. The word 'Itzamna' literally

"The Ancient Serpent Gods"

translates to lizard house or the house of the reptile."

There is also a rich history of Dragons in China and Japan.

"The ancient Dragon gods of the Far East were known to live underground and under the sea," Jason said. "They were said to have the ability to shape shift into a human form and interact with the population.

"In fact, the first Emperor of Japan, Jimmu, was said to be the grandson of the goddess Otohime, who was the daughter of Ryujin, the Dragon God. This means Ryujin was considered as the ancestor of the Japanese imperial dynasty.

"Many in the Far East are actually very proud of this rich heritage. The Emperors of China are said to also be the decedents of Dragons. These Emperors used the symbol of the Dragon to show their imperial connection, strength and power linking them to this Dragon lineage."

"Ancient alien theorists and translated evidence from the examination of ancient Sumerian texts say that these 'Serpent Gods' mated with humans and created a hybrid offspring.".

ANCIENT BLOODLINES

This offspring had human characteristics but were loyal to their Reptilian bloodline.

"It was decided these offspring would be the new face of what was to become the 'Kingship on Earth' also known as the rulers of Earth," Jason said. "Yet, the Serpent Gods remained behind the scenes using this kingship to rule."

Many believe this is the case today.

"There have also been suggestions, and not just by conspiracy theorists but by those who claim to have inside knowledge that the European Kingship, Royal families, and even the Presidents of the United States are directly connected to these hybrid bloodlines," Jason said.

"The reason these beings fear being discovered is that they are so few in numbers," Jason said. "The systems that have been set up allow them to be virtually invisible but still rule through their kingships around the world through their bloodlines. Many believe these beings live underground, protected from the eyes of most of the world and only known by an elite group of humans."

This group is known by several names, including the Illuminati and the Bilderberg Group – organizations that are alleged to be secretly running a world government otherwise known as a Shadow Government.

Secret underground bases have in recent years become a continuing topic of discussion among whistleblowers and conspiracy theorists.

"I have no inside knowledge if they exist but insiders have suggested there are hundreds of such bases known as Deep Underground Bases located around the world," Jason said. "Insiders and whistleblowers have also suggested the Greys are involved in these bases and are and have been working with the military for decades."

Is it not a little strange that the most powerful rulers of modern history, including today, have been linked directly to dragons?

"Even the Bible makes references to intelligent Serpents," Jason said.

"In the Garden of Eden, Genesis reveals Adam and Eve were there with a serpent. And this serpent spoke, walked upright and had arms and legs.

"A literal interpretation of the Old Testament also suggests the Anunnaki were the gods who descended from Heaven and (lay) mated with the (daughters of man) females to create giant offspring known as the Nephilim."

In the New Testament these beings are referred to as Dragons. Look closely at Revelations (12:7)

"Now war arose in heaven. Michael and his angels fighting against the Dragon; and the Dragon and his angels fought. But they were defeated and there was no longer any place for them in heaven. And the great Dragon was thrown down, that ancient Serpent, who is called Devil and Satan."

"The Ancient Serpent Gods"

IMPRISONED

"I have already indicated that my journeys have revealed that the Reptilians conquered many worlds in our galaxy," Jason said. "They took worlds through military force. These conquered worlds were used a resource planets and the indigenous population was either destroyed or enslaved.

"I've also been told the Reptilians were engaged in what has been described to me as the Great War and that it involved many star systems."

At the time of this intergalactic conflict the Reptilians had made their home base in our galaxy on a planet that once orbited between Mars and Jupiter, Jason said.

"This planet was known as Marduk," Jason said. "But an alliance of several different races that included the Pleiadians, Acturians and several others decided the only way to stop the Reptilians from spreading their war-mongering was to destroy their planet."

"Only a small group of Reptilians escaped and landed on Earth," Jason said.

"The destruction resulted in the formation of what we know as the asteroid belt but debris crashed into nearby planets, including Mars and Earth resulting in catastrophic environmental destruction," Jason said.

"To ensure the quarantine of our solar system a type of force field was set up around these planets so any remaining Reptilians would be trapped there and unable to harm any more planets or star systems. This shield was designed to prevent any of these beings from escaping this enclosure and preventing their consciousness from entering other dimensions beyond the fourth dimension."

In his research Jason believes that this Great War is closely similar to the Biblical story of the war that took place in Heaven.

"When God cast down the fallen angels out of heaven and bound them to the Earth to forever be trapped," Jason said. "It has been said that these fallen angels would be trapped on Earth until final judgment.

In Jason's view, the force field set up to quarantine the Reptilians on Earth is what is referred to in the Bible as the "Firmament" - the area of Heaven above the Earth

"It's basically what one looks at when they stare up at the night sky," Jason said.

Interestingly, in 1962 a series of high altitude nuclear weapon detonations at the height of the Cold War took place under a top secret project called "Operation Fishbowl," that was part of an overall secret program later revealed as "Starship Prime."

"The highest detonation was nearly 340 miles above Earth," Jason said. "These nuclear tests were conducted by the U.S. as well as Russia and they were done simultaneously.

"These weren't small explosions. They were 3.8 megaton detonations. The bomb dropped on Hiroshima was 20 kilotons. That means these high altitude tests were the equivalent of 3,800 kilotons – nearly 200 times the power dropped on the Japanese city in 1945."

Documentation indicates both the U.S. and Russia each detonated at least five of these explosions. This operation was classified at the time although details have now been declassified.

A much lower radiation belt was actually created when the U.S. detonated a nuclear bomb on July 9, 1962 in outer space - to see what would happen if such a weapon was detonated – under the codename Project Starfish Prime.

This 1.4 megaton detonation occurred 240 miles above Hawaii in the Pacific Ocean resulted in several unexpected results such as a powerful EMP (electric magnetic pulse) that caused widespread power outages in Hawaii and electrical surges in airplanes. The pulse also damaged several satellites.

While scientists weren't surprised by the EMP they were caught off guard when electrons from the blast lingered in space – instead of falling to Earth – and created an artificial radiation belt that lasted for many months.

The test proved one thing very clearly. In the wrong hands, a deliberate nuclear detonation in space could cripple a country with an EMP blast.

"The Ancient Serpent Gods"

The Flammarion engraving (1888) depicts a traveler who arrives at the edge of a flat Earth and sticks his head through the firmament.

But what were they really trying to do?

In Jason's view, the name of the secret operation provides a hint to its true purpose.

"Fishbowl refers to the Biblical Firmament or the force field that was set up around Earth perhaps millions of years ago," Jason said.

Were the governments under the direction of The Reptilians trying to use nuclear weapons to crack the fishbowl so that they could escape the fourth dimension barrier?

In 2014, Professor Daniel Baker and team of scientists from the University of Colorado discovered an impenetrable Star Trek-like force field encasing Earth about 7,200 miles above our planet.

Nearly 60 years earlier, a collection of charged particles, essentially radiation belts held in place by the Earth's magnetic field were discovered following the launch of US Satellite Explorer 1 in 1958. These belts became known as the Van Allen Belts. Scientists later learned there were actually two radiation belts, an inner belt stretching from 400 to 6,000 miles above the Earth and an outer belt from 8,400 to 36,000 miles above our planet.

Baker said about his study: It's almost like these electrons are running into a glass wall in space. "Somewhat like the fields created by force fields on Star Trek that were used to repel alien weapons. We are seeing an invisible shield blocking these electrons. It's an extremely puzzling phenomenon."

How did they explain this?

"The only explanation they could think of what that some type of force field exists and that it protects the Earth from these highly-volatile particles," Jason said. "Another scientists on Baker's study team, John Foster, said, "Yes, there is a hard, fast boundary."

In Jason's view, there might be another reason for its existence.

"Maybe it is also preventing something from leaving our planet," he said. "Again, is this the field set up by the beings who opposed the Reptilians?"

Many whistleblowers have come forward suggesting the Reptilians are stuck on Earth and can't leave but they are working with a select group of physicists and scientists to create technology that will open wormholes that will re-connect them to their groups in other solar systems," Jason said.

Insiders have suggested this is being done in secret under the guise of the CERN program in Switzerland, which is reportedly trying to create black holes.

"These whistleblowers believe that this is their desperate attempt to finally break from their Earth prison," Jason said. "Others theorize they have a more sinister motive. That this ancient and militaristic race is trying to open these wormholes in order to connect our planet with their home world in another solar system so their species can invade Earth and take over our planet."

Sure, this sounds like science fiction.

But what if it isn't?

"I don't have any first hand knowledge that this is happening but many insiders and whistleblowers have suggested it is," Jason said.

"The Ancient Serpent Gods"

According to Jason, the Reptilians exist in their physical form in our third dimensional world but mostly work —and exhibit control in the fourth dimensional realm of the mind and astral worlds.

"This is where the take over has really taken place," Jason explained. "By entrapping our thought forms, beliefs and emotions in the lower density dimensions, humankind has become trapped and unable to access higher dimensions.

"By holding our energies in the lower densities we provide an energy source to them in the fourth dimension. Essentially, our energy is a food source to them.

"Being in the third density we are held in the physical world but we still have access to the fourth density through out dreams. But some people are so deeply rooted in the third dimension that they have even stopped dreaming."

How many of you insist you never dream?

How many of you who dream also never remember your dreams?

"When we leave our bodies and enter into the astral realm we are accessing the fourth dimension consciously," Jason said. "This is the beginning of our awakening process starting to access and awaken to the reality of other dimensions. This is where we can witness this take over first hand and come into contact with these beings."

Remember the mysterious information that the hooded being wrote on Jason's wall indicting how the Reptilians deliberately severed the intergalactic web, preventing other worldly civilizations from traveling back and forth through our galaxy and the Earth.

"While the Great War has kept the Reptilians on Earth and cut off their access to their higher dimensional lives, the spider web connecting all worlds with access to higher dimensions was deliberately severed by the imprisoned Reptilians in an attempt to control humankind's spiritual development," Jason said.

"This severance has effectively prevented all of us experiencing who we really are - multi-dimensional beings."

In Jason's view, the "Fall" is essentially dimensional.

"As we descend into the lower densities from source we pass through various dimensions," Jason said. "We dilute our spiritual nature by descending to these realms.

"As our soul progresses on the path of enlightenment our consciousness and our awareness again ascends back through the higher dimensions back to source.

"But because our consciousness has been trapped by these fourth dimensional nets on Earth, our awareness, our soul is trapped in the vessel we call our bodies and we live in what is essentially a false reality where our beliefs and thoughts are implanted so that we can exist in this world.

"It keeps us trapped within this lower density in a constant cycle of reincarnation."

While the Reptilians are dimensional beings trapped in a third dimensional world, Jason has been told that most of them imprisoned on Earth have since lost their connection to their emotional bodies and therefore cannot ascent past the fourth dimension.

"The Reptilians believe the solution to ascending lays with humankind," Jason said. "By understanding our nature they can lean how to regain their lost capabilities."

But do they really want to?

"That's an interesting question," Jason said. "There is a sense the Reptilians now feel very comfortable in their current existence on Earth as soul catchers, as soul harvesters. As long as our energies, our consciousness, our souls remain trapped in an endless reincarnation as third dimensional beings on Earth they have an unlimited access to our energy to feed from."

WHAT HAPPENS WHEN WE DIE

In explaining this, Jason also needs to explain how the concept of faith and our death fits into the world most of us have no idea exists.

"We actually create worlds with our thought forms and beliefs," Jason said. "Our faith is very important and regardless of what faith we follow what we believe collectively will actually manifest in the spiritual world of death.

"For example, if we truly believe that when we die, Jesus will come

"The Ancient Serpent Gods"

and take us to Heaven, then that is the reality we will experience when we die as our consciousness leaves our body. The same thing applies for Buddhists and Muslims and whatever faith you follow."

It also works for being in Hell.

"People, who believe they will go there and face Satan when they die, will," Jason said. "All of this is totally legit.

"Essentially, for people who experience Hell, they have already feared while living in their current body that they will end up in Hell when they die because of all of the bad things they have done. And that fear will manifest itself when they die in this life.

"But it's not like they're trapped. These places are just the transition phase that is comfortable for you."

Jason has been called many times to other worlds as an enlightened being to help other dimensional beings with their transitional stage.

"They will look at me and see the being they're expecting to see," Jason said. "They're not expecting to see Jason so they won't see me in this form.

"They see me as a deity in their lives. The one they believe in. It doesn't matter what religion or faith you are, you see who you expect to see. Everybody is part of a soul group, a collective consciousness that creates their own world and reality," Jason said. "Beings from other world and galaxies do the same thing with their minds. This is precisely what happens when we die in this third dimensional world."

How often had you heard stories about people having near death experiences seeing their loved ones?

Perhaps you or your loved ones have ever wondered or absolutely believe your loved ones are waiting for you in another realm of existence when you die?

"This is exactly what happens," Jason said. "When your consciousness leaves this third dimensional world you will see who you want to see because their energies exist in this transitional realm.

"Remember, to ascend, you need to be in peace and filled with good karma and love. I can't think of a more beautiful way to enter this transitional realm than to be greeted by your loved ones. They are real because their memories, their consciousness is absolutely real.

"Our consciousness exists in multiple realms all at the same time, including this realm of transition."

So how does all of this fit in with the severance of dimensions beyond the fourth dimension?

"Because they have severed our ability to ascend to higher dimensions beyond the fourth dimension, we are all essentially trapped – and only able to incarnate back on Earth in the third dimension," Jason said. "So when we die, we ascend to this transitional realm where we can remain for seconds, minutes, years or hundreds of years, or thousands of years but we can only incarnate back on Earth and will always only be able to do this until we either learn how to ascend to the higher dimensions or the spider web of dimensions is re-connected."

Another mind boggling aspect of reincarnation is that we can also choose what time period to incarnate in,

"You can choose to insert yourself in the past, the present or the future," Jason said. "That's because time doesn't exist in the way we believe it does."

In the physical world a person can close their eyes and imagine they're some place. It's your mind that is putting all of these pieces together.

"But are you the one actually creating these images in a different level of consciousness," Jason said.

"The mind fills in the blanks. Every entity has a mind or a consciousness and awareness. In the human form, the brain doesn't hold your consciousness but it is the transmitter and receiver.

"Essentially it's like how we perceive 'the cloud' for our phones and computers. Our memories are held in the 'cloud of consciousness' and our brain accesses these memories and stores them in every cell in our body."

"The Ancient Serpent Gods"

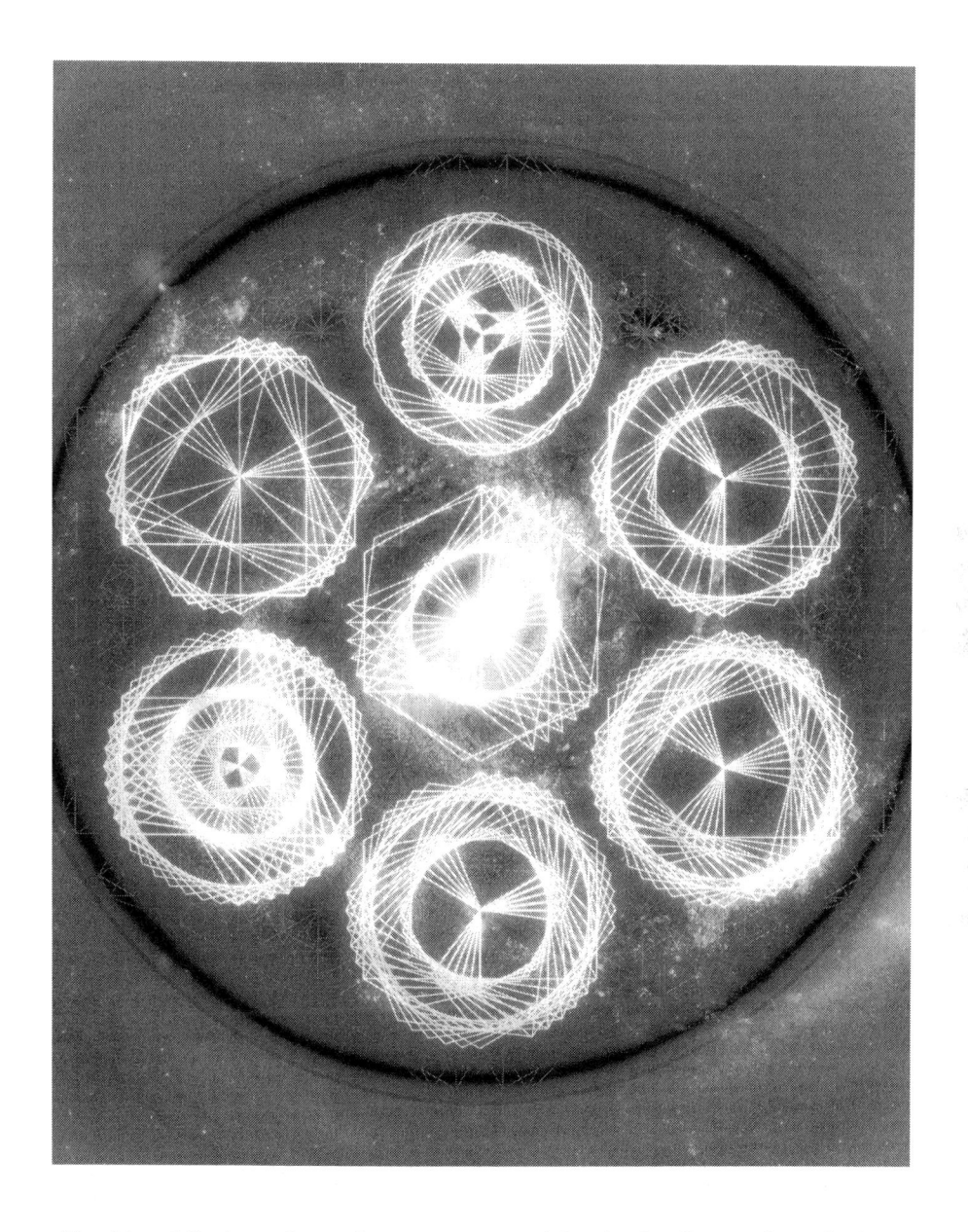

The Yosef Codes - Sacred geometry mandalas for healing and meditation.
Designed by Jason Quitt

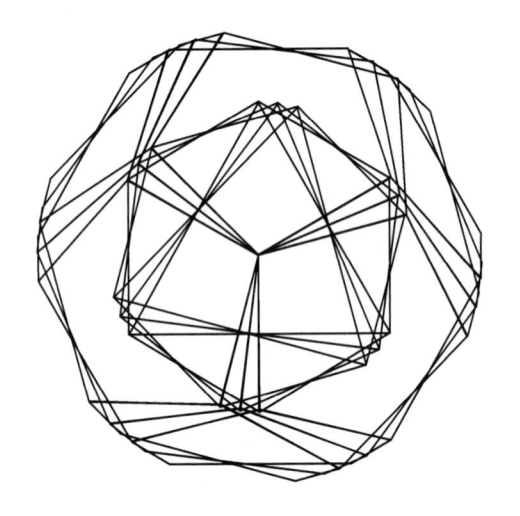

"The secret of change is to focus all of your energy, not on fighting the old, but on building the new."

- Socrates

Chapter 19
"Time Travel And Mind Control"

Jason has experienced numerous time traveling journeys.

So regardless what you believe, Jason insists he's living proof that time travel is not only possible but that all of us have the ability to do so – and one day we will understand what he means.

But what exactly is time travel?

And what role does it play in controlling humanity?

Physicist Albert Einstein believed time was actually an illusion – and that it also depended on how fast one traveled through space. He also believed time existed in the fourth dimension – not our third dimensional world.

In his theory of relativity, Einstein believed that time either slowed down or speeded up depending on how fast something moved relative to something else. For example, an astronaut piloting a space ship at the speed of light at 186,282 miles per second would age slower than somebody on Earth living the same period of time that it took the astronaut to reach his or her destination.

He also believed that gravity could bend time.

"We experience time as if we are moving forward through it," Jason said. "We call this horizontal time. In this perception of time we can make choices and interact with this reality to alter and change it."

This is the reality of cause and effect.

"What we do in the present will effect the flow of time in our future," Jason said. "This is one of our greatest powers to yield. This is where we utilize our free will.

"It is what we will that will manifest our future. We can do this on an individual basis and affect the way we navigate this world."

According to Jason, there are different kinds of time travel.

VERTICAL TIME

"This is how we time travel into other time lines of the future and the past," Jason explained. "This can be done within the mind telepathically or by leaving your body for an astral journey."

Being taken to many different future time lines is possible when you embark on vertical time.

"In vertical time you are only an unseen observe," Jason said. "You cannot affect the environment you are in. You can only observe and take it all in."

Vertical time traveling also can be used as a warning.

"For example, many people believe they have experiences of being taken into the future and shown apocalyptic events," Jason said. "But they aren't viewing an actual future carved in stone.

"This is what the future can look like if we follow the paths we have chosen. If we then go back to the present we can then change our path, which will alter the future.

Hieroglyphics depicting a helicopter, tank and flying ship in the Temple of Abydos, Egypt. Did the Egyptians have the ability to see into the future?

"Time Travel And Mind Control"

"This is why you should never predict the future because the future is constantly being written by the choices we make."

INSERTION TIME TRAVEL

"This is where you physically time travel either to the past or the future," Jason explained. "This is very dangerous and it's not something I would recommend.

"According to whistleblowers and many insiders, scientists and physicists have secretly been creating advanced technology capable of this type of travel.

"Some believe this has already happened. That our future selves have time traveled back into our past to try to correct our future. That the future they have come from is dying and the only way to save them is to correct the pitfalls of the past."

Interestingly, such an event is associated with the infamous Rendlesham Forest UFO incident, often dubbed as Britain's Roswell.

On Dec. 26, 1980 two U.S. military officers stationed at a RAF bases at Woodbridge and Bentwaters in Sulfolk, England claim to have seen a saucer hover, land and fly away.

One of the officers, Sgt. Jim Penniston, 26, claimed he touched a black triangular shaped craft and saw hieroglyphic-like characters on its surface. During regressive hypnosis in 1994, Penniston revealed he received a telepathic communication from the craft that indicated the visitors were humans from the future, who had traveled back in time.

"It's my belief higher beings live outside of what we call time," Jason said. "They can view all of this creation as one thing. They can then insert themselves in any part of the time line to interact, seed information, and try to shift the flow of time in different directions.

"Perhaps this is what most of us are. We are time travelers inserting our consciousness within the realm of time to try to shift and change our past and our future from our presence.

"This is how we should see ourselves in time. That we live in all times at once. That we are but one being having multiple experienc-

207

es throughout time space and dimension."

EXISTING FUTURE TIME TRAVEL

In Jason's view there is another time travel scenario possibility in play.

Consider the secret space programs.

"What if these secret space programs are actually something taking place in the future? That the future is really the present for them and that we are currently living in the past in a timeline that has already happened for those involved in the space program.

Wouldn't that explain how people such as Randy Cramer could serve for 20 years in the Mars Defense outfit but when he is returned he's still the same age that he was when he left?

These are just some more thought-provoking ideas to ponder on your journey of enlightenment.

According to Jason, there is another far more powerful way to alter the future, Jason said.

"This is through the collective consciousness of humanity as a whole." Jason said. "If all of humanity collectively got together and decided to live in peace in harmony with nature and to evolve into beings of higher consciousness this would be the future we would manifest collectively."

There are multiple time lines woven together at all times.

"These paths can be chosen and experienced. This is all decided by the choices we make together," he explained. "There are those, who are fully aware of this great power we hold within us. This is the power of free will to choose our future. In fact, there has been an all out war on our consciousness since our inception.

"Those who can control the minds of humanity can control the future. This is why we have "Government" the word itself meaning "Mind Control."

"The preface "Govern," means to rule, steer, command and direct while "ment," comes from the Latin word "mind."

"We are so mind controlled that we don't even know or understand the true meaning of the words we use. This control is programmed inside of us from many different angles."

According to Jason, religion is the most influential of these controls. One shouldn't confuse religion with having faith as Jason explained in the previous chapter.

"But religion is something totally different than faith and the belief in a higher source or God," Jason said. "It has worked for thousands of years without fail. This is a complete dumbing down of the nature of reality. It has made us give away our power to someone or something else."

"If they can control the narrative of your belief system then they can control you." Jason said. "If they can make you believe in their power, then in turn, your belief will make them powerful. In fact, the word "belief" can be changed to its true meaning. "Belief - to "will it."

When we believe something we will it into being.

So how does the concept of God or Allah, Buddha or Krishna or the Almighty fit in?

"The simple answer and one that might take awhile to understand fully or even accept is that we are all our own Creators," Jason explained. "We are always connected to source and through us we manifest and embody the source."

The purest manifestation of this source is expressed through the energy of love.

"Our creative power lies within our belief and faith," Jason said. "But through the programmed narrative of our controllers, we have turned religious organizations into the most powerful entities on the planet.

"If they wanted peace on this planet we would have had it. Truth be told, religions are what divide us and keep us in line."

But being religious and being spiritual are two different concepts.

"Religion teaches us in order to be saved and to achieve ever lasting life that we need to follow a particular religion," Jason said. "But the reality is for all conscious beings this power to have ever-lasting life is always within us. Most of us just don't understand or realize this to be true."

Were not the biggest wars throughout history done in the name of God?

Did not both sides believe they were doing the will of God?

How can both be right?

How can both faiths be true?

"But this is not the work of God," Jason said. "It's the work of power, greed and control. If a population gets too big to control, just send them off to war. If there are whispers of rebellion, start a war.

"The world has been in perpetual war for too long. We need to release these programs and choose to collectively come together to fight our true enemy – ignorance."

Remember how Jason revealed how the Reptilians and other beings "feed" from our energy of fear and anger.

Are wars and other violent-situations not causing us tremendous emotional fear and anxiety?

"As long as there are conflicts, these beings will always have a food source from our energy," Jason said.

Another way to alter our reality and control our minds is through the media.

"Media is the platform and narrative of this agenda," he said. "This is why we call TV shows "programs" because this is what they truly are. It is programming you to the idea of what reality should be.

"How you should think, feel and react to current events and politics. These are all staged and masterminded to follow a specific narrative and belief to push forward a future that is not our design. This is the matrix we need to unplug from."

TOKYO TRIP

During one of Jason's trips to Tokyo he had a sudden revelation.

"I was riding in a very full subway train and as I looked around I noticed how every single person was using their cell phones and were completely fixated on their screens," Jason said. "The subway was silent and since my phone didn't work in Japan I had the time

"Time Travel And Mind Control"

to look around and observer everyone tuned into their own reality.

"This is even worse for the new generation of children. They are completely glued to their games and social media via wireless technology. This is changing their developing minds into accepting false realities."

What makes this reality possible are the tools used to keep us in this state of consciousness.

"This is also done through the metals, chemicals and toxins that have been pushed on us for generations," Jason said.

"This is a fight for our consciousness. This is where we will find true freedom. Sovereignty can only be found within yourself when you take your power back. This power is the power to choose your own path, your own future by freeing your mind."

With this power we can dream a new future into being,

"This dream can be so strong that others will feel that reality around you," he said. "This is the greatest fear of our controllers. If people took their power back then the entire system and the reality they have woven would crumble."

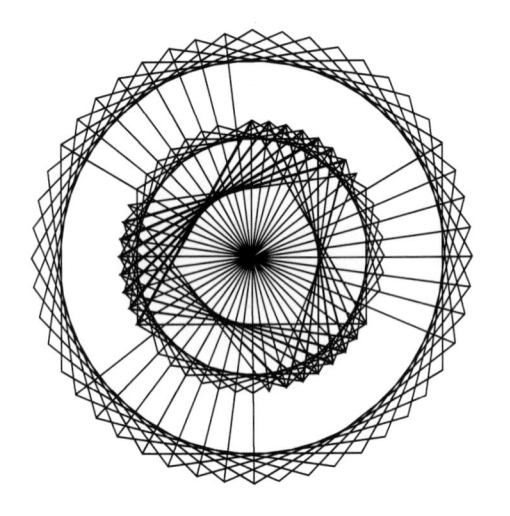

"Time is the soul of this world."

- Pythagoras

Chapter 20
"Atlantis The Untold Story"

Many people know the story of Atlantis.

At least they think they do.

Truth be told, the stories, the myths and what little recorded history is available, presents anything but a true picture.

According to Jason, Atlantis was real.

But it wasn't just a single island. It was a worldwide civilization that existed before the rise of Sumer and Egypt.

In fact, Jason experienced several different lives there, hundreds and perhaps thousands of years apart.

Atlantean civilizations were located throughout the world in places such as Central America, The Bahamas, the Atlantic Ocean, the Indian Ocean and of course, the most famous of all of locations on the Greek island of Santorini in the Aegean Sea.

This is why so many of today's mainstream archaeologists, historians and so-called experts have different opinions as to where Atlantis was located.

You see, they're all correct although in recent years much of the discussion about where Atlantis was located has centered on the Santorini location.

There's good reason for that because if there was such a place as

Forbidden Knowledge

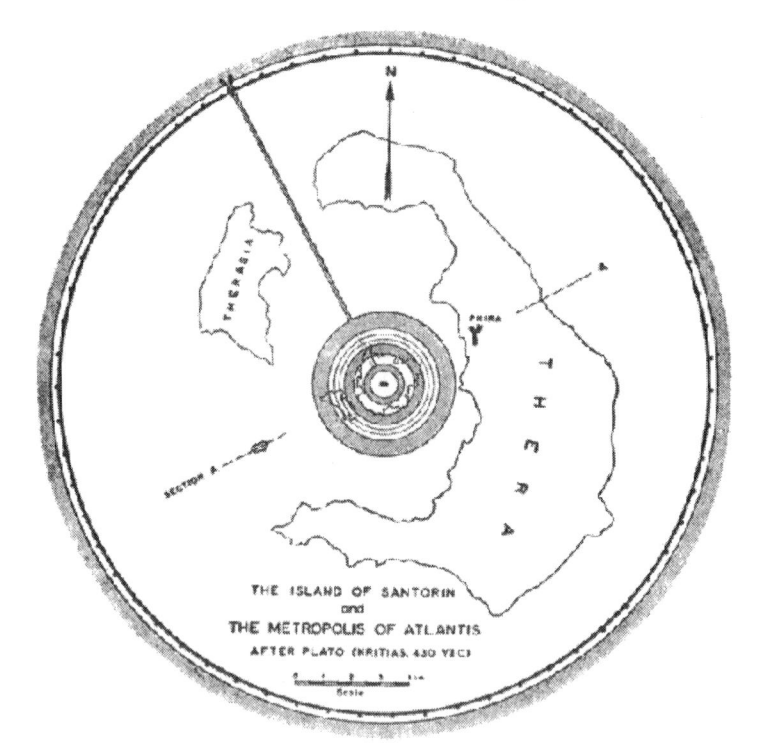

Atlantis depicted in the center of the Island of Santorini.

the world-wide capital of Atlantis, this is where it existed.

As mentioned earlier in this book, Atlantis was first described around the year 360 BC by ancient Greek philosopher Plato.

In fact, most of today's so-called experts on Atlantis have received their information from him.

Plato described Atlantis as an advanced civilization located "beyond the Pillars of Heracles" which today most likely refers to the Straits of Gibraltar.

Bordered by Africa and Europe and the modern day countries of Morocco and Spain, this is the gateway from the Atlantic Ocean into the Mediterranean Sea.

Arguments have also been made as to whether Plato referred to Atlantis being located in the Atlantic Ocean west of the Straits of Gibraltar near the Canary Islands and the Madeira Islands or further east into the Mediterranean Sea.

Regardless, according to Plato, Atlantis existed more than 9,000 years before he wrote about it in his work "Timaeus and Oritias."

The story of Atlantis was actually passed down through an ancient version of a jungle telegraph. Scholars say Plato heard about it from his grandfather, who learned about it from Athenian statesman Solon, who received his information from an ancient Egyptian priest.

You get the picture.

According to Plato, Atlantis was also an extraordinarily advanced society with paved streets, art-filled palaces, with thriving agriculture producing an abundance of food, water and wildlife. Its military was also far superior to any other civilization as was its engineering and construction skills that saw the building of integrated canals and sophisticated sewers and irrigation systems.

But as the legend goes, greed and corruption eventually overtook this utopian society. Its rulers set their sights on conquering other lands.

Then on one fateful day, a powerful earthquake followed by tidal waves not only sank the island where its capital city was located but also entirely destroyed other nearby mainland Atlantean communities.

While archaeological evidence of the existence of Atlantis remains largely yet to be discovered there is evidence that a highly-advance Atlantean-like civilization known as the ancient Minoans did exist on Crete, an island south of Santorini, before it and the Santorini vanished around 1650 BC during another cataclysmic event.

Also, Santorini was used as major sea port used by the Minoans.

Mainstream archaeologists have concluded this civilization was also destroyed by a giant tsunami as a result of an eruption of the Santorini volcano. It's believed this eruption was at least 10 times more powerful than the eruption of Krakatoa in 1883 in what is now known as Indonesia. Evidence suggests the deadly destruction killed more than 36,000 people and created several equally-destructive tsunamis.

Now, if Plato got his date wrong, it's conceivable the Minoans and the Atlanteans could have been one and the same civilizations and their destruction would have been caused by the same volcanic event.

But if Plato didn't make a mistake in the date then one of the biggest problems for mainstream scholars to accept concerning whether or not Atlantis existed is that our known recorded history suggests that humanity has only been on Earth since about 5000 BC.

Yet, Plato said Atlantis existed around 9600 BC, nearly 5,000 years earlier.

If that is true, then our entire recorded history is wrong.

One other interesting bit of information is that Plato made another less reported observation about Atlantis. He wrote that its inhabitants were half-human and half-god.

Was he describing the Anunnaki?

Now, according to Jason, Atlantis also wasn't the idyllic civilization portrayed in mythology and repeated by many mainstream scholars and historians.

"It was a very violent world," Jason said. "In fact, the world we live in today isn't much different than what it was back in the days when Atlantis was the known world."

"Many people have mentioned how the advance technology in play in Atlantis involved using crystals," Jason said. "But it might surprise you to know that all of our technology today is also based on crystals.

"Your computer and cell phone and even our satellites above Earth have crystals in them. It feels like a déjà view. This is why I believe we are all back here again in this time line dealing with the mess we are tangled in today.

"We are still collectively dealing with the karma we hold from the times of Atlantis. That's why subjects like Atlantis and Lemuria capture the attention of many people seeking the mysteries and the truth."

According to Jason, most of us have reincarnated with past lives, memories, and energies from Atlantis still active within ourselves.

"Atlantis was a very violent world with lots of bloodshed," Jason said. "Our world today is almost a mirror reflection of those past energies."

Those interested in Atlantis often focus on its last days leading to its destruction. Other than what Plato told us, very little information has ever been revealed about the beginning of this advanced

"Atlantis The Untold Story"

civilization and where it came from.

According to Jason, the original Atlanteans were not from Earth.

"They were from a distant star system," Jason said. "They traveled here through a portal under the waters of the Atlantic Ocean."

"Located in the Orion constellation their home planet was called Titanius," Jason said.

"This is where the myth of the Titans originates from," Jason said.

"Titanius was very similar to Earth except that it was much more a water world. The physiology of the original Atlanteans was much different than ours. Their bodies had a higher content of water within it."

"After coming through the portal they eventually came out of the waters of the Atlantic and intermingle with the then indigenous Earth populations," Jason said.

"They soon assimilated with them and then decided to move off the mainland to build the canal-city of Atlantis that we're all familiar with," Jason said. "Eventually this pure bloodline of the original

Oannes half man, half fish god that came out of the waters to give the Sumerian's civilization. Oannes was also the god king of Babylon. The Pope still wears the Oannes hat which represents these ancient gods.

Forbidden Knowledge

Atlanteans was mixed into the human populations.

"To keep these unique genetic traits of this bloodline active many ceremonies were held to remember their past history of where they came from."

"Part of the ceremonies of initiation of Atlantis was to return to the sea and to learn how to sustain themselves under water for long periods of time," Jason said.

"They did these types of initiations so that one day they might return back to the portal of their ancestors," Jason said. "There are many ancient pictures depicting this lost history.

"As their society grew using the knowledge of their ancestors they became highly advanced in technologically," Jason said. "They even started to connect with other star nations to trade information and technology. This was a very diplomatic type of relations.

"Some of these races we know today such as the Pleiadians, Sirians, Orionians, and Arcturians. Like their ancestors, the new Atlanteans also developed advanced space age and star gate technology."

"This is when many influences, greed and power started to infiltrate their society," Jason said.

"These great advancements were used to fight wars and create great weapons," Jason said. "It was because of this that many of these star nations eventually cut off all ties to the Atlanteans."

"One of the first star groups to do this were the Arcturians which was one of the most advanced civilizations in the galaxy," Jason said.

It's believed this alien race from the fourth and fifth dimension came from a constellation 36 light years away from our solar system. Even Edgar Cayce, the well-known psychic, talked about this race.

"This progression of technology and violence set in motion the fall of Atlantis," Jason said.

So what destroyed the island of Atlantis?

Was it sunk by a tidal wave caused by an earthquake that erupted naturally?

Did a cosmic event such as an asteroid strike the area, vaporizing Atlantis?

"Atlantis The Untold Story"

According to Jason, none of these things caused its destruction. Atlanteans themselves destroyed their island paradise.

"Many believe a natural event caused the destruction of the Atlantis," Jason said. "In fact, it was caused by the misuse of advanced technology that was being used to alter Earth's climate.

"This was set up using the Earth's grid, the existing pyramids built thousands of years earlier and advanced crystal technology. Using this set up they controlled the weather of the planet.

"It was also used by the Atlanteans as a weapon against other civilizations. It could create tidal waves, earthquakes and even volcanic activity or simply just to create a drought or a flood."

It's ironic people don't realize that we have the same technology today with HAARP. Today more then ever our climate is being modified and controlled.

"So in the end just like their predecessors before them in Lemuria, Atlantis destroyed itself," Jason said.

Are we destined to relive this karma in this time line?

Are we repeating the same mistakes we made in the past?

"This is why I believe many of us are here from that time," Jason said. "We are here to fix the mistakes we made and heal the karma we still hold deep within us."

Several years ago Jason had the opportunity to work with a 4-year-old child. His mother heard about him and thought it would be a good opportunity for son to meet him.

"He was a very scared child and he didn't want to talk with anybody," Jason said. "His mother explained how he only communicated with God, who spoke to him telepathically."

Initially, the little boy wouldn't talk to Jason.

"So I then told him to ask God why he was here to see me," Jason said. "He then had a conversation in his mind. Then he smiled and suddenly looked relaxed."

"The little boy then told Jason, "God said you will help me."

The boy then basically spilled his guts to Jason.

"I was very bad in Atlantis," the boy said. "I destroyed and hurt many people. I did something to the crystals. The towers and ships

219

exploded. I'm here in this life to fix those mistakes. That's why God sent me back here."

Of course, Jason was blown away.

"Despite being only 4 he had such clarity and purpose as to why he was here," Jason said. "His memories were very clear on the past life he once lived in Atlantis."

What really astounded Jason was that this child was providing him with information that the general public really had never been told.

"This was another true case of life after life," Jason said.

As indicated earlier, Jason lived several past lives in Atlantis.

According to Jason, Atlantis existed before the last Ice Age and had been thriving on Earth for at least 50,000 years before this last Ice Age.

This time table fits perfectly for mainstream scientists, archaeologists, historians, etc, who believe Atlantis never existed.

"That's because they don't want to admit there were thriving civilizations on this planet long before our recorded history," Jason said.

Jason was an ambassador to the Pleiadian counsel in Atlantis because of his many strong past lives.

"I had once lived as a Pleiadian," Jason said. "At that time there was much chaos with the population and the Earth grids.

"It was decided that the Pleiadians would try to help us shift our consciousness so that we could change the future we were destined to experience.

"This is when we received the information on the sacred postures. (I call them the Egyptian postures, but they actually first came here during the times of Atlantis.) These postures were devised so that when one practices them they could heal their energies and their karma.

"This works on the physical, mental, emotional and spiritual levels. They believed that by practicing these sacred movements we could change our energies and shift our consciousness. In turn our new energies would help heal and balance the Earth."

Humanity is very much connected to the Earth's grids.

"What we think and feel can actually alter the environment

around you," Jason said, "Many people took this practice very seriously, but it did not reach the audience necessary in order to make the changes needed.

"This is why we still have historical record of these postures found in Egypt. It is still found in the statutes and artwork. It is amazing how this information has survived right up to our time line.

"In fact, these statutes were fashioned by the priests and it was illegal for anyone to alter them. This was because they were trying to solidify this information into stone. You can see the same exact statute being produced over and over again. This was a way to keep this history alive."

During another past life in Atlantis Jason was a high priest, who worked closely with the King.

"This is when I fell in love with the King's daughter (now Monika)," Jason said. "We had a strong connection and love for each other but we could never be together because of the obligations we had chosen."

Jason also worked very closely with crystals in Atlantis.

"I was very much attuned to them," Jason said. "I could hear them speak telepathically with me. There were beautiful underground caverns with crystals coming out of the ground and walls. They had an aura and light emanated from them.

"They were very much alive. They were in communication with the other crystalline beings around the planet and off planet. They created a crystalline energetic grid around the planet that also connected to other grid systems out in space.

"This was the source of great power. Today some of these crystalline beings and grids are starting to reawaken and show themselves to people that have these crystalline strands still active in their DNA."

Jason remembers the last days of Atlantis and the tremendous fear and panic experienced by everybody.

"There were many boats and ships in the water to help evacuate the population," Jason said. "But it happened too fast and even many of the boats that had already fled got sucked into the waves

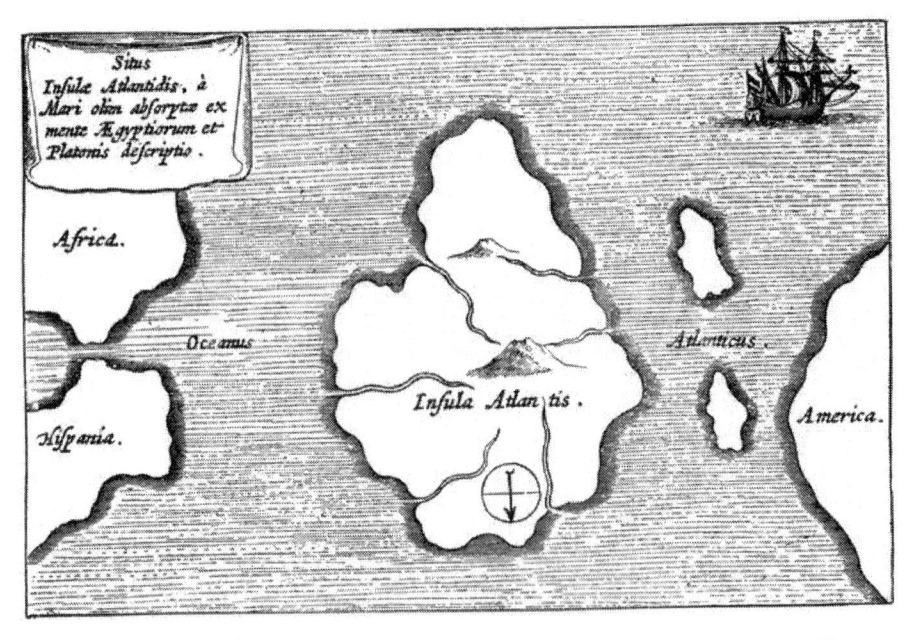

Map depicting Atlantis from a rare German book published in 1600.

and turbulence caused by the destruction.

"The earth shook violently with many earthquakes. This also created great tidal waves. Many survivors escaped to other populations and outposts on the planet."

According to Jason, those who survived made their way to what is today known as Egypt, Mexico and South America as well as numerous other locations on the planet.

"The great technology they depended on was nearly all wiped out," Jason said. "This is where you get the ancient Sumerian stories such as the Myth of Anzu, where these ancient gods fought over the control of these old technologies and weapons."

Were the ancient gods of our past the last survivors of Atlantis?

Did they have knowledge, technologies and a connection to the stars?

As indicated earlier in this book, in order to help balance the Earth's grid, the Atlanteans used their advance engineering and technology to construct additional pyramids and joined the ones built by a star alliance after the Reptilians were for all intents and purposes stranded on Earth thousands if not millions of years earlier.

Interestingly, Cayce predicted before his death in 1945 that Atlantean historical records and text were hidden in what he described as being a "hall of records" beneath the Egyptian Sphinx.

Such records would lend credence to Plato's story that the original knowledge for his work on Atlantis came from an Egyptian priest.

This secret chamber of Atlantean records has never been located despite several attempts by archaeologists to find it

Jason, however, believes he knows why these records have never been discovered.

"During my meetings with Thoth I was taken to a record vault in what I believed was located under the sphinx and pyramids," Jason said. "But I believe this vault, or hall of records, actually exists in the fourth dimension. Essentially, it's still there but being third dimensional beings, archaeologists can't access it."

Interestingly, Cayce predicted the records would be discovered in 1998.

Despite Cayce's insistence that records would be found in Egypt, he also predicted that evidence of Atlantis would be found in The Bahamas near the Biminis islands around 1968 or 69.

Incredibly, divers discovered what became known as the "Bimini Road" – a half mile perfectly-aligned road in the waters north of Biminis Island in 1969.

Forbidden Knowledge

Arkansas Quartz Cluster

Chapter 21
"The Living Crystals"

Jason has been drawn to crystals his entire life.

Actually, he has also been drawn to crystals in many of his past lives as well.

"Even as a young child my mother would take me to the local crystal store where I could look, feel and experience crystals," Jason said. "She would always buy me an amethyst because that was my birthstone.

"Crystals fascinated me with their complex geometry, their brilliant colors and varieties. Also, for some reason it always felt good to have crystals around. I actually can't think of a time in this life when I didn't have a crystal around. It has always been a part of me."

So it's understandable why Jason would get into the crystal business later on in this life.

But where did his obsession in this life with crystals begin?

"When I first started to have my awakening experiences and all different types of astral beings began to interrupt my sleep, I tried to find ways for these experiences to stop," Jason said. "At the time I really felt like I was being targeted by these astral beings.

"These intrusions were most unwelcome and started to seriously affect my day-to-day life."

Forbidden Knowledge

One day while searching online for help Jason discovered a website that suggested the most effective way to keep these astral intruders away was to set up a crystal grid around his bedroom using a man-made device called orgonite.

During the 1930s and 1940s Dr. Wilheim Reich used a Geiger counter to detect and actually measure the existence of etheric energy, which essentially is the life energy of people and objects. He called it "orgone."

Essentially, he believed that by stacking alternating layers of fiberglass and steel wool that it would attract and collect etheric energy from both beneficial and negative forms.

Using this principle, he claimed to have successfully healed patients of various ailments, including cancer, by having them sit inside a box that collected this etheric energy. Later this information would be used to create a man-made crystalline device called orgonite.

Jason was very intrigued by the website.

"This is a matrix of crystals and metals like copper within a fiberglass resin," Jason explained. "The website provided instructions as to how to put such a device together. I thought it looked easy enough so the next day I went to the crystal store and bought what I needed."

Jason purchased many quartz crystal points and started to make these orgonite pucks.

"They looked like hockey pucks because they were made in muffin trays," he said. "It took a couple of tries to get the desired result but I was happy in how they turned out.

"Then I proceeded to grid my room and house with them. I was surprised with the results. My astral intrusions actually were reduced.

"They were still happening, just not as frequently as before. For me this was a great victory. It was like I had found something that could help me."

Around this time Saundra's husband Neil became very ill and was hospitalized. Jason had read how orgonites were also good for health issues.

"The Living Crystals"

Orgonite generator Jason made to
grid around his house.

"So I made him two custom orgonites with different crystals," Jason said. "When I visited him in the hospital I gave them to him as a gift and told him how to use them.

"Neil recovered very quickly and for years afterwards he kept them in his jacket pocket. He swore by them.

"This gave me a real boost of confidence. Soon I started making large orders of these orgonites and selling them at my local crystal store. This was my introduction into the crystal business."

But Jason soon became even more obsessed with crystals. He went to all the crystal shows and shops looking for the next piece to add to his collection.

In June 2012, he was invited to the American Society of Dowsers for their annual conference in Vermont. He and Monika drove there and set up a small table in the vendors section with a couple shungite stones, pharaoh rods and his book on the Egyptian Postures.

"Across from us was a man in his late 70s selling quartz crystals from Arkansas," Jason said. "As I was setting up Monika was already over there looking at the crystals and introducing herself to this gentleman named LD.

As the show progressed over the weekend we had many conversations with him. He would continually come to our booth and gift us a crystal. By the end of the show he called me over to his booth. He wanted to show me something. Under his table he had a box that had the most spectacular quartz cluster in it.

"This was a showpiece fit for a museum. He looked at me and said, "I've been saving this crystal for you the entire show because I know you have the crystal sickness just like me."

By the end of the show LD had given Jason at least 20 stunning quartz clusters.

"As we left the conference LD told us to visit him in Arkansas whenever we wanted," Jason said. "We were more than welcome to stay with him for a week or two."

When they got home Jason placed all of his new pieces around his bedroom.

"I could feel the energy of my room shift," he said.

Arkansas crystals are sometimes referred to as Atlantean Crystals.

As indicated earlier in this book, crystals were once mined by Atlanteans because of their quality, strength and structure.

"There are many stories of the crystals and Atlantis and the great power and technology created from them," Jason said. ""This is one of the reasons why I have been so drawn to crystals. In many of my past lives I worked with crystals and experience their divine intelligence and power."

As indicated earlier, the Atlantean misuse of the power of the crystals contributed to the destruction of their civilization.

"Crystals were also used to predict and share this future outcome with the Atlanteans, who could hear the crystals speak," Jason said. "This gave some of them enough time to prepare for the inevitable collapse."

Now many readers will have a hard time comprehending how a crystal can be alive.

"In other dimensions stones are alive," Jason explained. "A stone resonates in a frequency range that higher being's consciousness is connected to.

"People might think a stone or a crystal is an inanimate object but they are actually alive in different dimensions and have life cycles.

"Let's say human's life span is 80 to 100 years if they're lucky. Well, a stone's life span could be millions of years.

"The Living Crystals"

Jason with an Arkansas Quartz Cluster.

"If you took time lapsed photos of a seed growing into a plant the seed would look as if it was totally alive. With a stone, we can't view this with timed lapsed photography because we would need to look at it for millions of years to see it move."

Because of his past connection to these crystals Jason also began to actually communicate with them.

"I first noticed it a night or two after I had brought them home," he said. "I would be sleeping and I would start to feel energy work being done on my body.

"Then I would get a flash of a vision inserted telepathically into my mind. What I saw was a quartz cluster hovering above my bed and rotating slowly. I felt energy waves going through my body.

"I started to even experience this when I was doing energy healing sessions on clients. As I would be working on them suddenly I would see a crystal floating above them on the table working on their energies. I started to really sensitize myself to the energies of these crystals.

"Even when I came home from a stressful day in the real world I felt them working on me as soon as I entered the house. It would feel as if all the bad energy that I had picked up during that day was being removed from me."

About a month after returning from Vermont, Jason called LD and thanked him once more for his generosity.

"At the end of the conversation he again told us to visit him. I don't know what came over me but before I hung up the phone I asked him if Monika and I could visit him the following week," Jason said.

"And just like that we were on an adventure down to the crystal mines of Arkansas. The energy there was amazing. We really got to know the local area and the people in the town of Mt. Ida, Arkansas.

Quartz crystal mine located in Mt. Ida, Arkansas.

"The Living Crystals"

"I took some extra money with me so I could bring back some boxes of crystals but I soon realized that the crystals had other intentions for me."

By the end of the trip Jason wound up emptying his entire bank account.

"This was clearly an out of my mind decision, but soon realized that it was something I had to do because the crystals wouldn't have let me leave without them," Jason said.

It was a 24-hour drive back home and along the way they decided to find a hotel for the night.

"But I was worried because my car was packed to the roof with crystal boxes and you really have to know where to stop on these road trips for safety," he said. "So we simply asked the crystals for help. Again, I know this sounds crazy, but that's what we did.

They asked, "We need to find a safe place for us to stay the night and that Monika is hungry and she's really craving the cheese cake factory."

Suddenly, Monika started to experience something incredible.

"She described how once we asked the crystals to help us she started to see them communicating with each other," Jason said. "She saw strands of light shooting out of the boxes to the cars on the highway next to us.

"Then they shot these strands into the neighborhoods we drove by."

They drove for about another 45 minutes when Jason looked at his GPS and realized they had been traveling in the wrong direction.

"We were even on the wrong highway," Jason said. "It was as if my mind had blanked out for me not to notice this. I freaked out. So we got off the highway at the next exit"

As they exited the highway they found themselves in what appeared to be a nice and safe neighborhood.

"I thought, "This is too perfect"

In no time they found a hotel that looked pretty nice and it was also located in what appeared to be a safe neighborhood.

"Monika and I went inside to see if we could afford to stay at this hotel," Jason said. "It turned out that the hotel manager's wife was also a Canadian. And because of the great conversation we had with him he gave us the room for half price.

"Then we asked if there was a place for us to eat. He then said there is a really good cheese cake factory one block away.

"Monika and I looked at each other and started to laugh. We knew this entire event had been orchestrated by these crystals."

When they got home Jason immediately called Nora and Saundra and told them about their trip.

"They both said the same thing to me," Jason said. "That there were more crystals waiting for me in Arkansas that I needed to bring them back to Canada.

"I laughed and thought that would be impossible. I told them that I had zero money left and that a trip like that would be very expensive. Not to mention the crystals also would cost me a fortune even at wholesale prices.

"But they insisted that I would soon be back there."

Knowing the crystals had helped him before; Jason decided to have a conversation with them.

"Again, I know this sounds crazy but I simply told them that if I'm supposed to go back to Arkansas to pick up their friends, then they needed to start calling out to people to buy them so I could make my money back.

"Incredibly, almost the next day, word got out to the community that I had this haul of crystals. Everyone was calling me and asking if they could come by and purchase them."

Jason not only made his money back but had enough funds to return to Arkansas and do it again. Incredibly, LD also phoned him the next day and told him that he had put aside another 20 boxes of crystals for him to be picked up when he returned.

"I couldn't believe the synchronicity," Jason said. "I laughed in disbelief of how this was all being arranged around me and how I was an active participant.

Jason told LD that he would see them again the next month.

"I'm still amazed at the power of crystals," Jason said. "But it was these crystals that led me to my next big discovery - Auralite 23."

"The Living Crystals"

Auralite-23 crystals are believed to be about 1.2 billion years old and are essentially found in the Boreal forest of the Canadian Shield north of Lake Superior. They were formed around the same time cellular life began on Earth.

Some believe meteors hit the Earth and their resulting impact brought rare metallic ores to the surface and were incorporated into Auralite crystals.

The number 23 is used because they contain as many as 23 different minerals including Titanite, Cacoxenite, Lepidocrosite, Ajoite, Hematite, Magnetite, Pyrite, Goethite, Pyrolusite, Gold, Silver, Platinum, Nickel, Copper, Iron, Limonite, Sphalerite, Covellite, Chalcopyrite, Gialite, Epidote, Bornite and Rutile.

It's believed these crystals help cure sleep disorders and their energy provides a deep sense of peace and tranquility.

"Again the crystals started to arrange things for me to be an active part of," Jason said. "It seems like these crystals choose certain people to become their guardians to help them move in the world to reach specific people.

"I have seen it and experienced it first hand many times. There is much intelligence, healing and magic in the crystal world."

Forbidden Knowledge

Metauralite Crystal

Chapter 22
"The Crystals Speak"

In 2012, Jason decided to sell some of his Arkansas Quartz at the Bancroft Gem and Mineral show.

This is one of the largest gem and mineral shows in Ontario. This is also where Monika would be called to a mysterious stone they had never seen until that day.

As Monika walked by one of the vendors she came across some small purple crystal pendants that looked very similar to amethyst.

"But these were not your typical amethyst," Jason said. "She was instantly drawn in and fell in love with the stone.

"As it turned out, these stones, known as Auralite-23, had just been discovered in Northern Ontario."

The stones are called Auralite because the location of the mine is very far north that you can see the Aura Borealis at night. The '23' is the number of rare metals and minerals found within the crystal.

This stone is said to be more than 1.2 billion years old.

"It's believed to have been created during a large meteor impact that hit the area of Sudbury, Ontario," Jason said. "This impact left very rare metals and minerals scattered all around that area."

Of course, Monika had to have one. So she purchased one.

A couple months later Jason and Monika were visiting one of

Forbidden Knowledge

Auralite 23 Crystal pendant.

Jason's crystal wholesalers and once again she was drawn to one of these stones. She also insisted she needed to purchase several necklaces to sell.

"We weren't going to leave until we did, so I purchased some choice pieces," Jason said.

In 2013, they returned to the Bancroft gem show to sell their crystals again. A couple of booths down from them a new vendor had set up an Auralite 23 booth.

"Monika pulled me out of my booth to check it out and it turned out that the owner of the mine from Northern Ontario was there and he introduced himself to us," Jason said.

"We started to talk and it turned out that Howard Pilsmaker and I grew up in the same neighborhood north of Toronto and we even ate at the same favorite restaurants in the area. Howard by then had moved out of the area to another city also north of Toronto. We exchanged numbers and I told him the next time he was in the city to call me out for lunch."

"The Crystals Speak"

Several months later Jason woke from a dream with an urgent need to call Howard.

"It turns out my intuition was on point," Jason said. "He picked up the phone saying, "How did you know I was coming into town today?"

They met later that day for lunch and went to one of their favorite bagel restaurants. Over lunch they discussed the crystal business and spirituality.

"It turns out we had many things in common and just clicked," Jason said.

Again, Howard said to him that if he ever needed Auralite-23 or was in his neck of the woods to call him.

Jason and Monika married in August 2015 and soon began looking for a house to buy.

"We looked everywhere for a new place to call our own," Jason said. "I even went out to Brantford to visit Bob Mitchell and he showed me some great places.

"But in the end we found a perfect place in another city. Excited about our new move, I remembered that Howard lived in the city as well. So I called him up and said, "Hey Howard, guess what? We're neighbors, I moved to your town."

Incredibly, it turned out not only were they going to be neighbors but Howard actually lived only a few houses down the same street as them.

What were the odds of that?

Around this time Howard had just received a new shipment of Auralite-23 from the mine.

"He had about 12,000 pounds of the stone stored in his garage that needed to be cleaned and repacked for the upcoming Tucson Gem and Mineral Show," Jason said. "I periodically popped in to check on his progress and had the opportunity to be the first person to see these stones after all the mud was washed off of them."

During one visit Jason was drawn to a particular stone among all the other new crystals that were spread out on the dining room floor.

"It didn't look as if it belonged with the rest," Jason said. "I picked it up and it was much heavier than Auralite. It was also very dark in color.

"It almost looked as if it was burnt. It was very different from Auralite."

Jason asked Howard if he could take this stone home to meditate on.

That night he lay in bed holding this new crystal.

"As I was starting to dose off I started to have a vision projected in my consciousness," Jason said.

In this vision he saw what appeared to be a long rope but it was covered with what looked like hard clay-like material.

"As I stared at this rope it suddenly twisted and the clay exploded off of the rope exposing a beautiful shimmering rope-like strands of light underneath," Jason said. "When the rope shattered it felt as if my entire body had shattered.

"I was shaken right out of bed. I asked what had just happened and then the crystal spoke to me telepathically.

"Be still, we are awakening dormant strands of DNA within you."

For Jason, it was clear.

"These crystals connected to very high dimensional beings," he explained. "They could work and communicate to me through this crystal."

Jason contacted Nora the next morning and explained what he had experienced. She had to visit him and Howard. She had to experience these stones.

Jason then went to How-

The amazing geometry of a Metauralite Crystal.

238

"The Crystals Speak"

ard to see if he had any more of these strange crystals.

"I needed to purchase all of them," Jason said.

Nora arrived the next day and almost instantly the crystal started to communicate with her.

"She was blown away by the messages and healing that these stones had connected to her," Jason said.

Nora received a message from the crystal later that night. Afterwards, she recorded it.

"I AM 15 Minerals, 4 Crystal Intelligent Strands of Auralite, beyond Super 7 and Auralite 23.

"I AM Titanium, Platinum, Plutonium, I AM Alkaline and I AM Electromagnetic Energies of Light Particles that will assist you in shifting the human form into a Crystalline ESSENCE of Electromagnetic Frequencies of Light.

"I AM aligning your Body at the Head, Hands and Feet into the Magnetic pulse of My Light Crystals. My properties work in clearing detoxing the body through the Head, Hands and Feet first.

"An Amplification of holding onto this Crystal detoxes the body and after a full hour session you will be fully infused of the Electromagnetic Vibrations in every Atom, in every Cell and every Particle of your Beingness will be Electrified by my 15 Mineral Essences of Intelligences.

"This Mega-Light Crystal and its Meteor Frequencies harmonizing the brainwaves are harmonizing into the Essence of these 15 STRANDS of Minerals.

"I AM activating the Pineal and IAM activating the Thymus where the Crystal Infinite Seedlings are becoming Aligned, Harmonized and Synthesized through these Minerals

"METAURALITE through SHEKINA Magnetics will fuel this

body, as it will Attune the body.

"For some more evolved and elevated Souls their Consciousness of their human form will begin to transfer into these heightened Energies of LIGHT PARTICLES of highest Intelligences from the Core of the Planet; into the heart beat as they Integrate and Permeate the frequencies of Ascension of the human body into a Crystalline Adam Kadmon Intelligent body when they are amplified and synchronized.

"Just sit with this ESSENCE, knowing that the many STRANDS of LIGHT PARTICLES humbly surround you so that you may receive their messages of LOVE LIGHT HARMONY.

"ALL IS OF LOVE, ALL IS OF PEACE and ALL IS PERFECTION."

From this message, they decided to name the crystal "Metauralite" because of the higher concentration of metals and magnetic energies within this crystal.

"I feel as if this stone just like the Arkansas Quartz arranged all of this with me," Jason said. "If I had not been there at that exact time, I would not have noticed this new species of crystals.

"It would have been lost in the tons of Auralite. There were just too many synchronicities associated with Howard and these crystals to ignore"

Jason later discovered that crystals seek out and choose guardians to help them move on the planet to people and places that need their energies.

"In fact, the being on the cover of this book is the dimensional being connected to these stones," Jason said. "As I was pondering what would the cover for this book be, this being appeared to me holding this scared geometry vortex of energy.

"This image was imprinted on me and the next morning I rushed to the computer to try to recreate it. The picture came out perfectly. It was exactly the vision I had been shown.

"The Crystals Speak"

"This is how these beings communicate with us. They can connect to us through higher frequency energies like these crystals, which ground their consciousness to this planet.

"They then connect to people who resonate with these frequencies,"

Since then Jason has shared these stones with many groups.

"I believe that these crystals are here for a very important mission," Jason said. "They are here to set up a new crystalline grid around the planet. This will help move the energies of this planet into higher fields of consciousness.

"It's as if these new grids of energies are allowing higher dimensional beings to incarnate and connect on this planet."

This is why the new psychic children being born today are called "The Crystal Children," Jason said. They are also known as "Star Children."

According to New Age believers, these psychic children began being born in 1990. They have a collective consciousness and are advocates of love and peace. They possess the gift of clairvoyance and healing and are born with a very caring and sensitive personality.

These children also don't react to fear. They are extremely connected to animals and nature. They are very artistic and often sing before they learn to talk. They dislike loud sounds and bright lights.

They also often stare at people for long periods and seem to communicate with their eyes, which are often larger than most children.

"These are very special children. They have etheric crystals throughout their body," Jason said. "These crystals activate as the child grows to maturity or through spiritual practices.

"These crystals create dimensional grids that bridge many worlds and beings together. This is part of the awakening process. Not just for the individual, but as a planetary body at large."

Forbidden Knowledge

Jason Quitt's original artwork of the multi-dimensional being that appeared to him in a vision while meditating with a Metauralite crystal.

Chapter 23
"The Reality Of Our Reality"

Ever wondered what human beings really are?

The question isn't meant to elicit a conversation as to whether our DNA is part extraterrestrial?

That's a given. Jason absolutely knows humanity's ancestry is from the stars.

The question is simply - what is the human body or the body of any extraterrestrial being?

According to Jason, we are all electrical beings.

"The key to life is electricity," Jason said. "This is the vital force that runs through us.

"It follows our circulatory system and is aligned by the iron in our blood. The more conductive our cells are the healthier we become and the stronger our electromagnetic field will be."

This is why populations of ancient civilizations ate manna - white powdered Gold.

"This was a superconducting material that was ingested in the body to enhance the amount of energy being conducted," Jason said.

"That's why gold was so important. This 'ormus' gold awakened and revitalized ancient DNA that has been in hibernation."

Being electromagnetic in nature, our bodies are divided by vibrations of the spectrum emanating from source,

"This is what we call dimensions," he said. "We are many strands of vibratory oscillation in a sea of frequencies.

"Humans are actually fourth dimensional beings living in a third dimensional world."

The key to navigation in these worlds is simply a matter of resonance.

"We can change our resonance with our minds and bodies," Jason said. "If we can shift our electromagnetic resonance we can have experiences outside of what we would consider the physical dimension such as astral traveling or out of body experiences."

In this physical dimension our minds and bodies function within a system of the Earth's magnetic field and the radiance of the Sun.

"These two systems drive all the chemical reactions and electrical impulses that make us human," Jason said. "Our physical brain resonates in tune with the Earth's ionosphere and is connected directly to the magnetic field that envelops all living things.

"This field of magnetism records our experiences, our thoughts and our emotions. This record is stored within the Earth itself and transmits out into the universe."

This is also the key to our health and our ascent into higher fields of consciousness.

"What we hold within us (thought forms, emotions, karma, ancestry, etc,) creates the reality we experience by holding our perception through our unique vibratory rates," Jason said. "These nets of energetic fields encompass our entire being which set us on our course in life. What we hold determines the paths we walk and the experiences we have.

"As humans we need to be in resonance with the subtle vibrations of the Earth and Sun through their magnetism and radiation. When we become out of sync with these natural rhythms we cut ourselves off from the life giving forces of creation.

"The Sun's light feeds every cell of our body and the magnetic field syncs all our biorhythms. The combination strengthens us and builds our energetic bodies."

"The Reality Of Our Reality"

Our environment is made out of two charges - negative and positive ions.

"The Earth is not neutral," Jason explained. "It is actually slightly negative. But the air around us is mostly positive. Humans thrive in environments consisting of negative ions. Negative Ions relax us, heal us, and give us life."

Negative Ions are found everywhere in natural settings near water such as waterfalls, rivers, lakes, oceans, streams and throughout forests.

"Positive ions, however, actually take our life away," Jason said. "These are mostly found in artificial environments such as inside of an office building or house. This causes body stress and even ages us.

"We start to build positive ionization in our bodies when we are not grounded. When we are physically not connected with our feet to the Earth our body builds up positive ions. This weakens us and our immune systems."

Ever feel like you're drained of life after a long day at work?

"That's because all of the energy built up in your body," Jason said. "When we put our feet on the Earth we create an electromagnetic circuit.

"The Earth's negative charge pulls the built-up positive charge out of our body. This is why we feel so full of life when we go on vacation in natural environments.

"This is amplified when we stand and face the sun light. By doing this we energetically start to cleanse and heal the body, our mind and emotions because these forces will sync up all of our biorhythms and feed every cell with life giving energies."

When you look at the artwork of ancient Egypt you will notice how the people are saluting the Sun and aren't wearing anything on their feet. Also, they hardly wear any clothing.

"This allowed the sunlight to touch their skin directly," Jason said. "With the right postures and prayers they were performing an ancient form of alchemy of the body. Using the energies of nature they could transform themselves and the energetic nature of their bodies using these postures.

"Egyptians didn't wear head dresses, gold jewelry and gemstones placed on their bodies for fashion. This was used to adorn the body with superconducting materials such as gold. The gems would vibrate with different frequencies.

"Together placed on the right parts of the body they could shift their resonance to send and receive information dimensionally through their minds. They could also then travel out of body and enter into other worlds.

"This is done by the ancient tradition of the shamans, who use sacred plants to communicate with spirits and leave their bodies for healing and wisdom. Plants containing psychoactive alkaloids change the brains chemistry, which tunes the brain into other frequency ranges."

This is why many people on psychedelic drugs often have encounters with mystical beings, aliens, and entities. The plants shift their perception of reality and tune it into another dimensional stream.

"But these realities are as real as ours even if we can not perceive it with our naked eyes," Jason said.

"These sacred plants have the power to change our perception of reality and even have out of body experiences. Some of these plants can have a very positive effect on our brains as if they are somehow rewriting our neural pathways to let go of addictions and obsessions."

Did you know Magnetite and Silica crystals are found in various tissues in our bodies?

Did you know there are also crystals in our brains?

"You see, we have the ability to tune into other dimensions using the crystals in our body," Jason said. "This is the exact same concept as a radio. Radios use crystals to capture the electromagnetic waves out of the environment and translate them into electricity."

Just like we can with radios, humans have the ability to change these stations in our minds.

What if our organs worked in this fashion?

"We basically have an antenna that receives and sends information through the biology of the brain and other organs," Jason said. "And it's the geometry of these crystals that determines our reality."

"The Reality Of Our Reality"

If you can change their geometry you can also change your reality.

"Reality as we know it in a physical sense is wrong," Jason said, "Because nothing is actually physical. Everything is energy being arranged by non-perceivable dimensions.

"When you zoom into reality we find more space than matter. In fact, we can zoom into our reality until it becomes a quantum reality.

"It is almost like there is infinite dimension no matter which way you look. Up or down."

This is the world of fractals known as the holographic universe. That everything that we know is merely a holographic projection of conciseness itself.

"This is how we can explain dimensionality," Jason said.

For example, let's examine our dream world.

When we are dreaming does it not seem like another reality?

Do you have a body?

Can you feel pain, pleasure and emotion while in a dream state?

"The answer is yes," Jason said. "In fact, many ancient cultures believed the dream world was the connection to the spirit world. Today, we discount our dreams as nothing more than our brains working things out as we sleep."

How do we then explain an alien abduction case when the person claims to be taken on a ship where experiments are done on them?

"In these experiences they have a body and feel pain," Jason said. "But how can this be when the person is physically still laying in bed fast asleep."

How can this person claim that they are in two places at once?

"This is why so many discount these experiences as being nothing more then dreams," Jason said.

The truth is – it's something else entirely?

"These experiences are happening dimensionally," Jason said. "This explains how people can be in two places at once. You see, the physical universe is one of many perceptions of what our mind can navigate. Even though we experience our reality from our senses, they are only translated into electrical impulses that our brains interpret.

"If our mind changes its resonance it also changes its reality, just like waking and dreaming."

But how does this explain how some abductees claim they felt pain while under going medical experiments?

"It's the same reality that amputees experience," Jason said. "Even after an arm or limb is removed they absolutely have a sensation of still feeling their missing limbs until their mind realizes the limb is no longer there.

"The same thing occurs with abductees. The event is so shocking that their conscious mind still feels pain even though their physical body is still lying in bed.

"Many of these other beings we call astral, entities, aliens, ghosts, angels, gods actually do exist. They are not figments of people's imagination.

"They simply exist outside our perceivable reality. They exist in a world – in a dimension that is just a change in vibration."

There is something else we need to consider.

What if we have a body that can navigate in all these dimensions?

"The fact is, we do. And it's the key to understanding, who and what we are," Jason said. "We have another body that can navigate in all the other dimensions."

So when our mind awakens in the astral realm we are actually still in a body that is still in our third dimensional physical body.

"This astral body is governed by a different set of laws," Jason said.

When Jason has his outer body experiences, he uses his mind to separate his astral body from his physical body.

"It is almost like you are making a duplicate of yourself in another dimension." Jason said. "I needed to be out of my body to see and experience these beings. Even if my physical body is lying on my bed asleep, my astral body is conscious and having experiences that are as real as being fully awake."

Many experiences happen in the dimension of the mind during dreaming. This is probably used the most in contact cases. Using the mind and telepathy a dream like environment can be set up to have a meeting.

"This is the easiest and safest way for contact to be made," Jason ex-

"The Reality Of Our Reality"

plained. "As an example you are having a dream and suddenly you are kicked out of the dream and pulled into another dream. In the dream you are in a new environment and your mind is fully conscious.

"In this state, a being then enters the environment and starts to speak with you. Then you are awoken right after the experience in the physical world remembering what had just occurred. These dreams are a contact to other beings on other dimensions of time and space."

Some of these dream experiences are so vivid and real that sometimes it's impossible to figure out if it was a physical experience, memory or dream.

"This often happens when a loved one passes," Jason said. "Many people report how their loved one visited them in a dream to say goodbye. This has happened to me with both my grandfathers after they passed.

"My first experience came about a month after my mother's father passed. He came in a dream and said goodbye to me and that he loved me. I was so happy to see him, I hugged him and didn't want to let go.

"When I woke up from the dream all I could smell was his cologne in my room. That smell stayed with me the entire day. That was my confirmation that it was a real encounter."

When Jason's father's father passed he was awoken in the middle of the night by a voice in his head.

"It was my grandfather and he said I love you and I'm proud of you."

Jason immediately called his father, who had been staying over night at the hospital.

"My father picked up the phone crying saying "how did you know? How did you know to call right now? Your grandfather just passed away." Jason explained.

He told his father that he had said goodbye and he loves us.

"This is away for our loved ones to speak to us once they have left the physical world," Jason explained.

"Our dreams are an access point to the spirit world. And it's through the sleep state that we can change our brainwaves so we can leave our body and travel to other worlds of time and space."

THE RESONANCE SECRETS

Resonance creates a bridge between time space and dimension.

During Jason's research into ancient Egypt he came across information dealing with metals that were used on the body to heal. Many of the ancient cylinders found were made of copper and zinc.

"When these two metals are combined they create a micro electric current," Jason said. "This is how a galvanic cell battery is designed.

"When you hold a copper cylinder in one hand and a zinc cylinder in the other with your bare skin you are creating a current of electricity in the body. These cylinders can be seen clearly in the artwork and statutes of Egypt.

"They were used in conjuncture with postures to charge their bodies up and strengthen themselves on all levels."

Copper and zinc bracelets have also been found in Egypt and throughout the world dating far back in antiquity.

"When I was in Vermont at the American Dowsers Conference an Egyptian Master named Aaron Singleton told me that when you wear these types of bracelets it helps block negative energies from entering your body," Jason said. "He demonstrated on Monika. He projected a negative energy through her hand. She said she felt pain starting climb up her arm.

"Then Aaron put the bracelet on and tried again. She said she could feel his energy but it did not pass her wrist. This was a great demonstration, but I already knew there was a very magical property produced when these two metals are used together."

After this teaching Jason was determined to find a bracelet that contained just the right amount of copper and zinc to create this micro current of electricity. It took some time but he found a company in South Africa that manufactured them.

He ordered a shipment to test them out. As soon as the shipment arrived he instantly put one on his wrist to feel its effects.

"The Reality Of Our Reality"

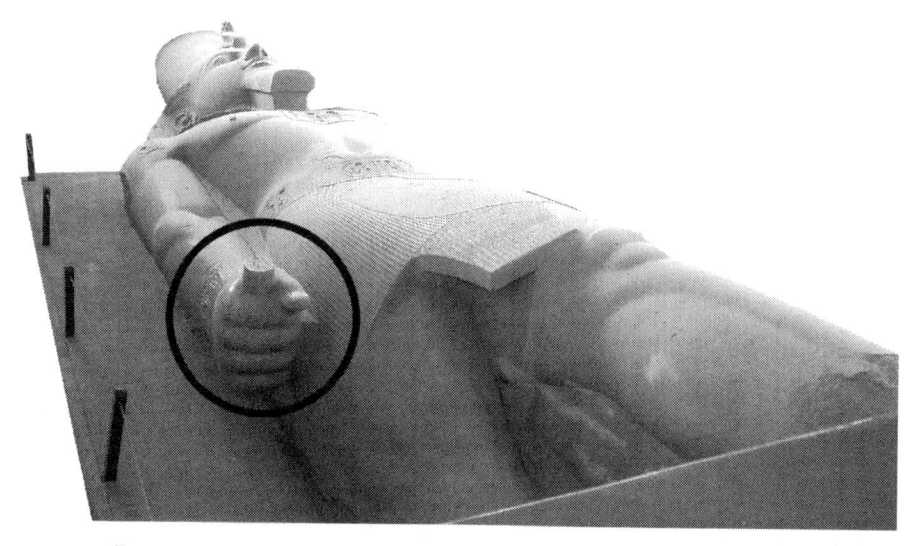

Ramses II statue clearly showing the copper and zinc rods.

"My body began to heat up," Jason said. "I knew this was the effect of more energy through my body boosting blood circulation."

That weekend Jason was invited to a friend's cottage in Northern Ontario. He slept with the bracelet on during his first night there.

"That night I had an unexpected visitor," Jason said. "I was awoken in the middle of the night by a very warm and loving energy. I could feel it radiating through my body.

"So I left my body to see who was with me. Sitting on the end of my bed was a being that had the features of Grey alien but distinctly different. Its skin was almost luminescent with slight feminine features.

"Her aura flowed around her with brilliant sliver and copper waves of energy that sparkled. There was no conversation or messages between us. All I felt was love. I just sat there for some time just gazing at this being and enjoying its company."

When he woke the next morning he recounted the night's events.

"I realized something. It was the copper and zinc bracelet," Jason said. "The energy of those metals resonated with this being and she came to see who was connecting to her energy.

"I remembered that the brilliant aura I saw around this being was the same colors as the bracelet. Being in the right resonance can create a bridge through time, space and dimensions. This is how we travel."

According to Jason, this is what is known as the "law of resonance."

"Remember, what we think and how we feel creates a resonance around us," he said. "The field of resonance we create is sent out into the universe and it's this resonance that pulls people and experiences into our lives.

"You need to remember you are responsible for what you project. It is part of your creative power. If all you feel is anger or believe everyone out there is trying to rip you off, and then the universe will continue to put you in situations where you have set these intentions in motion."

Have you ever met someone, who is always angry and every day of their lives something happens to them that just makes them angrier?

Are they creating that cycle?

Or are they continuing to hold that pattern around them by resonating in that field of anger?

"We need to take responsibility for what we choose to resonate with," Jason said. "If we choose to resonate with love, learning, peace and joy these emotions will attract certain entities and beings to us.

"It's the same if we choose fear, anger, greed and hate. These emotions will attract a different type of being or entity.

"This is where free will comes into play. We can choose who and what we want to resonate with."

Chapter 24
"Life In Another Body"

While Jason remembers some of his out of body experiences, most of the time he awoke only knowing he had been somewhere but without much of a conscious recollection.

"I wanted to know why I wasn't allowed to remember everything," Jason said.

As indicated earlier in this book, most of the time during his travels he would simply be an observer. He could float around and check out everything but wasn't allowed to inter-act.

"There was a time in my journeys where I would leave my body 20 to 30 times a night." Jason said. "At least that's what it felt like.

"I would leave my body, and then I would feel a pull on my being. I would see a portal open up in my room and I would be pulled through it. It would feel as if I would be projected light years away traveling at fantastic speeds.

"It was like I was entering a black hole, which acted as a wormhole to other places in time and space. I would feel myself going through these portals but then my consciousness would snap back into my physical body."

Jason became increasingly frustrated.

"I knew I was leaving my body and I knew I was traveling

through different portals to unknown locations," Jason said. "But all of these experiences had no memories attached to them."

For months Jason repeatedly asked the beings to allow his consciousness to remain awake and to be totally aware of what was happening during these journeys.

One night he got his wish.

"I was allowed to experience the entire journey as "Jason," he said.

Not only did he find himself on another world but his consciousness ended up in the body of a young boy.

However, before that happened he found himself traveling through space and aware that his consciousness was traveling to another constellation.

"I asked them where they were taking me," Jason recalled. "They replied – to the Pegasus Constellation."

As he traveled through space he eventually became aware of a planet that appeared to be covered in ice except for the part around its equator region. From space, the equator region was distinctly green.

"The poles were massive," Jason said.

Jason recalled being dropped down onto the planet. He soon found himself not only inside a school but his consciousness was implanted in the mind of a young boy.

"Picture that you're traveling through space and then suddenly you are projected into a living and breathing being," Jason said. "I'm still Jason but now I'm inside this child. I'm literally a different child on a different planet in a different world far away from Earth."

Jason was obviously excited.

"It was so cool," he said. "I'm in a classroom with other kids and I'm turning to other kids and asking them to tell me who I am.

"I'm literally disrupting a class on another world."

This isn't surprising.

You see, Jason was never the best of students.

In fact, he wasn't particularly interested in school growing up and missed many classes, much to the concern of his father and mother and of course, his teachers.

"I wasn't a great student. To me, school was a joke," Jason said.

"Life In Another Body"

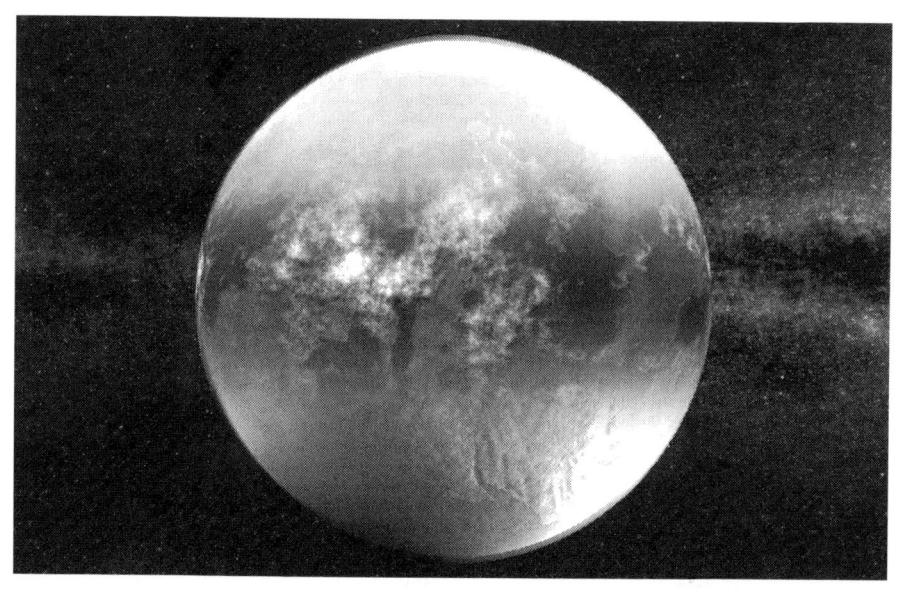

Ice planet Jason was taken too in the Pegasus Constellation.

"I would skip classes with my friends. By the end of the school year I probably missed about a month's worth of classes."

Despite missing so many classes he still obtained high grades.

"I got kicked out of Math. It was like reading Chinese to me," he said. "For the life of me I couldn't understand Math or French. But I still passed even though I never studied anything. If they gave me a month to do an assignment I would wait until the night before it was due to complete it. But I would always get good marks."

Being dyslexic also didn't help. He wound up being put in special classes.

"If I had a month I couldn't do it. But if the pressure was on, I could do it," he said. "Forget about reading, I just bought the movie or Coles notes (Cliff Notes).

In high school his real focus was on music. He played in several bands.

Despite being a troublemaker, or perhaps the class clown, Jason never revealed the mysterious things that had happened to him when he was younger.

255

"I basically kept all of that to myself," he explained. "The fact is that I didn't really feel it was important to tell anybody. I just put all of my weird experiences in the back of my head and forgot about them. They were fresh in my mind when my experiences happened but after awhile they just became memories."

Indeed, it was understandable why Jason was so energized when he found himself inside a strange child's body.

"As I was talking to all the kids around me I could see the teacher was looking at me really weird," Jason said. "Then all of a sudden I got up and ran out of the classroom. I went looking for the library because I just had to see their books."

But before he got the chance, the beings took him out of the boy's body and returned him to his home.

"I guess I was causing too much of a ruckus," Jason said.

It would later make sense to him.

"We live many lives simultaneously, which is why we don't usually remember," he said. "By allowing me to experience in real time the life of that boy I was really intruding on another life stream and neither I nor anybody has the right to do that.

"The fact is, that little kid might actually be me in another life stream in another existence on another planet but he has his own consciousness stream. But we both come from the same essence, the same spirit, the same soul.

"Essentially, I believe I was given the chance to experience this – and recall everything – to prove to me that we are all multi-dimensional beings. That we live many lives throughout time and space – all at the same time."

In other experiences, Jason was taken to other planets in other worlds in order to help heal beings that were connected to him.

"Something new started to happen to me once I started to progress in my healing and astral traveling, "Jason said. "I would start to be called to other planets to help other beings in their healing.

"There was one being in particular that I had a resonance with. I'm not sure who this being is to me. Perhaps, he was me in another life stream."

"Life In Another Body"

Despite resembling what many people might describe as a tall Grey, Jason knew the being wasn't one of those entities.

"It lived in a cave in a desert environment," Jason said. "Its skin was almost salmon pink color and very weathered."

Jason sensed the being was afraid and had been hiding in a cave for protection.

"It was as if someone was hunting him," Jason said. "I have been called many times to this being and each time I would send him energy in his time of need."

Monika has even seen some of these beings come into their bedroom to wake him up.

"One night she was really frightened by one of these beings," Jason said. "She heard something walk into our bedroom and when she opened her eyes she saw a being that she described looking like Darth Vader from Star Wars.

"He was breathing through some type of respirator system that covered his face. I calmed her down and just told her that this was normal for me and that these beings have been calling on me for help or a healing."

According to Jason, this also happens in the spirit world where souls that are stuck there need to have their energies healed before they can ascend into the spirit world.

"Many times I would wake with these types of beings presenting themselves to me," Jason said. "I would just open up a portal to the upper world and call on my guides and angels to assist this being in healing. Within an instant the beings are transported away into the spirit world.

"The physical body is our connection between the worlds. It gives us great power when wielded the right way."

According to Jason, we all have the ability to heal.

"We are the portal between the worlds," he said. "We are the doorway and the bridge between all worlds and dimensions."

Forbidden Knowledge

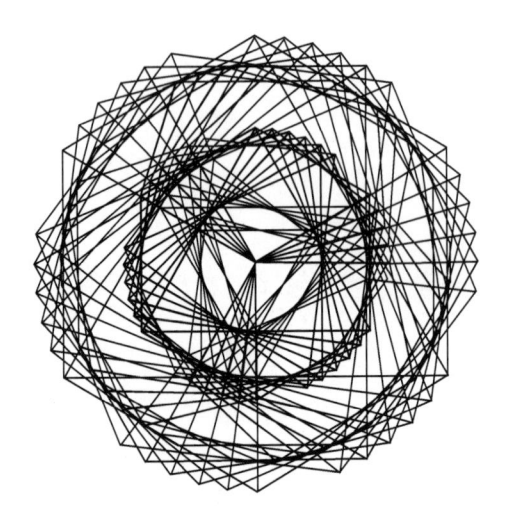

"Those who are able to see beyond the shadows and lies of their culture will never be understood, let alone believed by the masses."

- Plato

Chapter 25
"Forbidden Archeology"

Our history isn't what we have been told it is.

Not only has Jason experienced this first hand during his journeys but he believes tangible and irrefutable evidence has previously been discovered throughout our world that indicates the Earth has undergone several different historical periods long before what we believe and have been taught.

So why are mainstream scholars, archaeologists, historians and scientists so willing to ignore this evidence?

"The answer is simple," Jason said. "To acknowledge this evidence would destroy the existing narrative and essentially re-write our history.

"The fact is our history isn't what we think it is. Ancient discoveries, skeletal remains and artifacts, many of which most people have no idea have been discovered just don't fit the historical narrative that has been drilled into us."

For example, we have been taught that in pre-historic times Dinosaurs ruled the world and that mankind didn't evolve until nearly 65 million years had passed.

If this is true, then how do you explain the incredible discovery made between 1944-50 of more than 33,000 clay, ceramic figurines

Forbidden Knowledge

Acambaro artifact discovered by Waldemar Julsrud depicting humans riding dinosaurs.

buried in the outskirts of the Mexican city of Acambaro, Guanahuato that included instruments, pottery, monkeys and – dinosaurs?

Some have dated these artifacts from 2500 BC and if this is true then how would an ancient culture even know about such animals as dinosaurs?

The initial discovery was made by 69-year-old amateur German archaeologist Waldemar Julsrud and some of the artifacts actually depict humans riding dinosaurs.

As the story goes, Julsrud was a merchant, who stumbled upon some of the figurines while riding his horse. He hired local farmers to dig up what turned out to be a treasure drove of artifacts over the next seven years.

Of course, some mainstream experts have concluded these figurines were simply fabricated by the locals in order to attract tourists.

But the reality is that as of 2016 nobody has been able to prove they are fakes or true ancient artifacts of a culture that pre-dated the Aztecs by more than 3,000 years?

The question remains. If the artifacts are real then it clearly indicates humans and dinosaurs roamed the Earth at the same time and some how the ancient artisans, who created these ceramic figurines, knew this.

"When new discoveries, archaeological sites, artifacts and even skeletal remains are found – and they don't fit our taught historic narrative - a series of events take place," Jason said. "The mainstream scientific community and governmental departments ignore these new revelations, collect them and hides them away never to be seen again.

"Or the powers simply announce the discovery was found in a known historical period even though the common sense evidence suggests this isn't the case.

"In fact, finding such artifacts often end the careers of prominent archaeologists and scientists. Just by simply making a discovery known that goes against the collective narrative will often end in ridicule and being pushed out their profession never to work again. This has happened to many professionals in these fields and is unfortunately a common story."

But the 1944 Mexican discovery isn't the only one that goes against mainstream thinking.

"The famous Ica stones found in Peru show many different species of dinosaurs with humans," Jason said. "There are more than 15,000 such artifacts."

Like the Mexican discovery, this one has also been ridiculed by mainstream experts as a hoax partially because the cave where they were supposedly discovered has never been revealed. The stones have also never been scientifically examined.

These are all good reasons to be skeptical.

But are they really fakes?

The collection of round stones allegedly discovered in a cave near Ica, Peru not only shows the Incas hunting and fighting dinosaurs but some also depict them riding them as a form of transportation.

Forbidden Knowledge

Inca Stone discovered by Dr. Javier Cabrera Darquea depicting various dinosaurs.

Stone engraving of a Stegosaurus on the wall of the Ta Prohm Temple.

Other stones depict Incas using what look like telescopes and performing surgery or perhaps, a sacrifice.

The stones became a world-wide phenomena in 1966 when Peruvian physician Dr. Javier Cabrera Darquea left his practice and opened the "Engraved Stones Museum" where thousands of the stones are now on display.

Since, then several local farmers have revealed they created the stones to sell to tourists.

Were these local farmers told to say this?

Were they paid to say this?

Nevertheless, Dr. Cabrera has maintained the stones are real and are evidence that the Incas inter-acted with Extraterrestrials.

On display in the National Museum of Cambodia are historical relics discovered in Angkor, Cambodia.

Among the artifacts from the Khmer Empire of the 9th to 124th dynasty is what appears to be a stone carving engraving of a Stegosaurus on a wall of the Ta Prohm temple.

This temple was built as a Buddhist monastery in the 1100s and this particular carving initially became known when it appeared in books

"Forbidden Archeology"

Various pictures of giant footprints left in stone from around the world.

written by Claude Jacques and Michael Freeman in the late 1990s.

"I'm not suggesting this carving proves dinosaurs were around at the time the relics were carved but it does seem to indicate that the ancient cultures were aware that such animals lived," Jason said. "Again, how could they have known this?"

Let's now examine the mystery of giant footprints that have been discovered throughout the world.

In Asia, there is a story told about how Lord Hanuman, the great devotee of Lord Rama, left his giant divine footprints in sol-

263

id stone as he landed in various countries. Hanuman was believed to have been a Hindu god and a central figure in the Hindu epic Ramayana. He is also one of the most revered figures in Hindu mythology.

"These footprints date back millions of years," Jason said.

"They have become shrines and altars of prayer and ceremony throughout Asia.

"But these footprints are found worldwide fossilized in stone. Some of these footprints defy logic. They are four-feet long and have been dated back to an astonishing 300 million years."

Fossilized dinosaur footprints have also been located along side human footprints in the limestone beds of the Paluxy River near Glen Rose, Texas at the Dinosaur Valley State Park. The dinosaur footprints were discovered in the early 1900s.

"Once again, mainstream experts have concluded these giant human footprints are simply a fake and case closed," Jason said. "Is it just as possible they refuse to consider what the alternative would mean? That man and dinosaur existed at the same time?"

"In South Africa near the town of Mpaluzi there is a four-foot footprint that is believed to be more than 200 million years old," Jason said.

"This footprint made headlines after author, researcher Michael Tellinger brought attention to this find on the Internet," Jason said.

The footprint embedded in granite stone in a remote area of the country was initially discovered in 1912 by Stoffel Coetzee, a local lion hunter.

"Adding to this discovery is the fact that an upper leg bone with a hip was found in the early 1960s in the mines of northern Namibia that would have had to belong to somebody standing more than 12 feet tall," Jason said.

"Experts have determined this bone clearly shows that giants existed in Africa more than 40,000 years ago."

"But stories of giants aren't new to our world," Jason said.

"In fact, we have been talking about giants since we first started to record history," Jason said. "Documented stories of giants are

"Forbidden Archeology"

found throughout the ancient texts of Sumer, Egypt, and even in the Bible.

To quote from Genesis 6:4

"There were giants in the earth in those days; and also after that, when the sons of God came in unto the daughters of men, and they bare children to them, the same became mighty men which were of old men of renown."

The stories of giants reach every culture on the planet regardless of race or location.

"These stories are deeply embedded in our consciousness," Jason said. "Many truly believe that at one time giants walked the Earth. In fact, besides giant footprints, giant skeletons have been discovered all over the world. But just like artifacts that don't fit into the narrative they often go missing without a trace."

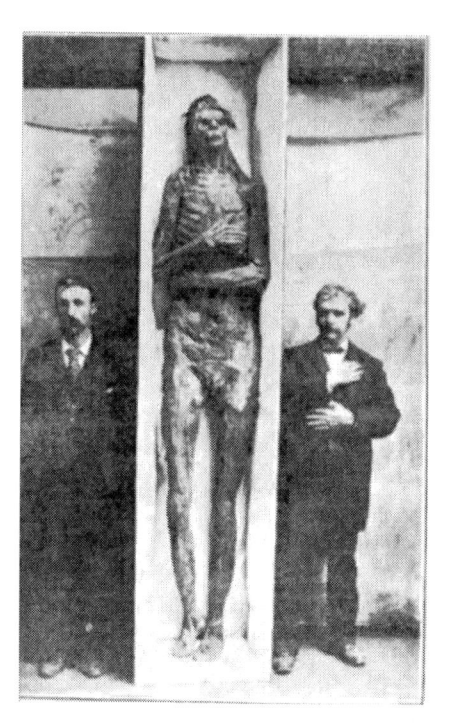

Historical pictures of giants published in newspapers.

But we don't have to look far. Many of these giants are found right here in North America.

"There have been numerous published stories and documents regarding these discoveries," Jason said.

One such case was published in the New York Times on Dec. 20, 1897. When a Wisconsin mound was opened and explored a nine-foot skeleton was discovered.

"Two other skeletons were also discovered in this area. One was 7 ½ feet tall and the other was 8 feet tall," Jason said.

"Interestingly, reports of these discoveries, essentially evidence that a lost race of giants once lived in the area, have largely been ignored," Jason said.

"Besides their height, what made these skeletons that more unique was the fact they had a double row of teeth," Jason said. "There have been hundreds of these documented cases of ancient burial mounds holding remains of giant skeletons, including some up to 12-feet tall."

Stories written around the time of their discovery also indicated they also had six fingers and six toes and their skulls were elongated.

Now here is something to think about.

How many of you have ever gone to a museum and saw a giant skeleton?

"Isn't it interesting there are no such displays despite all of the documented evidence, including newspaper stories that wrote about these incredible finds," Jason said. "Is there any truth to the rumor that many of these giant skeletons remain hidden away in the vaults of the Smithsonian Institution?"

Are they hidden because to admit they exist would totally go against the government-driven mainstream historical narrative?

"The history we have been taught in school and in our text books is designed to fit a fabricated history," Jason said. "Mainstream experts hold on to their beliefs so strongly that they refuse to believe anything that doesn't fit the narrative they were taught and the one they continue to perpetuate."

"In the late 1950s a 47 inch femur bone was discovered in

"Forbidden Archeology"

southeast Turkey during road construction in the Euphrates Valley," Jason said.

"This meant it had to have come from a 15-foot giant," Jason said.

Reports suggested many tombs were uncovered containing remains of giants.

In 1988, Swiss archaeologist Gregor Sporri photographed a mummified Egyptian finger that measured 16-inches long and was alleged to have been found by a grave digger near the Giza pyramids.

"Again, this would mean this Egyptian stood 16 feet tall," Jason said.

"Another giant skeleton found in County Antrim, Ireland was over 12-feet tall," Jason said.

A photo of this appeared in the Dec 1895 issue of Strand Magazine in England. As the story goes it was allegedly discovered by a prospector looking for iron ore. Reports suggested this giant also

Ancient Egyptian artwork that depicts many different sizes of humans.

had six toes.

Very little is known about this discovery, including whether anybody ever tested it to see if it was a real skeleton.

Skeptics often point to this one as also being a hoax.

A 19-foot-six inch skeleton was discovered at Lucerne, Switzerland in 1577 under an overturned Oak tree. But nearly 200 years later a mainstream scientists announced the bones were that of an elephant.

Was he correct was this just another cover-up to prevent our history being re-visited?

"Another 30-foot giant skeleton was discovered in 1613 in Rhone," Jason said.

As this story goes, stonemasons were digging a well near ruins of the Castle Chaumont near the Rhone and Isere Rivers in France when they discovered bones of a giant.

"The list goes on and on. It seems that finding giants is actually a common occurrence," Jason said. "It's just not made public anymore.

Who were these giants?

They aren't just found in one localized area, but virtually all over the planet.

Was our world once populated by giants?

"Many artifacts from Egypt and Sumer clearly depict different sizes of humans standing beside each other," Jason said. "One very well-known artifact shows giant Egyptians standing side by side with full grown Giraffes."

Were these just artist interpretations?

Or were they documenting reality?

Is this archaeological proof that many different sizes of humanoids existed on Earth in our ancient history?

"But ignoring the reality of giants is pale compared to what mainstream experts have refused to acknowledge about pyramids," Jason said.

"In some cases, ancient sites have virtually been ignored by the mainstream," Jason said. "Pyramids have been located all over the planet.

"The problem for mainstream archaeologists and historians is

"Forbidden Archeology"

that some of these pyramids date further back then anyone would like to admit."

Take the discovery of the Bosnia pyramid for instance.

"It's the largest pyramid ever discovered and is roughly twice the size of the Great Pyramid of Giza," Jason said. "Ancient tunnel systems and tools have been discovered at this site.

"But the entire complex is believed to be about 25,000 years old, far older than our civilization is supposed to be.

"Tests have also indicated this pyramid emits an ultrasonic frequency that can be measured around the frequency of 28 kHz."

"An ancient pyramid was also discovered in China in Qinghai Province," Jason said.

"What makes this find so unique is that within this structure lays many iron pipes," Jason said. "These pipes have been dated back 150,000 years."

But of all of the ancient pyramids, one that completely re-writes our known history is the discovery of megalithic constructions in Crimea, Ukraine in 1999 by former Soviet military man Vitaliji Gokh.

If the dating is correct, then this structure and others, pre-dates the time when pre-historic dinosaurs roamed the Earth.

"It's been claimed that this is the oldest structure ever to be discovered dating back to a mind numbing 65 million year of age," Jason said.

150,000 year old iron pipework found in a Chinese Pyramid.

Bosnian Pyramid is estimated to be over 25,000 years old.

269

Forbidden Knowledge

London Hammer artifact dates back 450 million years.

Gokh also discovered these structures were emitting three beams of energy at the frequencies of 900x109 Hz, 500x109Hz, and 10x109Hz.

According to reports, Gokh discovered a giant pyramid of nearly 148 feet and more than 236 feet wide. Also, there were hollow chambers inside, including a mummy.

The site is still under excavation but reports suggest nearly 40 pyramids and other structures have been located.

"Of course, mainstream archaeologists have yet to recognize this extraordinary discovery," Jason said.

"There has also been a tool that was discovered that simply defies logic," Jason said.

Known as the London Hammer, this tool was made of iron and wood and found embedded in solid stone.

"This object dates back to a date that is simply impossible for mainstream experts to believe," Jason said. "The layer of rock surrounding this object is from Ordovician period which is around 450 million years old."

Jason once came face to face with an historical contradiction

"Forbidden Archeology"

while vacationing on Manitoulin Island in northern Ontario, one of his favorite places.

He was visiting the historic Sheuiandah Centennial Museum and as he looked around he came upon a small photo hanging on the wall with the caption, "On this site Thomas E. Lee of the National Museum of Canada found advanced tools dating back to a culture that once lived on the island 125,000 years ago."

"Now if this statement is true then the entire theory of the migration of our ancestors out of Africa using the ice as a bridge to cross over to North America would be absolutely untrue," Jason said. "If the land bridge theory is true then the first people to come to North America would have to have done so 13,000 years ago. Recent scientific claims have suggested this land bridge migration took place 19,000 to 22,000 years ago."

"But Thomas E Lee's historic discovery was ridiculed by mainstream experts and he was basically ridiculed right out of his job and into prolonged unemployment," Jason said.

"No reputable publication would use him," Jason said. "Many authors rejected his discovery and all of the artifacts discovered suddenly vanished. Even the director of the National Museum of Canada was fired for even suggesting that his discovery should be published. Others who worked closely on this case also never worked again in these fields."

According to Jason, this isn't a unique case. The same kind of professional assassination has happened to many others, who have dared to go against the established history.

"The risk to go against the common view is just too great," Jason said. "The history being taught to us is used to program us into a false reality so that we can be controlled.

"If you take away a culture's history you can assimilate them into a new society with new beliefs. This is what the Church tried to do with the Native Canadians in their residential schools. They tried to break all the connection to their roots in the name of religion."

"Canada and the United States tried in the past to systematically destroy the Native population because they didn't share the same view of the world," Jason said.

"Ideology and belief is the greatest threat to this world when it is based on fear, greed and control," Jason said. "That's why many archaeological finds have been swept into obscurity because they just simply don't fit the mainstream historical narrative."

So do we remember a time far in our past when we once walked the Earth with dinosaurs?

If so, then how old is our history?

"In one of my journeys I was shown a hologram of the Earth," Jason said. "I watched the Earth reverse in time at fantastic speeds. I saw the Continents move and shift.

"I saw the Earth when it was one giant continent. There have been many cycles of the Earth over a time span of millions of years.

"In fact, I have clearly been show at least five different times of Earth's history."

Jason has a very strong connection to two different sites at two different times of Earth's history.

"I have felt the call to travel back to these sites," Jason said. "They have a great connection and mystery to me. I'm not entirely sure their purpose but I feel like I have been there many times before."

"One is a temple located in a time when the Earth was just in its beginning stages of development," Jason said.

"It was a fire world," he said. "The sky was always dark and there were no signs of vegetation. It was strictly a rocky environment and I could see lava flows glowing out of the ground in the distance."

"The temple appeared to have been constructed out of rocks of red clay and were very archaic looking," Jason said.

"There was a strong force that I felt. It was very sacred," Jason said. "There were long steps that led up to the temple.

"The rooms and hallways were lit by fire. It was a very warm environment. It felt as if this place existed millions of years in our past.

"I call this the Temple of Fire."

Every time Jason has journeyed to this temple he has always been alone. Even though there are no signs of any other human-like beings he always senses a strong presence.

"Forbidden Archeology"

"I can almost hear very low vibrations as if there were people chanting ancient mantras," Jason said. "But I never saw them. Only this sound filled the temple."

Another site that Jason has continually been drawn to appears to have existed around the time of Atlantis.

"Maybe 50,000 years in our past," Jason said "There are many water ways and islands. But when I'm called there this ancient site is just ruins. There isn't an active civilization."

At the side of mountain facing an ocean Jason saw many ancient pillars carved out of the side of this mountain.

"I always feel as if both of these ancient places mean a great deal to me and that they hold some great importance to me," Jason said. "But I have no idea why.

"Perhaps both sites once served a very important purpose. But the answers have yet to be provided to me."

So was mankind or a different version of mankind present in all of the various Earth stages Jason has viewed?

Do we still have these memories buried deep within us?

Can we still access them?

"Our hidden history doesn't just go back thousands of years," Jason said. "This history extends back into the millions of years.

But the big question remains.

Are we ready to uncover the hidden history of our planet?

Forbidden Knowledge

Ojuelos de Jalisco artifact showing spaceships, planets and beings with alien features that are performing a sacrifice.

Chapter 26
"Unacknowledged Artifacts"

In early 2016, Jason received a telephone call from Howard from the Tucson Gem and Mineral show.

Howard said he needed to talk to a man named Mark Russell, who had introduced himself while viewing the Auralite crystals in his booth.

It turns out that Mark currently lives in Mexico where he has been documenting thousands of unacknowledged artifacts from the area around Ojuelos de Jalisco. It's a colonial city of about 12,000 in the state of Jalisco and some 280 miles northwest of Mexico City.

The city dates back to 1569 when it was founded by Spanish conquistador Pedro Carrillo Davila as a military garrison to protect people against the Chichemecas warriors. History tells us that unlike the civilized Aztecs these warriors were wild, nomadic hunters, who generally didn't wear any clothing and fiercely resisted the Spanish intrusion into their territory and the silver the Europeans wanted to mine.

What makes these artifacts so incredible is their content and motifs.

"They seem to show many different beings, including some with elongated heads as well as UFOs, advanced technology, planets, black holes and worm holes," Jason said.

Forbidden Knowledge

Ojuelos de Jalisco artifact showing spaceships, planets and beings with alien features.

Jason had never heard of these artifacts but if what Mark told him in their phone conversation was true then this was one of the most significant archaeological finds ever.

They would prove beyond any reasonable doubt that other worldly beings existed and that they interacted with ancient human cultures.

But there was a big question.

Why had he never heard of them before?

Surely, one of the many alien documentary television shows would have done a piece on them?

Mark explained to Jason that these artifacts have been found in numerous caves in the area for hundreds of years. He even invited Jason down to Mexico so he could see them first hand.

"Unacknowledged Artifacts"

"He explained there are about 50 square miles of ruins and caves that are still yielding new artifacts every year," Jason said. "He said there are so many artifacts that many people in the area want to open a museum for them."

A few days later Mark sent an email that provided Jason access to his (Mark) hard drive with more than 7,000 high quality images of the artifacts.

Some of these images have been produced in this book.

"These images completely blew me away," Jason said. "These unique pieces ranged in size from a half and inch to a couple of feet.

"If this was a hoax, it would have taken an entire army of people to pull it off."

But the big question still remained.

How come no one has ever come forward with this discovery in a public way?

The reason, according to Mark, was that nobody wants to listen or believe this discovery is authentic.

"In fact, he said area scientists and government officials have completely ignored the artifacts," Jason said. "In previous years someone tried to display these artifacts in a local museum but military officials removed them and took them away."

If this is true, one has to ask why?

Did the government not want the outside world to know these artifacts existed?

Was this another case of mainstream experts not wanting to acknowledge our history isn't what we have been led to believe it is?

"Incredibly, some of these artifacts have simply wound up as conversation pieces on coffee tables," Mark said.

Some have also ended up in the personal collections of interested people who have come to the area after hearing about them from locals and in recent years from Internet sites.

Indeed, these artifacts are starting to garner more interest via the Internet but usually the info is second hand and published via blogs or Facebook.

The fact remains, to be the best of our knowledge, there has never been any scientific, archaeological, historical or government announcement of this amazing discovery.

A few Internet articles suggest that in 2012 the Mexican government had publicly revealed their existence although a search of Google failed to provide any article reporting this had in fact happened.

In fact, only one legitimate researcher has ever written anything official about them.

Austrian Klaus Dona managed to obtain many of these artifacts and has been meticulously studying them since 2010.

According to Dona, a local farmer found more than 3,000 arti-

Ojuelos de Jalisco artifact showing spaceships, planets and beings with alien features.

"Unacknowledged Artifacts"

Ojuelos de Jalisco artifact of an alien head with what looks like a star map.

facts deep within one cave that had previously been sealed for more than 100 years.

"Out of these 3,000 artifacts, supposedly 2,500 of them are made out of stone while the other 500 are made out of a unique form of ceramic called kaolin, a clay material now used in making ceramics and fireproof materials," Jason said. "Some of these pieces are also made of gold and silver."

"He has conceded the find seems too good to be true but it hasn't prevented him from studying them," Jason said. "He has run many different scientific tests on them and has come to the only conclusion he can – that they are genuine."

However, because some of the pieces are so preserved, most mainstream experts have written them off as fakes.

Truth be told, it's easy to come to such a conclusion because some of them really do look almost too perfect to be thousands if not hundreds of thousands of years old.

"I'm still a bit skeptical," Jason admitted. "On the other hand similar artifacts although not in such great number have been located throughout the world among ancient ruins and wall carvings. So in some sense this discovery isn't unique.

"There are many Mayan, Aztec, Inca, Hopi, Egyptian, Sumerian, etc. artifacts found that tell the story of visitors from space interacting with the human population.

"Stories in their ancient text and wall drawings and artifacts have even suggested that these star beings brought or created humankind. In fact, some of these cultures have even claimed to have originally come from the stars.

How does one also explain the mysterious if not incredible depictions of what appear to be airplanes, tanks, and perhaps even a submarine and helicopter discovered in 1848 on a ceiling beam at the ancient Egyptian temple in Abydos built by Pharaoh Seti some 3,000 years ago?

Mainstream experts have dismissed these strange objects. They are hieroglyphics that have been re-carved and re-surface over the ages and only appear to represent military machines that couldn't have possibly existed during the time of their discovery never mind thousands of years ago.

But these unusual carvings were again brought to world wide attention in the 1990s when a tourist snapped some photos and later distributed them on the Internet.

So what are we to make of this?

If they are a fake, they're an elaborate fake and for what reason would somebody even attempt to do it?

Ancient Egyptians depicted what they saw.

Are we to believe such flying machines actually existed in ancient Egypt?

Or is this proof that time travel technology was known to at least some of the ancients and they carved what they had seen

"Unacknowledged Artifacts"

during journey into the future?

Among the motifs Jason found extremely fascinating from Mark Russell's collection are the ones with scenes of cone-headed beings appearing to be exiting a space ship and holding an infant with the same features.

"Many more show other beings that look more humanoid wearing what appears to be space suits and holding an alien-looking child in the air as a UFO flies above them." Jason said.

"There are also scenes of these beings sacrificing an infant during celestial events. You can clearly see comets in the sky with planets and UFO's. These types of scenes are depicted on hundreds of these artifacts."

Who are these beings?

"They're not just one species," Jason said. "The depictions involve numerous types of beings. Many have the typical elongated skulls that have been found all over South and Central America."

If these artifacts are genuine then what are they trying to tell us?

What are the many ancient cultures where such artifacts have been discovered trying to tell us?

"They all seem to have a similar story regarding our past," Jason said.

"Throughout our ancient history myths of these beings are said

Ojuelos de Jalisco artifact showing spaceships and beings.

to arrive from other worlds and interact with different human populations during different time periods.

Was it these other worldly beings that taught our ancient ancestors architecture, math, religion and spirituality?

What if it wasn't just one alien species that has been doing this but many different beings from different star systems and dimensions?

What if the truth is that some of these beings even lived among the indigenous populations and interbred with them creating an entirely new being?

What if these beings deliberately genetically-altered the native population to create a new hybrid species?

What if some of these same inter-galactic races never left Earth and they are still her interacting with us, waiting patiently for the right time to publicly announce themselves to the world?

Is this what humankind is waiting for?

"These questions ultimately will lead to one very important theological question," Jason said.

What if these beings come here claiming to be our Creators?

What would we do in that scenario?

For Jason, these questions have been an integral part of his enlightened journey.

"The real truth is that nothing can claim ownership over you," Jason said. "Even if your body was created by other worldly beings no being has authority over you or your actions.

"Freedom is maintaining the sovereignty of your consciousness. This is your power in these realms.

Chapter 27
"Our Anunnaki Connection"

Many have come forward with their theories about what is known about UFOs witnessed by millions around the world.

The Internet is filled with so-called experts. Late night talk radio shows continually provide listeners with the latest information.

Conspiracy theorists have gained dedicated followers throughout the world.

Fake photos of aliens and space ships have been created by Photoshop and other computer-generated means.

But amidst all of this are some very exceptional people, who have put their reputations on the line in order to provide the real truth.

Two such trailblazers are Robert Dean a retired Command Sergeant Major of the US Army and the Honorable Paul Hellyer, the former Canadian Minister of National Defense.

While working for the military in Europe in the mid-1960s Dean claims to have seen a document called "Cosmic Top Secret," which essentially revealed the existence and recovery of numerous crashed alien craft and bodies.

Hellyer, once Canada's Minister of Defence, has publicly revealed a global cover-up of the existence of aliens and their influence on our society.

They have also claimed knowledge of the existence of at least four known species of extraterrestrials have and continue to visit Earth.

"In my view, these men are among the highest-ranking whistleblowers to ever come forward," Jason said.

"But while these courageous men have revealed what they believe – and know – they are only just scratching the surface about the reality of what aliens really are," Jason said.

According to Jason, far more than four alien species have visited this planet in the past and are continuing to visit Earth on a regular basis.

"These alien beings are not only physical but also have the capability to travel multi-dimensionally through time and space," Jason said. "Some of these beings have been interacting with us for thousands of years, perhaps millions of years.

"And at least one group looks entirely human. You would not even know if you were sitting next to one right now."

According to Jason, governments not only have hidden this fact from the populace for decades but governments and the military are extremely concerned that at least one species is walking and blending in with humanity on Earth.

"They simply have no way of knowing which humans are really not human," Jason said. "There is a good chance some of them also hold high ranking positions in governments and the military. This fuels our government's paranoia."

For many years now governments and scientists have understood that human beings are composed of multiple genetics from at least 12 different extraterrestrial races.

In February 2001, researchers working on the Human Genome Project revealed that 97 per cent of non-coding sequences in the human DNA – otherwise known as junk DNA - was the genetic code of extraterrestrial life forms.

In simple terms, the human genome consists of two sets of 23 chromosomes and each parent contributes these genetic building blocks. But 97 per cent of our genomes have no known purpose.

What this discovery essentially means is that our evolution isn't what we have long believed it is. That somewhere along our evolu-

"Our Anunnaki Connection"

Ancient Sumerian artifact depicting the Anunnaki as giants.

tion extraterrestrial DNA was used with existing human DNA to create an entirely new human species.

According to Jason, our alien genetics enables all of us to have abilities, gifts and connections that we are completely unaware of.

"Many Experiencers have been told that human beings are very special and unique in the universe," Jason said. "This is why many of the abduction cases have a strong genetics side to them."

This is why an extraterrestrial race known as the Anunnaki played such a crucial role as our creator gods.

"These were the geneticists, who created the humans we know today to serve the gods," Jason said.

According to ancient texts, the Anunnaki were a race of god-figures who existed in ancient Mesopotamia among the Sumerians, Assyrians and Babylonians, the oldest known civilizations on Earth

Another way of saying this is that they were a race that existed at the time of our current existence as a species on Earth. As indicated earlier in this book, Jason has been told there are many different civilization eras on Earth dating back millions of years.

Mainstream archaeologist and historians are in agreement. There is no known evidence of any civilized society before 3300 BC to 750 BC. Evidence suggests there were pockets of cultures as far back as 8000 BC but no organized societies such as what eventually rose in what is today the country of Iraq.

The name Anunnaki suddenly became well-known in modern times when the late author and economist, Zecharia Sitchin proposed this extraterrestrial race had genetically manipulated mankind. His theory has since been adopted by numerous ancient alien theorists

Ancient alien theorists believe the Sumerians were the first civilization on Earth to come into contact with the Anunnaki, who arrived on Earth from a planet in another Galaxy. Their mission was to mine gold and other minerals.

In his 1976 book "The Earth Chronicles," Sitchin's translation of the ancient Sumerian texts revealed how the Anunnaki came to Earth to mine gold that was needed to repair their home planet's atmosphere. According to the tablets translated, the Anunnaki came from a planet named Nibiru, which is supposed to circle our Sun every 3,600 years.

Some believe this planet will appear as soon as August 2018 and lead to a catastrophic extinction event similar to what happened 65 million years ago.

Jason has been told that these so-called Anunnaki gods went on to establish cities and kingdoms throughout Earth.

But the story of them being from a planet named Nibiru might simply be an ancient work of fiction to sell their story of ruler-ship.

"Despite this, at no time have I ever been given any information about Nibiru or have even heard of this planet during my journeys," Jason explained.

"The gold that they would mine might have had other purposes as a resource," Jason said.

"Gold is an amazing element. It can be used as a superconductor of electricity. It can also be a shield against radiation," Jason said. "Gold would be the kind of element needed to travel through space.

"Our Anunnaki Connection"

"Many also believe gold can be turned into a chemical substance that would reverse the aging process so these beings could maintain virtually endless lives in harsh new environments.

"They created religious doctrines, priesthoods and monetary systems," Jason said. "They even waged wars between different populations in their names.

"This has been well documented in ancient Sumerian texts, the Vedas and even recounted in the stories of the Old Testament. We are still living in the same systems set up by these beings."

Based on some ancient text writings, Jason also believes the Anunnaki also had Reptilian traits.

"The bloodlines of Royal families that claim rights and privileges over the population believe these ancient gods are their ancestors through blood," Jason said.

According to ancient text, the Anunnaki stood 9 feet tall.

"Also, that in the distant past these beings interbred with the human population," Jason said. "Their offspring became the first kings and queens of this world. This is the bloodline they try to trace back to. This is also where we get the term "Blue Bloods" from; these gods had more copper in their blood, which made their blood blue when oxidized.

"Human beings have been modified genetically for at least the past 400,000 years but this experiment is much more ancient then the Anunnaki. Our real history of civilizations on this planet dates back millions of years."

According to Jason, there were many reasons for genetic intervention and not all of these reasons are sinister.

"Some groups like the Anunnaki wanted to create the perfect obedient worker so they could live as gods while the humans provided everything for them," Jason said. "They were even used to mine for resources such as gold for these beings. This is where we have inherited our lust of gold from".

As it turned out, Earth is quite diverse in its resources and this is another reason why there are so many visitations from other worldly beings. They came to take resources from this planet.

"We are not just talking about minerals and metals," Jason said. "It turns out that genetics are the most valuable resource in the universe. And Earth is quite diverse in many different types of life. We truly are the Garden of Eden."

According to Jason, humanity was altered in the distant past when Earth was undergoing tremendous climate changes.

"It's my understanding that if humanity didn't receive this genetic upgrade we would have not survived these Earth changes," Jason said. "This is why there was a mass extinction of other humanoid species such as the Neanderthals.

"Many species just suddenly vanished from our historical record. Climate changes brought many sudden challenges to the Earth's populations. They suffered from starvation, pestilence and disease, which overtook them quickly."

Several geneticists now believe that some of these ancient humanoids survived and that they are a part of us now.

"It seems that in our distant past the human populations interbred with these other species," Jason said. "This enabled these long extinct races to carry forward through hybridization.

"This is also the case now with the so-called alien/human hybrids. Many groups are trying to create the perfect mix of genetics to create a new species."

Jason understands there are many reasons for this.

"Hybridization is a way for another races to integrate into a society," Jason said. "They include traits of the indigenous population so they have the ability to fight infections and acclimatize to a different environment."

In December 2015, Jason had an unexpected experience.

"I was taken to interact with a hybrid child that was around 1 or 2 years of age," Jason said. "When this child was placed in my arms I knew instantly he was somehow connected to me.

"I was told his name was Michael."

But every time Jason looked directly at him he would experience tremendous pain and pressure inside his head.

"It was almost as if this child didn't want me to look at him di-

"Our Anunnaki Connection"

rectly," Jason said. "This child was incredibly psychic. I sensed that he was already in telepathic resonance with me.

"He looked very much human with brown hair and fair skin. The only thing off was his big eyes and head. I knew he was a hybrid child. He needed to be held by me for some reason, but as I tried to look at him I would experience this great pain."

It was at this point that memories began entering his consciousness.

"It was an understanding of the Greys and their hybrid programs," Jason said, "I started to get angry. I became upset and thought this child was part of the Grey hybrid program."

"The anger built up within me and with my telepathic thought I projected to this child - "I hate you" - and as I did, this child suddenly became weak in my arms," Jason said.

Immediately, Jason found himself transported back and he awoke in his bedroom.

"I really don't know why I had this reaction and I hope no harm came to this child," Jason said. "I just couldn't shake the feeling that I had been taken advantage of.

"Maybe that was just my human mind and fears bleeding through. Perhaps I screwed up and this experience was something entirely different. I hope I can figure this one out soon."

Another reason for hybridization is to create a new species that would have a strong connection and allegiance to their creators.

"This is similar to the story of the Anunnaki and the gods of the past," Jason said. "Other types of hybrids are already on Earth but like me they are here for other reasons.

"They are here to shift the consciousness of this planet so they fully understand the position we are in. There has been too much deception and too many wars for too long. It is time we wake up and understand the war that has been waging behind the scenes for thousands of years."

Jason has also been told that many star beings incarnate on Earth so that they can inhabit a human form.

"Once they are in possession of this form these beings come to Earth to pick them back up," Jason said. "These beings do this so they can seed other worlds with the human form.

"At a certain age in childhood these star beings abduct these children and take them to another world under what is known as a seeding program."

Essentially, what this means is that many abductees are literally being taken because they lived as these aliens in another life.

"They are being examined by their own race," Jason explained. "But there have also been backdoor deals allowing human abduction as a resource in return for governments receiving advanced technology."

Such agreements were mentioned earlier in this book.

"We need to wake up and realize how precious life truly is," Jason said. "How gifted we are to be living on this Garden of Eden. This world can enable us to grow spiritually and awake our gifts and abilities so that we can truly know who we actually are.

"This is the greatest gift of all. To know thyself. We are not what we believe we are. We are something much greater. There is so much potential within us that we can not only shift ourselves and our planet but we can affect mass change throughout time and space.

"This is a power we have been programmed not to access or even believe. It is well past the time we start to remember our true nature. We are multi-dimensional beings emanating from source. We are not a body. We reside in a body. We are not separate from source, and we can reside both in time and outside of time."

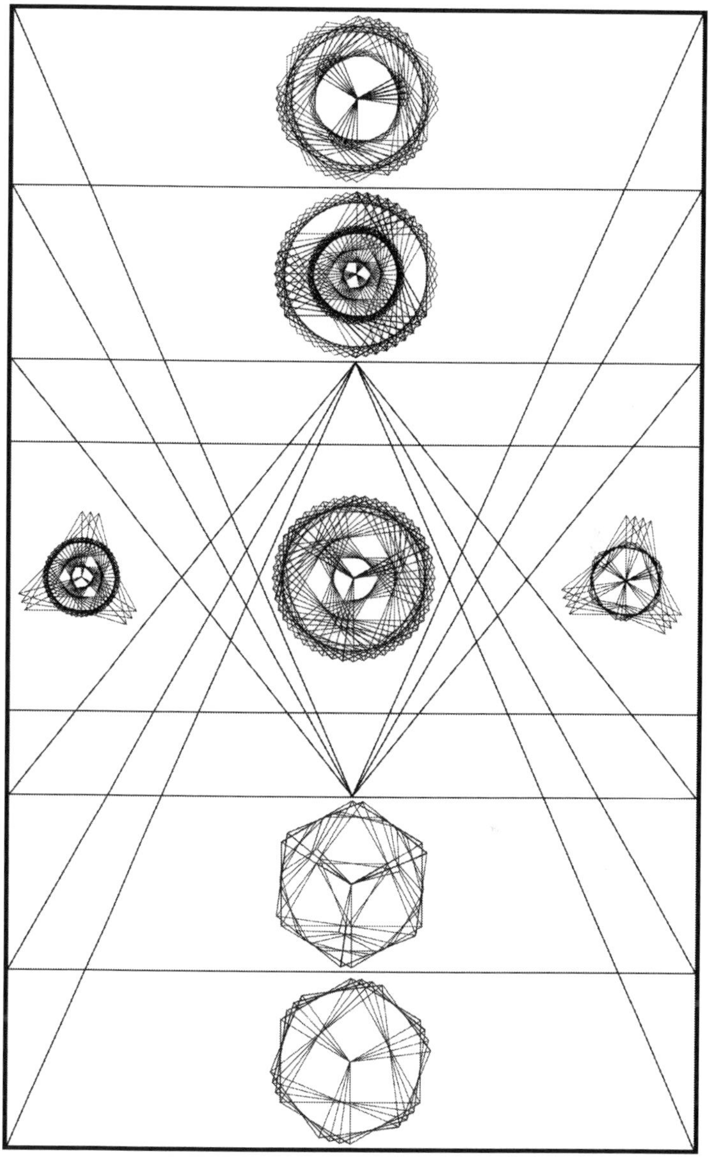

Forbidden Knowledge

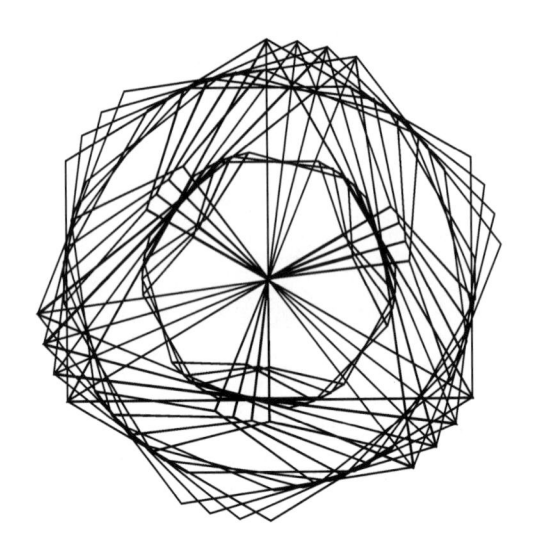

"You never change things by fighting the existing reality. To change something, build a new model that makes the existing model obsolete."

- Buckminster Fuller

Chapter 28
"The Greys"

As an incarnated being, for all intents and purposes, Jason would also be considered an alien.

He has lived many lives as a human on Earth but he has also lived as other worldly beings and has existed in other dimensions.

Admittedly, this concept is mind boggling.

But it's important to understand that many other aliens other than the species Jason is directly connected to – really do exist.

This brings us to the topic of "The Greys."

Who are they?

What are they?

Why are they here?

In all of his journeys, past and future time travel, incarnations and encounters with alien life forces, Jason has never had any direct contact, communication or experience with what most people would recognize as the short Greys with large dark oval eyes.

"Perhaps this is a blessing," Jason said based on what people, who have encountered them, have reported."

That's not to say he hasn't come across Grey-like beings with similar features such a large eyes, huge heads and slender, almost stick-like bodies, fingers and toes.

"But they didn't appear to be the common Greys that so many people have encountered or described," Jason said. "The ones with large oval black eyes, spindly thin bodies, long fingers and huge egg-shaped heads."

Jason's lack of encounters with the type of Grey most people know is interesting particularly when UFO research indicates more than 50 per cent of all encounters reported involve these type of Greys.

The truth is – there really isn't just one type of Grey and how this creature became fixed and embedded in the human experience is a story that doesn't seem to have a precise answer.

Although Grey-like beings have been discovered among the artifacts of ancient cultures such beings really never became part of our modern experience until the 1980s.

So when did the term "Grey" become common in alien discussion?

That question isn't as easily answered as one might think.

One of the most well-known abduction cases of modern times was the Betty and Barney Hill incident of Sept. 19, 1961. However, their abduction story was never made public until 1965 and even then they never used then term "Grey" to describe the beings they encountered.

Curiously, their descriptions of the beings they encountered have changed over the years depending on who is telling their story and what site one reads on the Internet.

To set the matter straight we went to the best source alive – Kathleen Marden, the Hill's niece, who co-authored the book "Captured-The Betty and Barney Hill UFO Experience" with Stanton Friedman, an internationally-renowned author/researcher and physicist.

Marden said her relatives definitely never used the term "Grey" to describe the beings they encountered although their descriptions of the beings were very similar to what most would consider to be a Grey.

"There were two types of beings, one taller than the other," Marden wrote in an email for this book. "They had large, slanted eyes, mostly black with some yellow where our white is.

"Their arms and legs were spindly but they had barrel chests. They were hairless and had very small noses. They were also dressed

"The Greys"

Betty and Barney Hill

in black, tight-fitting attire."

This was basically the description of what Betty and Barney gave while under hypnosis, Marden explained.

According to Marden, her aunt also had nightmares and in them she described the beings as having a more human appearance than the ones she actually recalled seeing when hypnotized.

The New Hampshire couple initially saw a UFO and experienced missing time while driving back home from Montreal.

Betty reluctantly reported the sighting when they got home. At the time, neither she nor her husband knew they had been abducted but they couldn't figure out why they were 30 miles further down the road or why it had taken longer than it should have to get home.

Betty also reported their sighting of the UFO to the nearby Pease Air Force Base, which at the time was also the home of the

509th Bomb Wing. Co-incidentally, this was the same 509th Bomb Wing that had been based at Roswell in 1947.

Under hypnosis conducted by Dr. Benjamin Simon, a well-known Boston psychiatrist, Betty and Barney each described being abducted by beings, taken to spacecraft and undergoing medical experiments before being returned to their vehicle.

Just as incredible was the fact that Betty mentioned how the aliens had told her they were from the Zeta Reticuli star system – a star system that wouldn't be discovered until eight years later in 1969.

Although Dr. Simon believed the Hills "believed" they had this encounter he concluded no abduction ever took place. In his view, Betty's mind had created dreams of abduction and Barney adopted her ideas when she told him about her nightmares following the incident.

Interestingly, Project Bluebook also concluded there was insufficient evidence to determine what the Hills saw and even suggested they probably were looking at Jupiter.

Really?

The planet Jupiter?

Does anybody with an intelligent mind believe the Hills mistook a planet for an alien space craft?

Nevertheless, we know one thing for certain. The Hills never used the term "Grey."

So where did the term "Grey" come from?

Well, it seems clear the Grey image although not necessarily the term "Grey" became forever embedded in our psyche once Whitley Strieber's book "Communion" was published in 1987 with the startling image of an alien on its cover.

Strieber described having several alien encounters with beings that people around the world would eventually call "Greys" in the book that became a New York Times best seller.

For Strieber, his abductions began in 1985 over the Christmas holidays in an isolated cabin in upper New York State. After going to bed he suddenly awoke in the woods near the cabin. He had fragmented memories and decided to undergo regressive hypnotism.

While under he recalled being abducted, floating up into a space

"The Greys"

ship where he would encounter four different beings, including the one depicted on the cover of his ground-breaking book.

Also during his regression he recalled undergoing medical experiments, including having a needle inserted into his brain and blood removed from a finger.

Of course, his regressionist refused to believe that he had been abducted by aliens. He diagnosed him with having temporal lobe epilepsy, a condition that can cause hallucinations.

Strieber has always believed he experienced a real event and his book led to numerous people recounting similar stories throughout the world. Interestingly, the haunting alien on the cover, whom he described as "thin, frail with haunting back slanted eyes, was female.

However, in "Communion," Strieber called the beings "Visitors" not "Greys." In 2007 Strieber published a fictional account of an alien takeover under the title "The Grays."

Was this the beginning of people calling these aliens Greys?

Remember, the general public really didn't know much about the 1947 Roswell UFO crash in New Mexico and the alleged recovery of several small beings until nearly 40 years later when several books were released, including "The Roswell Incident," written by Charles Berlitz and William L Moore in 1980, "Crash at Corona," written by Stanton Friedman originally published in 1992 but updated since and "The Day After Roswell," written by U.S. Colonel Philip Corso in 1997. All of these books revealed how the incident actually happened, that a military cover-up occurred and that sev-

Forbidden Knowledge

Alien iconography is commonly found in the mainstream.

eral aliens, dead and alive were captured.

By then, these beings were forever called "Greys."

The truth is – there isn't one single alien species known as the Greys. Some researchers have suggested there are as many as 16 different sub-species of Greys.

In Jason's view, the vast majority of alien species are humanoid-like.

"I'm led to believe that many of these humanoid alien species that have interacted with Earth fit into this category," Jason said. "But there's no doubt whatsoever the Greys are the single most depicted alien of our modern age."

Why has this type of being and image gained so much popularity?

"We live in a culture of abductions," Jason said. "Thousands of cases are reported every year. Most of them also involve the Greys.

"Most if not all claim their abduction experiences are physical and that they were taken out of their bedrooms into a space ship, placed on a medical-type table and then experimented on."

These experiences are anything but pleasant. Some Experiencers remain traumatized and suffer mental breakdowns. Only through

"The Greys"

deep hypnosis can these traumas be retrieved.

"Some of these cases involve physical evidence of the abduction," Jason said. "Many have woken up from these experiences to find strange wounds and markings on their bodies. Some have even recovered implants placed in them by these beings.

"Many of these implants have been studied with the most bizarre results. Documented cases indicate the implants contain a mix of metals and biological materials."

Is this so the body doesn't reject them or develop an adverse reaction to them?

Are they tracking devices?

"Documentation has also indicated some of the implants have magnetic properties," Jason said. "There are cases where small magnets actually stick to an Experiencer's skin.

"Also, in some of these cases, radio frequencies that can be measured seem to emit from the implants."

This is not just happening to farmer's out in the middle of nowhere. This is happening worldwide. In fact, it's estimated millions of people worldwide have been abducted or have had alien encounters and visitations.

"Indeed, this doesn't appear to be a rare occurrence," Jason said. "This is now part of our human experience."

So how many Grey-like species actually exist?

It depends on who is presenting the information.

Sgt. Clifford Stone, a controversial insider, has claimed to have knowledge of more than 80 different species, including 16 that are related genetically to the Greys. Stone claims he spent 22 years in the U.S. Army as a member of an elite top secret crash retrieval team and was used as a telepathic communicator with several of the alien survivors.

Stone also claims the intelligent life that has been visiting Earth bypasses known physics to travel here and that technology recovered from the many crashes has enabled governments to tap into far superior advancements than we have been led to believe exists.

Even if as many as 16 different Grey-like species exists, most

UFO researchers believe they all belong to one of six or seven specific genetic groups.

All have one common characteristic. They are hostile.

SHORT GREYS

This is the most popular of all Grey species. Some UFO researchers call them Zetas or Zeta Reticulums because they are believed to originate from the Zeta Reticuli star system.

Most Experiencers have described them as having grey skin and between 2 ½ feet to 5 feet tall with large hairless heads and large dark slanted eyes, an extremely thin body with very skinny arms and legs. Their hands have either three or four fingers. They have slit mouths and tiny nostrils and no ears.

Their communication is entirely telepathic. Some believe they are biologically-engineered unemotional entities, more machine than alive, and always seem to be controlled by another species. Many believe this type of Grey is really the worker bees of other species but they have the ability to control an abductee's mind.

Some abductees have also reported encounters with even smaller and equally hostile Greys standing no more than 2 feet tall.

TALL GREYS

Not to be confused with the "Tall Whites" these Greys are usually described as being 7 to 8 feet tall and are believed to play a key role in the hybridization of humans. Some UFO researchers also call them "Orion Greys" because they are believed to originate from a planet in the Orion Constellation.

Tall Greys are also believed to be the species that inter-acted with U.S. President Dwight Eisenhower during the alleged meeting of 1954. Based on Experiencers recounts, the Tall Greys seem to play a key role in abductions carried out by the short Greys. Most abductees wouldn't describe either the Short or Tall Greys as being benevolent although the Tall Greys often seem far less aggressive or hostile. This species is also believed to be the race that creates hybrids from human eggs taken during female abductions and are also responsible for the removal of growing fetus during the early months of pregnancy.

CROSS-BRED GREYS

Some UFO researchers are convinced The Reptilians and various Reptilian-like species such as the Draconians either have Grey genetics or that Greys have Reptilian genetics and are in fact the result of ancient hybridization between the two species.

Regardless, these are warrior species and are one of the oldest species in any time line and have ruled and conquered planets throughout the ages.

On Earth, some believe they are behind the Shadow Governments that control everything on Earth without the knowledge of most human beings.

According to those who have encountered this species, they are at least 8 feet tall, extremely muscular with scaly, green reptile-skin with large yellow eyes with lizard or cat-like pupils.

Some also believe this species is behind the Grey abductions

But while the Greys seem connected to most abductions some Experiencers have also reported other alien beings playing some kind of role as well.

"These beings often appear to either be working with the Greys or controlling them," Jason said. "Interestingly, some people have also reported seeing humans or at least human-looking people involved in the abductions and experiments.

"More often than naught the description of these human-like beings resemble a species known as the Nordics or Nords or Pleiadians. They are usually described as being male and female, Caucasian, and 6 to 7 feet tall with strikingly long blonde hair and blue eyes."

The term "Nord" has been used to describe these extraterrestrials because they resemble Scandinavians. Most abductees have suggested Nords are a benevolent race of beings commonly associated with spirituality and enlightenment.

"Despite this description, some people still have reported seeing Nords working or directing the Greys during their abduction experience," Jason said.

Some UFO researchers have suggested that U.S. President Dwight D Eisenhower secretly met with a group of Nords at Edwards Air Force Base in February 1954 to forge a treaty that would have resulted in advanced technology being provided in return for the U.S. agreeing to eliminate its nuclear arsenal. As the story goes, Eisenhower refused this olive branch and eventually struck a deal with one of the Grey races allowing abductions to take place in exchange for technology.

Is this the reason why governments have never admitted ETs exist?

"Of course, no such meeting or agreements have ever been publicly acknowledged." Jason explained. "The Nords are also known as the Pleiadians because they are believed to come from the Pleiades star system.

"Even though I have been told that I lived as a Pleiadian in one of my past lives I have never been provided with any information about if this supposed meeting ever occurred."

"Reptilian and Insectoid beings have also been connected with the Greys," Jason said.

"In fact, these are the most common species seen on space ships with the Greys and like the ones involving the Nords, the Reptilians and Insectoids seem to be directing what the Greys are doing." Jason said.

Also, abductions don't always take place in an alien space ship.

"What makes these cases even more bizarre is that many Experiencers report being taken to underground bases where these beings are experimenting on them," Jason said. "And again, often, they report humans and military personnel being in these locations."

Are these Experiencers hallucinating?

Could our military secretly be involved in these abductions?

"Thousands of women have also come forward revealing their eggs were taken from them during their abductions," Jason said.

"The Greys"

Is this part of a world-wide alien hybridization program?

"Many have also recounted stories of being impregnated by in vitro fertilization," Jason said. "Some claim they have even had sexual relationships with these beings.

"These beings then come within the first month of pregnancy to extract the child. These are incredibly traumatic experiences for these women. Some have even claimed to have undergone this horrific experience since childhood."

Experiencers have even seen and interacted with their own hybrid children while on board space ships or in underground facilities.

"It seems as if these children need to have some connection to their mothers in order to maintain their health," Jason said.

Jason's mother has recounted her own abduction from a "dream-like" state.

"She claims that she remembers being levitated off her bed in the basement and up the stairs to a ship," Jason said.

The beings encountered by his mother were similar to the ones former Lockheed Martin senior engineer Boyd Bushman revealed before his death in August 2004.

Like all whistleblowers, Bushman's claims have been ridiculed and dismissed by mainstream experts.

Nevertheless, Bushman alleged that he not only had first hand knowledge that aliens and UFOs were at Area 51 but that he had pictures to prove it. His photos showed a being with a large head and five toes, five fingers and webbed feet. He claimed 18 were at Area 51 helping with reverse engineering and that they lived to be nearly 300 years old.

But there was a big problem with his photo. It looked similar but not exactly like an alien doll previously sold at K-Mart. However, according to what has been purported to be a real polygraph test, Bushman told the truth when asked questions about aliens, and their anti-gravity technology.

So who are these Greys?

And why do so many people believe the Greys are doing the nasty work?

Just think about this for a moment.

Suppose the entities really doing most of the abductions have subconsciously placed in the minds of abductees that this is what the alien looks like?

"The Greys have become such a common alien that nobody would really question an Experiencer if they claimed this is the species abducting them," Jason said. "Based on what Experiencers have reported, it's absolutely clear that whoever is abducting them can manipulate their surroundings and scenarios to the point reality and non-reality is blurred."

Several people, including former U.S. Sgt. Jim Penniston, have come forward claiming they are, in fact, us from the future.

"That they are dying and need our genetics to help save what we have become," Jason said. "To save what mankind has evolved into from extinction."

In December 1980, Penniston was among the U.S. military stationed at RAF base at Woodbridge and Bentwaters in Sulfolk, England who claim to have encountered a black triangular craft in the forest.

Penniston claimed he not only touched the craft but also saw hieroglyphic-like characters on its surface. He also claims his mind was later bombarded with a binary code

During regressive hypnosis in 1994, Penniston revealed he had been told the visitors were humans from the future, who had traveled back in time.

"The Greys"

In 2010, the binary code was translated with the startling results.

Experts have concluded the message essentially revealed that the craft piloted by time travelers from the year 8100 on an exploration mission with longitude and latitude co-ordinates.

"Some have also claimed that the Greys are a slave race from Zeta Reticuli being controlled by the Reptilians," Jason said.

"Many believe the Greys are nothing more than clones or biological automatons controlled by the Reptilians and the Nordics to do their work," Jason said. "In my view, this is the most plausible explanation although it still doesn't explain the underground bases people have reported being occupied by these beings and human military personnel."

Many whistleblowers have come forward claiming there are many alien/human underground bases hidden all over the world.

If the Reptilians aren't solely in control could there be collusion among all of these alien groups and Earth governments?

Interestingly, isn't this the underlying theme of the X-files TV series?

Is it possible that many of these abductions are being done by the military using reversed engineered antigravity crafts?

Is it possible the military is simply blaming aliens, particularly the Greys because humans already have been conditioned to fear the Greys?

"Many believe this is closest to the truth," Jason said.

But for what means?

What is the ultimate goal??

"Some believe that our entire world is under the control of these beings," Jason said. "That the Earth has already been taken over by these beings."

Remember what Laura Eisenhower said in her appearance at the World UFO Congress in 2014 and indicated earlier in this book – that an invasion has already taken place but governments don't want us to know about it.

Every time Jason thinks about this an image and line from the famous "Smoking Man," from the X-Files continually pops up into

305

his mind, "The date has already been set."

Indeed, many believe this take over has been in the works for a very long time, Jason said.

"The date that is believed to be the final nail on the coffin is around 2030," Jason said. "But this is just speculation."

Jason is absolutely convinced these beings have been part of humankind's experience for thousands of years.

"There is plenty of evidence to support this," Jason said. "There are times in history when these beings are present and times when they are not."

What if the disclosure movement is the final preparation for the time when they become present again?

Are we being prepared through the media that if this event does take place in our future we will be ready to accept this take over?

"Again this is just speculation and theory based on testimony of whistleblowers and Experiencers," Jason explained.

There is another type of contact that is very manipulative and strange.

"In these cases, an individual appears to have been chosen to be the only connection to a particular race of beings," Jason said. "These people claim to be the only ones in the world with the correct information and everyone else is spreading disinformation.

"Some of them will even provide proof of their contact to substantiate their claims.

"What is troubling about these contracts is that the beings claim that no other alien species has ever visit Earth accept for them. That only this chosen person knows the truth about the world and them. And if anyone claims otherwise, then they are delusional or spreading disinformation. "

One of the most famous of such cases is the Billy Meier story. The Swiss-born Meier claims to be in regular contact with ETs he calls the Plejarens but likely are the Pleiadians. He claims they exist in a dimension just slightly off kilter from our own.

He also claims to have visited other worlds with these beings

"He has collected amazing evidence of his alleged contact," Ja-

"The Greys"

son said. "Many people, including some very well-known UFO investigators and authors have dismissed Meier but in my view, I believe him. I believe this is a true case of contact."

But it's the content of his message that concerns Jason.

"It's almost as if these beings are giving Meier and others about 95 per cent of the truth with 5 per cent disinformation," Jason said.

A similar claim was made by an individual known as "Cinta ej Narat" in Bob Mitchell's book "What if? Close Encounter of the Unusual Kind."

She claimed the Greys were actually a species called the Ataracu from the Orion Constellation and that they created mankind from inter-breeding an intelligent ape-like species from their home world with one that existed on Earth.

She also claimed the Ataracu were the only alien species to ever visit or interact with humankind and were the ones who built the pyramids and provided technology to ancient cultures.

She also claimed the Ataracu are a benevolent race and have been deliberately marked as evil and sinister by Earth governments.

"By claiming they are the only ones with this message they essentially become "prophets" for these beings," Jason said.

So why have so many of these types of cases suddenly popped up in modern times?

Why are we being confused with so many different claims and counter claims?

What if there really has been genuine contact from races of beings who want to help us get out of the mess we

King Atalanara - the Supreme Commander of the Atarcun in a drawing sketched by Cinta

307

are in?

What if this genuine contact has been happening to people all over the world?

"If these other beings know this is happening, wouldn't they try to implant and seed false information throughout the world," Jason said. "This would certainly cause mass confusion as to what is truth and what is disinformation.

"This would cause inaction within the contact community and would lead to in-fighting as to who is right and who is wrong."

Such arguments about what is true and what is false have exploded with the Internet.

"Each side is able to get their fix," Jason said. "Beliefs from either side are easily backed up or refuted and there is so much information and disinformation that most people have no idea what really is true or a hoax.

"It's as if we have become a fly caught in a web and we can't see that we are actually in a vast forest."

Regardless of who is right and who is wrong we have to look at the overwhelming evidence from the thousands of abduction cases.

"This is not fantasy," Jason said. "There is too much irrefutable evidence that something is going on without our consent. And there seems to be five main players – The Reptilians, The Nordics, The Insectoids, Humans – and of course The Greys, whoever or whatever they are.

"But the big question remains." Jason said. "What is their ultimate game and are they all working together?"

Again, let's look at what Laura Eisenhower suggested at the World UFO Congress.

Based on what insiders have told her, a Military Industrial Extraterrestrial Complex (MIEC) has been using an alien technology-driven super computer, including the HARP chem-trails and Artificial Intelligence mind control to create a world-wide ecocide and genocide.

Within this scenario, this secret group has overseen the construction of hundreds if not thousands of self-sufficient underground

"The Greys"

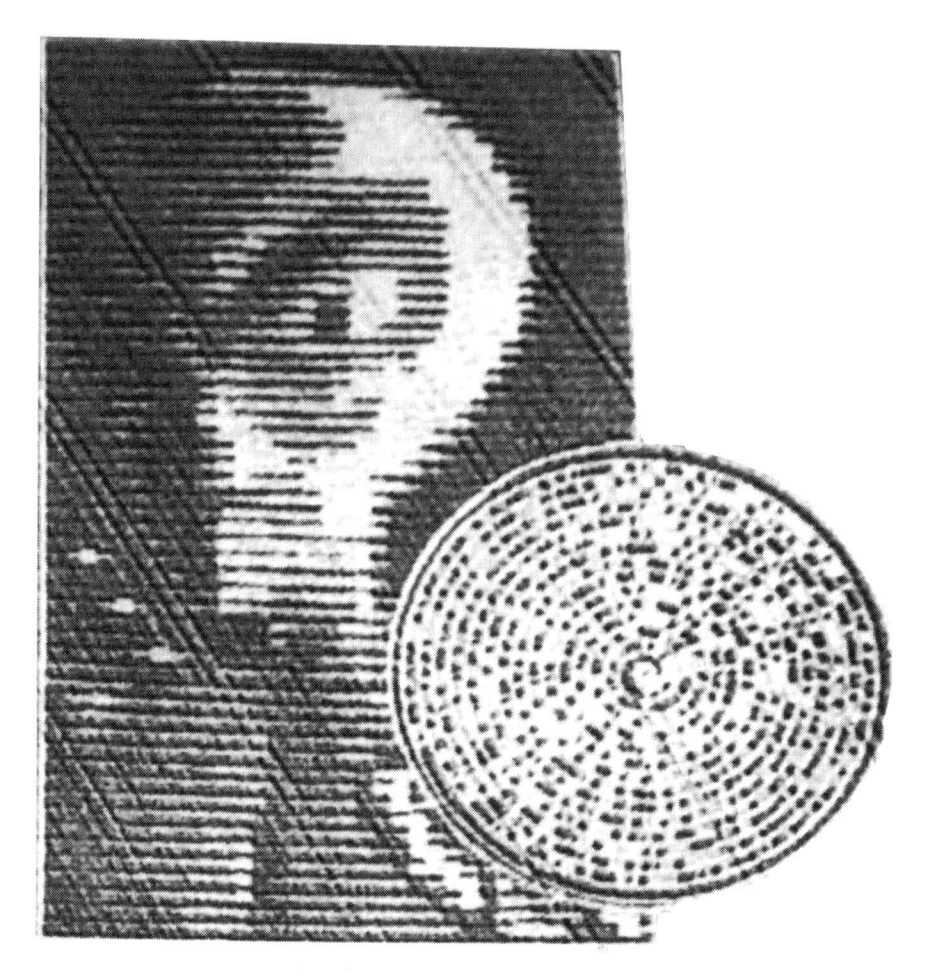

2002 Crop circle showing a Grey Alien. Three stars of Orion and a coded message on a disc.

The decoded message:
"Beware the bearers of false gifts and their broken promises. Much pain but still time. There is good out there. We Oppose deception. Conduit closing."

tunnels, virtual cities, for an elite selection of the population and elite officials.

Insiders have told her that the Greys and perhaps a Reptilian-Grey alliance are also closely connected to this world-wide conspiracy. But the Pleiadians remain here to prevent this from happening.

Insiders have also suggested to Laura Eisenhower that robotic Greys are also working with the military in the abductions of humans. In fact, most of the abductions have involved the military making it look as if the populace is being abducted by hostile aliens.

Laura Eisenhower also presented an even more alarming possibility based on what she has been told. That the medical experiments being conducted by the real Greys are being done in order to hybridize Earth with human-Grey beings that one day will be completely controlled by The Reptilians.

What if this is true?

As Jason was working on this chapter he received the following message.

"In the hermetic laws there is an important principle of Polarity.

"Everything is dual. Everything has poles. Everything has its opposite. Like and unlike are the same; opposites and are identical in nature but different in degree.

"Extremes meet and all truths are but half-truths and all paradoxes can be reconciled."

In his view, we are all part of the whole and within this whole we experience duality.

"We might think there is separation but when we change our perception we clearly see we are both the light and the dark," Jason said. "This is the Law of One.

"The two play an endless dance. It's just like the rising and setting Sun. Life feeds off of death and death feeds off of light. The only way they can exist is to be in perfect harmony with one another.

"When people ask me who and from where beings are attacking them, I give them the truth."

According to Jason, the beings that have attacked him and have come to him are actually himself in another form coming to teach him a new lesson.

"Each experience positive or negative awakened my consciousness to new truths, knowledge and gifts," Jason said. "Many of these experiences were painful and I suffered through them, but I survived and I'm grateful to still be learning."

"The Greys"

Like Jason, Laura Eisenhower also believes the only way for humankind to win this fight is to create a positive shift in the energies of our world.

Almost as if Laura was speaking Jason's language, she gave the following message to the world UFO group,

"We have abilities beyond our wildest imagination. It is time we recognize the benevolent forces and vastness of our Multi-dimensional Cosmos, that we are mirrors of Multi-dimensional beings."

When Jason initially had the experience with the hooded being that came into his bedroom to reveal his past lives, they imparted a very important lesson.

"They said that they would send these beings to me so I might learn how to navigate these worlds," Jason said. "I didn't understand at the time that he meant they were to test me.

"I didn't understand that these being had arranged for all of these experiences, even the most horrific ones, to test my will.

"I don't regret what happened to me but I also don't wish them on anybody else. But now I look back with great love and know these beings were my greatest teachers."

They taught Jason through experience and he was required to interact with all of them in order to remember who he actually was and in fact, who we all are.

"I needed to be taught how to navigate these worlds as a multi-dimensional being," Jason said. "This is what all of us are becoming in this world."

During his journeys Jason has been told there are many higher beings incarnated on Earth.

"We are all here as the "Checks and Balances," which keeps the balance between the light and the dark," Jason said. "This is the true war of the sons of light and sons of darkness. It is a never ending battle.

"But I wouldn't even call it a battle. It's more like a dance, the dance of opposites yet identical in nature but different in degrees.

"When I would face these beings I knew they had come to me because I was ready and strong enough to be their equal opposition. When we hold that view we can only have respect, love and gratitude for that being, no matter whom or what that being is."

On one of his journeys to an alien world, his consciousness experienced being in two different beings at the same time.

"I was the predator and the prey," Jason explained. "The pray resembled a purple koala type being but with a trunk like an elephant," Jason said. "It had black eyes and stood about two feet tall.

"This creature was sitting and meditating."

The predator resembled a walking anglerfish and was dark blue and about 4-foot tall.

"As this predator approached, the pray entered into a hand posture mudra while meditating," Jason said. "The predator then experienced a painful high pitch frequency in his head and then ran away seeking shelter.

"At that moment I was both the prey meditating and the predator experiencing the pain. This prey had developed some type of psychic defense from this species."

According to Jason, we all face much opposition in our world, ones we must overcome in order to proceed down a new path on our journeys.

"Some of the beings currently on Earth are hybrids that are here to shift the consciousness of those around them," Jason said. "They have always been here with us since our beginnings as a species.

"They have always incarnated with us to bring new teachings, gifts and knowledge to push humanity forward. This is to keep our oppositions in balance."

As indicated earlier in this book Jason has been guided on how to heal his energy in order to become who he is today.

"I needed to learn how to shift and change my energy so I could prepare myself for my journey," Jason said. "This was my catalyst to face my fears and grow.

"The practice of the Egyptian postures and Qigong is what I used to see my goals through. I learned that our energy bodies were weak and could be easily manipulated and even possessed.

"That the only way to protect ourselves was through healing and strengthening our bodies so that we can take back control of

"The Greys"

our conciseness."

As we heal ourselves we begin to know ourselves. Your consciousness is yours and by it you are always connected to the source.

"The spark of creation is within us all," Jason said. "The body is merely the temple to hold our light. This body is our vehicle that allows us to navigate these worlds.

"We are here to insert our conciseness within these realms to grow and experience ourselves by working out our karma. We are here to express our divine nature through our experiences. As we grow we start to shift and change the environment and people around us. We have a great power within us to dream a new world into being."

The truth we seek evolves with our perception of reality.

"What I know today as truth will evolve into a deeper understanding as my perceptions of that truth will inevitably start to change as I grow," Jason said. "Learning is never over. It's the questions of life that drive us forward.

"Not knowing is our motivation that propels us into the future. We are the only mystery we need to figure out. All our answers reside within this vessel. All of this information simply reminds us to look within to find our true answers.

"What we see outside of us is just our reflection."

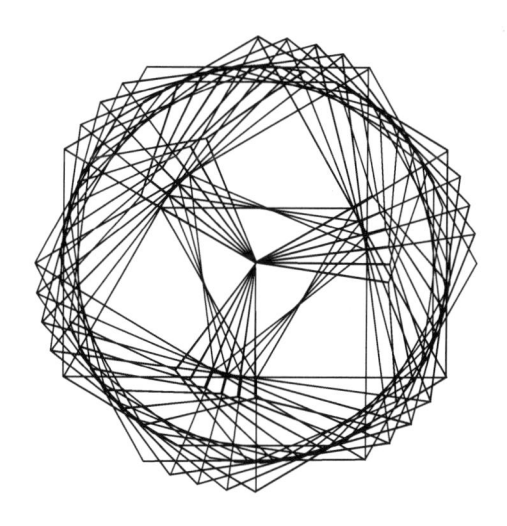

ABOUT THE AUTHORS

Jason Quitt is a graduate of the Institute of Energy Wellness, and a student of Algonquin Shamanism. Jason has been training and working with many teachers, shamans, and traditional healers from around the world.

Jason is also the author and teacher of "Egyptian Postures of Power - Ancient Qigong System" & "The Yosef Codes - Sacred Geometry Codes For Healing." Jason combines these methods and modalities of energy medicine, shamanism, and dowsing to assist those on their own personal paths of healing.

www.thecrystalsun.com

Bob Mitchell is a Canadian author and journalist, who covered crime and sports for The Toronto Star for more than 35 years.

He's the author of seven books, including three UFO books.

His first UFO book – "INCIDENT AT PLEASANT RIDGE – A CANADIAN UFO MYSTERY" was published in 2014. His second UFO book "INTRUSION-ALIEN ENCOUNTERS" was published in 2015.

His third UFO book "WHAT IF?

CLOSE ENCOUNTERS OF THE UNUSUAL KIND" was released in November 2015.

He is also a field investigator for MUFON based in Ontario and an executive with MUFON Canada.

He has also written three true crime books.

"THE CLASS PROJECT-HOW TO KILL A MOTHER" was initially published in March 2008 and updated in April 2013. It's the story of Canada's infamous Bathtub Girls, which was turned into the "Perfect Sisters" motion picture.

He is also the author of the true crime book "DEADLY DEFIANCE"- the story of a Canadian honour killing and "IN PLANE SIGHJT:BEFORE 911" – the story of an American black militant, who was on the run for 30 years after pulling off the only successful airplane hijacking in Canadian history.

He is also the author of "GRAVE DECEPTION" – murder mystery novel inspired by a true crime. Mitchell also continues to be a freelance journalist and media consultant.

Mitchell has appeared on numerous radio and television programs talking about his UFO books and has spoken at numerous conferences and events, including the Alien Cosmic Expo in Brantford, Ontario and the Rose City Paracon conference in Windsor, Ontario.

He continues to shop a horror/thriller screenplay.

Mitchell is also a co-founder of Toronto News Wire Services @TorNewsWire

Bob Mitchell can be reached via email at bobmitchellwriter@gmail.com or @ThePitBull123.

His website is bobmitchellauthor.simplesite.com

Forbidden Knowledge

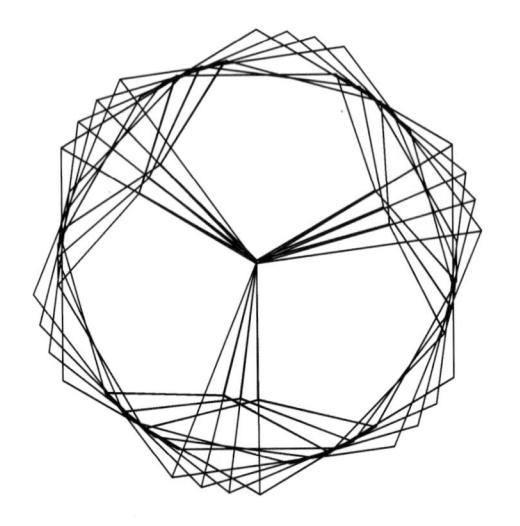

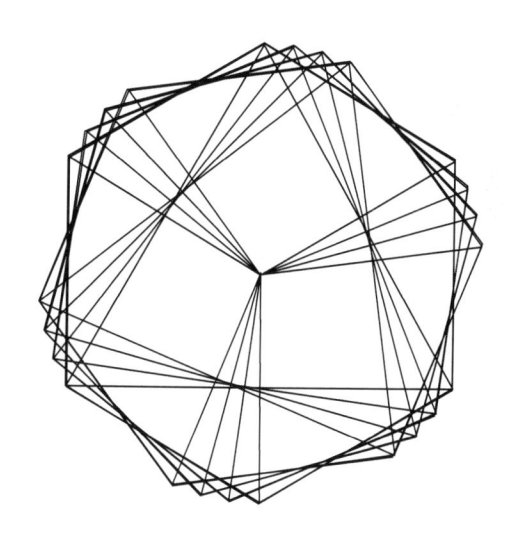

3 Golden rules for positive thinking

1. **Day dreaming** about pleasant stuff positive - to overight the negative thoughts

2. **Always Smile** - if you have smiley outside it affects the inside

3. **Posture** - keep good posture, head high, shoulder even. Poor posture affects the negative. When talk to someone look in people's

4. **Eye** - to have confidence

5. Accurately observe nature without judging

Ideas for positive thinking

6. Spend outdoors as much as you can, you need the sun - it programs your body to reprogram your cell

7. **Shout/Sing out loud** - a name you live - to loose up the stress, feel free - laugh, sing loudly